SWISS MEN OF LETTERS

Twelve Literary Essays

SWISS
MEN OF LETTERS

Twelve Literary Essays

edited by
ALEX NATAN

OSWALD WOLFF
London

1970

108164

SBN 85496 064 3

MADE AND PRINTED IN GREAT BRITAIN BY
THE GARDEN CITY PRESS LIMITED
LETCHWORTH, HERTFORDSHIRE

CONTENTS

List of Contributors

Fernand Auberjonois, European correspondent of *Toledo Blade* (USA).

Guido Calgari, Professor of Italian Literature, Federal Institute of Technology, Zürich.

Martin Esslin, Head of Radio Drama Department, British Broadcasting Corporation (BBC), London.

Mrs. Liliane Fearn, Ph.D., Senior Lecturer in French, Birkbeck College, University of London.

J. R. Foster, M.A., Assistant Director of Recruiting, Civil Service Commission.

Werner Günther, Emeritus Professor of German Literature, University of Neuchâtel.

Charly Guyot, Emeritus Professor of French Literature, University of Neuchâtel.

J. M. Lindsay, Ph.D., Professor of German Literature, University of St. Andrews.

Dr. Andri Peer, Lecturer, Kantonsschule, Winterthur.

H. M. Waidson, Ph.D., Professor of German Literature, University of Swansea.

W. E. Yuill, Ph.D., Professor of German Literature, University of Nottingham.

Preface

by ALEX NATAN

The literature of a nation reflects the history of the country concerned. Although Switzerland is only a small nation she can look back upon a long and fascinating history. The Swiss Confederation was not brought about in any spectacular way but can best be described as the end product of prevailing common sense which welded four distinctly different ethnic groups together and safeguarded their independent cultural development. The ways and means of this achievement were complicated and intricate, and mirrored successfully solutions which the rest of Europe, facing similar problems, never mastered. In this indigenous evolution of Switzerland the reader will find the explanation why there is no history of Swiss literature but a history of the literatures of all four national languages, each of which can claim special and adequate attention by literary historians. While the literature of other countries brought the testimonies of literary achievement forward like a huge wave which began in times immemorial, reached the present and flows on into the future, one feels rather inclined to speak of four different rivers in Swiss literature, each taking its own and individual course.

To orientate the reader it will be well worth his while to remember that 70 per cent of the Swiss population dwell in cantons which have German as their mother tongue. Out of a total population of six million Swiss approximately 4.2 million form the German ethnic group. The "Suisse romande" has 1.5 million inhabitants belonging to the French ethnic group. The Italian part comprising the canton Ticino and a number of adjacent valleys in the Grisons totals approximately 200,000 inhabitants while the Rhaeto-Romanic group, entirely confined to the Grisons, numbers hardly more than 50,000 Swiss. Reference must also be made to the existence of a Swiss dialect literature which nowadays flourishes predominantly in the German-speaking parts of Switzerland, mainly because here the population, irrespective of social standing and upbringing, uses the dialect for everyday purposes. The existence of numerous local idioms, the result of much geological stratification of the Alps, supports this trend towards an increasing variety of dialect writing. This situation does however not rule out that many poets and writers continue to write both in High German and in the vernacular.

Countries which, like Switzerland, are in the fortunate position of being the focus of different cultures naturally also produce a many-sided and stimulating intellectual life. It has frequently been commented upon how many Swiss writers, irrespective of their racial origin, display a distinct tendency towards a pedagogic didacticism. It does not therefore come as a surprise that some of the greatest writers were also teachers of distinction. Such an attitude shows faith in progress and faith in the moral fibre of man. "That the idea of humanity is particularly deeply rooted in Switzerland can be partly explained by the fact that Swiss territory stood longer and stronger under the influence of Roman culture and thus of the Christian-classical world of thought than all the rest of Germany" (A. Zäch).

Guido Calgari goes one step further when he asserts that "the intermingling of literature with politics, morals and traditions is a basic characteristic of Swiss literary creation". He too, like other observers before him, stresses the fact that very few Swiss authors have ever been mere writers who dwelled in an artistic ivory tower. They were all citizens of their country who took their political duties seriously. The typical Swiss writer is always prepared "to take a stand in a fight for ideas, for the cause of his own country, for the furtherance of social principle . . . All this, no doubt, limits somehow his artistic freedom, but on the other hand provides him with a guarantee of morality : a position lacking perhaps in imagination but showing nonetheless the Swiss sense of civic-mindedness" (Guido Calgari).

These seem to be cogent reasons for a closer acquaintance with the main currents of Swiss literature. This volume of essays is therefore a selective attempt of introducing some important literary developments in Switzerland. They should serve as an introduction to the interested reader who will also find a bibliography which will pave the way to more detailed and more exhaustive studies. Although some of the essays in this volume, notably those dealing with German-language writers, have previously appeared in various volumes of the series *German Men of Letters,* we could not leave them out of a book wholly devoted to Swiss literature. They have been revised where necessary and their bibliographies have been brought up-to-date. We cannot do better than reprint by way of introduction an essay by the foremost Swiss literary historian Professor Guido Calgari.

The Editor and the publishers are greatly indebted to "Stiftung Pro Helvetia" for their support in the production of this book. They also wish to place on record their indebtedness and gratitude for the active interest and unstinting help received from the cultural attaché of the Swiss Embassy, London, Dr. Paul Stauffer. The book owes more to him than words can express.

Introduction
The Literatures of Switzerland
by GUIDO CALGARI

Switzerland is remarkable among countries divided by differences
of language or nationality in that the Swiss live and work together
in peace despite their four languages and cultures, which they
have no intention of merging or of subjecting to any hierarchical
scale of priority. On the contrary, each group makes every effort
to preserve and foster its own particular cultural heritage. There
are three official languages : German, French, Italian; for thirty-
one years recognition has been extended to a fourth language,
regarded as a national if not an official tongue, the Romansch
spoken by fifty thousand inhabitants of the Canton of the Grisons.
The Confederation does not recognize linguistic groupings as such,
it recognizes only the "Cantons", which are political and historical
entities—each with its own legislative body and government. Consequently there do not exist in Switzerland linguistic or cultural
conflicts. In German Switzerland there are spoken a wide variety
of different dialects all together designated by the term *Schwyzer-
dütsch*; these dialects were established in medieval times and have
survived owing to the isolation afforded by the mountainous topo-
graphy of the country. German Switzerland is fiercely proud of its
dialects, as of all the traditions, customs and usages that distinguish
it from Germany. However, newspapers, publishers of books, repre-
sentatives to the Federal Assembly in Berne, the higher courts and
the schools employ standard High German (Schriftsprache). As for
French Switzerland, it has forgotten its former dialects and Pro-
vençal influences, except in a few tiny districts, and exclusively
employs the official language, which is identical with Parisian
French. In Italian Switzerland the native residents among themselves speak Lombard dialects but write Tuscan, and this tongue,
i.e., standard Italian, is increasingly supplanting the local dialect.
In Romansch-speaking Switzerland various idioms are employed
which are basically the Late Latin speech current at the time of
Charlemagne (a native of the Engadine, Giuseppe Planta, librarian

in chief of the British Museum in the eighteenth century, demonstrated its very close resemblance to the text of the *Strasbourg Oath,* which confirmed the division of the Carolingian Empire in 842 !). This language has deep historical roots in the same medieval Latin Christian culture that gave birth to the perfected tongues and glorious literatures of France, Italy and Spain.

The existence of a variety of languages in Switzerland has served greatly to encourage philological study, recent examples being the *Linguistic Atlas of Italy,* the monumental *Etymological Vocabulary of the French Language* and the four "glossaries" of the four national idioms, one for each region of the country. As for the literatures, it is necessary again to bear in mind fundamental regional divergences; we are not confronted here simply by a question of form; the German-speaking Swiss display in their history, their traditions and their mentality a distinctly autonomous ethos moulded through the long centuries of political experience different from that of Germany and of economic and social conditions that have been just as different. This means that they will not seek in Germany or in Austria the writer to represent them and to express their philosophy of life; they have their Gotthelf and their G. Keller; they can even imagine, with Th. Mann and György Lukacs, what German literature could have become "if, in 1848, the democratic revolution had triumphed in Germany—as it triumphed in Switzerland—and if Germany had had G. Keller as an admonitory voice, a reproach and an inspiring example" . . . It appears that French-speaking Switzerland finds itself in a different position with regard to France and that it tends to identify itself with Paris; nevertheless, it too has a political and religious tradition distinct from the rationalism and the Catholicism of France; its Calvinism, its long association with German Switzerland, its romantic nineteenth century, the influx of so many political refugees, of so many free spirits from everywhere and the influence—finally—of the ideas of J. J. Rousseau, "citizen of Geneva", have all in a certain way deflected French Switzerland from the rationalism of France. Romansch Switzerland, by the very fact that it employs a language which is "national" only in Switzerland, is more entitled than any other region to speak of an indigenous original literature. It is only Italian Switzerland that does not possess a cultural heritage proper to it alone; its conception of life is Lombard, its author is the Lombard, A. Manzoni. Nevertheless, in the nineteenth century it produced an uninterrupted line of political writers, from Stefano

Franscini to G. Motta, who revealed to it the reality of Switzerland, and his teaching lives on in the character and the civic discipline of the people.

Thus it is not possible to speak of a Swiss literature, which is something that does not exist. One must think in terms of literatures, or of the *four* literatures of Switzerland and attempt to isolate a "Swiss outlook", to discover "constants" in the expression of the Swiss ethos, features common to the literary men of the different linguistic regions, features which are the outcome of a common history, of a similar political education, of the same love for the severe majesty of the mountains or for freedom, at times, of a similar mission of cultural mediation among the various European countries surrounding Switzerland. In short, the Swiss attitude is a moralistic one. As a reaction these qualities also give rise to a centrifugal effort, a tendency towards a cosmopolitanism that turns its back on "Swiss" themes to grapple with universal problems—in the bosom of the three great literatures: German, French, Italian—and even ventures on criticism, which can be stringent, of the Helvetian ideal, which is frequently charged with egoism and a narrow spirit of conformism.

The "Swiss" Outlook

The traditional moralism of the literatures of Switzerland which has always maintained a certain seriousness and respectability, accounts among other things for the greater importance attached to the essay than to imaginative works, to works of history, ethics and criticism than to poetry or narrative writing. To explain this cool reflective bent it is not necessary to cite André Gide, for whom *"every Swiss carries within him his glaciers"*. This moralism accounts for the numerous works illustrating "the apprenticeship for life", Keller's "Grüner Heinrich", for example, all those novels describing the development of a young man and ending in an apologia for the family, the native place, tradition, the old verities discovered to be sound after the disillusionments or the excesses of life in the great world. Another characteristic is the "political" penchant which always makes the writer feel "available" for mobilization, as it were, for the contest of ideas and always at the service of the politics of the country; another is the love of nature and of the mountains, the Alps (this is the heritage of Rousseau and Haller and Gessner), the sources of freedom, and the love of the solidly built farmstead (Gotthelf) and of democracy and the political institutions of the Confederation (G. Keller, Toepffer);

finally, these writers all have a very human and concrete, as it were, "mundane" religious sense, which consists in assuming one's own responsibilities (Rousseau, Vinet, Pestalozzi). In medieval times only German Switzerland can be said to have had a literature, thanks to the Abbey of St. Gall and the love poetry of the "Minnesänger" in the Manesse Manuscript in Zurich. In French Switzerland there was a certain cultural inertia that is all the more astonishing if one thinks of the intensity of contemporary life in some French regions, in Provence, Picardy, Limousin; however, there did appear one outstanding figure in Othon de Grandson of sufficient renown to be translated by Chaucer as the author of the "most beautiful ballades" of France.

The Golden Age

In the history of Swiss thought the culminating centuries are the sixteenth, the eighteenth and the nineteenth. The rise of the towns, on the one hand, which took the lead over the original rural Cantons, and Swiss military prowess, and, on the other hand, the Church Councils convened on the frontiers of Switzerland (Constance, Basel), the foundation of the University of Basel, and later the Reformation are all factors in the intellectual awakening of the Swiss and the revival of learning : it suffices only to recall the names of Erasmus (professor at Basel), of Th. Platter, of that extraordinary Faustian figure Paracelsus, of Zwingli, Vadianus, Niklaus Manuel . . .; humanists, theologians, political leaders and dramatists dedicated their entire energy to the triumph of their faith and of their city. In this period, French Swiss literature enters the field of controversy for the first time, led by its theologians and the Reformed jurists. In the Grisons Romansch literature commences (a rustic "chanson de geste" and the translation of the Bible; later on there will appear the monumental *Bible of Chur* (financed by George I of England); and even in the areas of the Ticino subject to Switzerland men of letters appeared with works in Latin and in Italian. The eighteenth century brought the *Enlightenment* with Zürich as its centre and with J. J. Bodmer as its guiding spirit, who introduced Milton, Shakespeare and Dante to the German-speaking world. Along with Dean Bridel in French Switzerland, Bodmer at this time fostered the idea of a Helvetian literature (language was of secondary import for these men; it was ideas, themes, sentiments that could contribute to the rise of a "Swiss" art). Both Rousseau and Salomon Gessner celebrated the cult of nature, the noble savage, the "wisdom of the heart" and prepared the way for Lavater and Pestalozzi; even more, they herald the Romantic movement. Nevertheless, Switzerland did not produce great romantic artists, except for the "English painter" J. H. Füssli, who did all his work in London, haunted by midnight visions and by the Swiss legend; the English called him *"the wild Swiss"*, the people of Zürich "der Londoner Füssli". The nineteenth century saw the demolition of the dream of Bodmer and Bridel : while political theorists sought to tighten the bonds among the different parts of the Confederation, to create a more compact body politic (hence the political reform of 1848), the literary movement was, rather, centrifugal, characterized by a return to the regional cultures. At the same time, men of letters were concerned with problems of form, i.e., aesthetic values. Literature, after its long engagement in the Protestant-Catholic struggle, then in the heroic national legend, and later still in moral criticism and the Helvetian ideal, finally strives to serve beauty. It was at last realized that to produce works of art it was not sufficient to "think well" but also it was necessary to "write well"; as Ph. Godet put it, "a badly written book is never a good book". Despite this return to the original literary impulses, there was still a profound concern with national themes : liberalism, democracy, the modus vivendi among the national groups of Switzerland, all reflected in the work of Gotthelf, Keller, Rambert, Olivier, Vinet and even Amiel, certain pages of whose *Journal intime* were the favourite reading of Tolstoy. However, there was a group of great writers who sought their myths and heroes elsewhere than in Switzerland : Spitteler, C. F. Meyer, the two Monniers, and, in our own day, J. Schaffner, Blaise Cendrars and Francesco Chiesa, three writers who naturally feel at home in the great literatures of their respective languages, German, French and Italian. There are, finally, "uprooted" writers, lost in the flux of German life or in Paris, such as Cherbuliez and Rod in French Switzerland.

Contemporary Writers

In the Grisons Romansch literature celebrates local history or becomes obsessed with the melancholy theme of the emigration; a "nouvelle vague" of poets is taking its inspiration from the themes of the literatures across the frontiers and is expressing itself in a very modern form. Italian Switzerland, following the example of Chiesa, has produced in the last few years a fine group of story-tellers and lyric poets, essayists and historians. French Switzerland too, with Ch.–Ferd. Ramuz and F.–Gonzague de Reynold, possesses a group of poets, novelists and critics of outstanding excellence; several of them enjoy world-wide renown, such as Cendrars, already referred to, or Gehri, or the founder of the Théâtre de Mézières, René Morax. German Switzerland, the most important region economically and the one with the largest population, is producing copiously both in the literary language and in dialect, the former being of primary interest to the foreign student. There are storytellers like H. Federer, M. Inglin, Cécile Ines Loos, Regina Ullmann, Nobel Prize winner Hermann Hesse, lyric poets like Albin Zollinger, Max Pulver and the young Siljy Walter and playwrights and novelists, such as Max Frisch (translated into all the principal languages) and Friedrich Dürrenmatt (whose plays are performed from America to Japan).

Switzerland, in short, is not merely a picturesque land, a holiday mecca or an industrial country alone; nor is it simply peaceful and devoid of problems, but it is a country in which the life of the mind and its expression in literature have always been taken with great seriousness.

(It was with deep regret that we heard of Professor Calgari's death while the book was in the press.)

Henri-Frédéric Amiel

Henri-Frédéric Amiel

by LILIANE FEARN

AMIEL is a strange case, and perhaps a unique one, in the history of Letters.

A not very distinguished professor of Philosophy at the University of Geneva, he published nothing of outstanding value in his lifetime. His literary reputation, which stands high among connoisseurs, rests entirely on the posthumous publication of his *Journal intime,* which he had kept sporadically from 1839 and regularly from 1847 to 1881, the year of his death.

To this is added another strange circumstance : the *Journal* has never been published in its entirety. All that we have is a series of "anthologies" (which will be described later). Successive editors have given us their personal selections. An attempt, made twenty years ago by the Swiss publisher, M. Pierre Cailler, to publish the *Journal* in its entirety was abandoned after the third volume (it was to have forty). The only way open to a fervent reader is to go to Geneva and read the MS in the Bibliothèque publique et universitaire where it has been deposited. It is a daunting task, for the MS totals 16,900 pages.

Born in 1821, Amiel belongs to a religious generation rich in meditative and introspective writers, some of whom also used the journal as a means of expression. Nearest to him in time and character is Senancour, whose Obermann offers so many similarities with Amiel : lassitude, feeling of incompatibility, inaptitude for practical life, search for an ideal, refuge into nature and reverie. This mournful book left a deep impression on the adolescent Amiel. Then there is Maurice de Guérin, who died in 1839 aged twenty-nine and whose *Journal* Amiel read much later, in

Author's Notes:
1. For the reader's convenience I have mostly quoted Amiel directly in English. The passages I am quoting in French are those in which I wanted to preserve the artistic quality of the style.
2. My references are mostly to the Bouvier edition in three volumes, but I have occasionally made use of unpublished passages, quoted here and there by commentators.

January 1866, commenting that the artistic and poetic aspect of it is much more apparent than its philosophical content, and regretting this fact. Regretting, also, that Maurice de Guérin had not given us more details about his daily life, his readings, his occupations etc.

One cannot level the same criticism at Amiel's *Journal,* which is extremely rich and can be read in a variety of manners. It is a chronicle of daily life, a meditation on life, a collection of "poems" on nature, a series of critical articles on literature or philosophy, a self-portrait, a story of several attachments, etc. It is, nevertheless, a work for the "happy few" and requires a certain amount of patience on the part of the reader, for it is slow and repetitive—just as life is.

The collections which the reader has at his disposal are varied, but only the most recent ones are on the market. In chronological order, they are :

—*Fragments d'un Journal intime,* précédés d'une étude par Edmond Scherer, 2 vols. 1883–4, (582 pages).

—*Fragments d'un Journal intime,* précédés d'une étude par Bernard Bouvier, 3 vols. 1922, (1111 pages).

—*Philine: Fragments inédits du Journal intime* publiés par Bernard Bouvier, introduction par Edmond Jaloux, 1927 (294 pages).

This selection is centred round a sentimental attachment of Amiel which lasted for ten years.

—*Journal intime.* Introduction et notes de Léon Bopp. 3 vols. 1948, 1953, 1958.

This is the first attempt to publish the full text. The three volumes cover the years 1839–50 and total 566 pages. The publication was discontinued.

—*Journal intime de l'année* 1866, édition intégrale. Introduction et notes de Léon Bopp, 1959 (560 pages).

—*Journal intime, L'année* 1857, éditée et présentée par Georges Poulet, 1965.

Taken all together these six major collections represent about one fifth of the whole *Journal.*

Each collection represents an improvement on the preceding one, not only because the text is richer, but because the Introduction is more detailed. The Scherer edition (1883) hardly has anything about Amiel's life. He appears as a pure spirit who has no biography. The Bopp editions are particularly useful in that M. Bopp has been able to identify several persons whom Amiel names only with initials. And yet, he himself resorts to initials in certain cases which he considers delicate. In his 1948 edition he writes: "We have replaced by initials the names of people about whom Amiel makes unkind remarks" (p. 16)—this sixty-seven years after Amiel's death! And in his 1959 edition, after revealing that "Philine" was Marie-Andrienne Favre, he refuses to give the surname of the man she married in 1853 : he is simply Jean-Philippe-Gabriel P. (p. 23)—this seventy-eight years after Amiel's death. Is this prudence de rigueur in a small city?

Henri-Frédéric Amiel was born in Geneva on September 27, 1821. His father was a Genevan citizen of French descent; his mother, Caroline Brandt, came from Canton Bern and spent her childhood in Aarau, in the German part of Switzerland. She used to call her son Fritz, and in his youth Amiel often signed his letters to his family with this name. Gide, discussing in his autobiography, *Si le grain ne meurt,* his mixed origin (his father Southern French, his mother Norman) propounds the idea that only people issued from the same race are capable of "powerful affirmations"; those born of mixed blood can only become artists and arbiters. I don't know if this theory always proves to be true, but it fits in the case of Amiel.

When he was eleven, he lost his cherished mother : she died of tuberculosis. Two years later, he lost his father, too. Unable to recover from the loss of his wife, he killed himself by throwing himself into the Rhône. This double tragedy was bound to affect an impressionable child very deeply. Fortunately, Henri-Frédéric and his two sisters were brought up by an uncle, Frédéric Amiel, and his wife Fanchette, who had five children. He lived seven years with this happy and lively family. But some part of his psyche had been irremediably damaged.

His studies at the Collège de Genève, then at the Academy, were brilliant and uneventful. In 1839, at eighteen, he began his first diary. He completed his studies by a long stay in Germany, 1844–8, where he studied at Heidelberg and Berlin Universities and formed lasting friendships. He was happy : he enjoyed his freedom and the intellectual ferment of university life.

Soon after his return to Geneva the Chair of Aesthetics at the Academy fell vacant. He applied and was appointed in 1849.

A few years later, in 1854, he was nominated to the Chair of Philosophy. Thus began a career which he followed dutifully but not very
successfully. Not being a natural talker, he read his lectures from
notes, and the result was dull. Several times, through the press, his
students asked him to modify his method. In vain. He was not a
very open man, and found the contact with students difficult.

He never married, although he attracted, through his good looks
and distinguished personality, the attention of many young women
who would have been happy to marry him. His *Journal* is full of
agitation concerning this grave subject. With perfect frankness
Amiel confesses that he is tortured by his sex, and yet does not
dare to make an irrevocable decision and marry : "Sexuality has
been my Nemesis, my torture ever since childhood. My extraordinary timidity, my violent desires, my ardent imagination, my
pernicious readings in adolescence . . . the fatal attraction which
I exerted later on delicate and tender women : all this proceeds
from a false notion of sexuality. This error has poisoned my life"
(February 25, 1861). He exhorts himself to "take the plunge" even
though it might be repugnant! This event happened in October
1860 with "Philine", Marie Favre, a young, pretty, passionate
widow of thirty. Amiel was by then thirty-nine. But the experience
was "sans lendemain", although the platonic relationship continued
for ten years, torturing Philine who fell deeper and deeper in love.

In 1867 he got engaged for a short time to "Perline", Marie-
Anne Droin, a clergyman's daughter. But nothing came of it. Yet
another friend was Fanny Mercier, fifteen years younger than
Amiel, the headmistress of a private high school for girls, whom
he called la Seriosa, la Fida, la Stoica. She called herself, half-
jokingly, half-sadly, his "widow"—his widow, without ever having
been his wife. Her fidelity was rewarded, but in a rather frightening
way : Amiel bequeathed his *Journal* to her. He had judged her
with perfect acumen. She undertook the formidable task of reading
the enormous MS and preparing a first selection. Many passages in
the *Journal* concerned her and she must have been gratified to
find how much he valued her friendship, if not her looks : "Is
there anybody better made for heroism than this poor little
Calvinist without any looks, but whose inner being is a flame?"
(July 5, 1875, unpublished).

In general he attached great importance to rare moral qualities
in women. Sex cannot be envisaged unless it is accompanied by
the highest moral guarantees. His numerous descriptions of the
perfect woman bring a smile to the lips until one realizes that it is

precisely his tragedy that he cannot accept sex *per se*. Whenever he is tormented, he tries to exorcise the "demon" by lofty thoughts, prayer, work. After a crisis, he writes :

"The invisible wind has changed its direction, the sensual miasmas have been blown away like the emanations of a swamp. I had to prepare a lecture for tonight, and work has restored my spirituality. From nature I return to morality, from appetites to conscience. I climb up the mountain and find again the healthy air and the high spirits which I had missed for several days" (*Philine*, September 28, 1860).

Gide calls this type of exercise "faire de l'alpinisme moral". There is plenty of it in the *Journal*. One wonders whether Amiel ever realized that the apathy and lack of will of which he accuses himself regularly and painfully were due to this constant repression of sex.

Up to a point the *Journal* is the diary of a discontented man. The incapacity to act, the flight of time, the lack of direction, the approach of old age are leitmotivs of the *Journal*. Nobody is more severe on Amiel than himself. But let us leave the plane of every-day life and reach the plane of the spirit : everything changes. The malady of will appears like the malady of the pearl-oyster. Without it, Amiel would have been a professor similar to many others, efficient and satisfied. Because of it, he is able to secrete his life's work, his *Journal*.

Outwardly, Amiel led a very quiet, well-ordered life. The only events were journeys in Switzerland and abroad. He visited London in 1851 and 1862. A political incident in Switzerland brought him, indirectly, a little fame. The principality of Neuchâtel had been under Prussian domination for more than a hundred years when it joined the Swiss Confederation in 1848. Nine years later, in 1857, the King of Prussia tried to re-assert his rights. This caused great alarm throughout the country and Switzerland mobilized. Amiel, who wrote verse with ease, but without great talent, felt moved to write a patriotic hymn (with music), and it was an immediate success. It figures to this day in the song books of the Swiss Primary Schools, under the name *Roulez, Tambours*. When Amiel published the piece in one of his collections of poems, he called it *La Guerre sacrée*. Nothing is more incongruous than to see this peaceful citizen, a philosopher who had numerous friends in Germany, and who himself had never done any military service for reasons of health, exhort his compatriots to take up arms and "mow down" the enemy. He often commented, in the *Journal,* on the fact that he had different egos. The patriotic ego was one which did not suit him well.

For a long time, he lived in the same large house as his sister Fanny, who had married a clergyman, and took his meals with them. The couple came to resent this obligation and Amiel reluctantly moved out or, as he says, "emigrated". He noted, with his usual frankness : "I cannot hide from myself the fact that I am beginning a completely new period in my life, when I shall have to stand entirely on my feet." He was forty-eight.

His health, which had never been very strong, began to decline in 1879. He died of bronchitis on May 11, 1881, after a long illness which he bore courageously.

The Journal

Amiel began his *Journal* sporadically when he was eighteen, in 1839. But the *Journal* proper begins on December 16, 1847 and ends on April 29, 1881, thirteen days before his death. During these thirty-four years Amiel made regular entries, sometimes several entries in one single day, as the *Journal* began to be more and more the confidant of his perplexities.

The total comes to 174 Cahiers which Amiel grouped into 13 cardboard portfolios tied up with black tape. Each Cahier bears the extreme dates accurately recorded, and often some quotations which have the purpose of serving as exhortations for the period to come. So much care seems to point to a desire for publication. But Amiel felt unequal to the task. He practically never re-opened a Cahier, except when he wanted to read some passages from a recent one to one of his women friends. "This enormous jumble is of no use to anybody, not even to its owner" he wrote on April 22, 1876. In his will he suggested a posthumous publication of his various works in six volumes, three of which should be devoted to extracts from the *Journal*. The MS of the *Journal* he bequeathed to Fanny Mercier, the "pauvre petite calviniste" of whose devotion he was sure. During the following year, she spent night after night reading the never-ending manuscript. One cannot but be moved by the thought of this virtuous lady of forty-five who had worshipped Amiel "as a master and a guide" and who now discovered his failings, his sentimental attachments and his sexual problems. But she persevered, read the *Journal* to the end, copied by hand a number of extracts, and sent them through an intermediary

(Bernard Bouvier, then only a student) to the famous critic Edmond Scherer in Paris. He had lived in Geneva in years past, Amiel had admired him, and Fanny Mercier thought that he was the only man whose authority would "launch" the book. At first Scherer did not even want to cast an eye on the extracts : "I have known Amiel : he never succeeded in anything he did." One thinks of André Gide, thirty years later, refusing the manuscript of Proust's *Du côté de chez Swann* for the *Nouvelle Revue Française*. But Bouvier insisted, Scherer read the extracts and wrote to Fanny the next day : "Send me as much as you can from the *Journal*." Thus began a friendly collaboration between the modest teacher and the acknowledged critic. It is pleasant to think that without Fanny's efforts Tolstoy would never have known the *Journal*, which he was to declare to be his "livre de chevet". But from a purely literary point of view her collaboration was not entirely beneficial. She chose only the noble passages and suppressed the rest. She even corrected the style where she thought it too familiar. Bouvier quotes, in his Introduction, some amusing amendments : "J'ai rêvassé jusqu'à m'endormir" became "J'ai rêvé la tête dans mes mains"[1] and "J'écris en manches à côté de ma fenêtre ouverte"[2] was simply omitted, as too little decorous for a professor.

There is no doubt that for Amiel the *Journal* is a mode of life. From time to time he pauses and asks himself of what benefit it is. And he answers : "It is my dialogue, my society, my companion, my confidant. It is also my consolation, my memory, my victim, my echo, the repository of my experience, my psychological itinerary, my protection against intellectual rust, almost the only useful thing that I can leave behind" (September 20, 1864).

This poses the question of the value of the *Journal* for us, its readers. It lies in its author's frankness and deep psychological insight, which take us through an astonishing voyage of discovery.

First, it offers us the rare spectacle of a man who has the heroic courage to show himself as he is. The *Journal* is, among other things, a scrupulous *Amiel par lui-même*, to use the felicitous title of the series of self-portraits initiated in recent years by a French publisher (Les Editions du Seuil, Paris). But the portrait is not concise : it is endlessly re-drawn and completed. And it is not flattering : more often than not, it is a self-accusation—perhaps the result of a Calvinistic upbringing.

"My friends—those of the old guard—are, I'm afraid, disappointed with me. They feel that I do not do anything, that I deceive their expectations. I, too, am dissatisfied. What would make me inwardly proud appears to me inaccessible, and I fall back on little nothings, trifles and distractions. I have as little hope, energy, faith and determination as ever, yet I read, I speak, I teach, I write. But it is as a sleep-walker" (September 20, 1866).

"What a lot of time wasted, good God! since the end of June, say, this last year, these two years, five years! I do nothing but coming and going, wandering, planning, postponing, daydreaming, tinkering, idling, without any precise aim, any certain hope, any clear idea. Listlessness, restlessness, instability, discouragement; that's the story of all my life" (November 12, 1869).

"What a singular fellow I am! I abhor governing my life, having a will. Acting is a torture. I love neither dependence nor freedom. I know not how to hope or to decide. I would like to be dispensed from being, for I do not fit in with the world. I do not believe in happiness, I expect nothing from the future. I have neither compass nor lighthouse, nor haven, nor aim. I do not know what I am, what I owe, what I am still capable of. Loving, thinking would be the wish of my nature, and I must act, which I execrate!" (July 3, 1874).

Amiel is particularly candid in the analysis of his amorous comportment. He does not show himself at his best, he is timorous, undecided, selfish, slightly comic. But he tells the truth. He prefigures Proust, who, in his portrait of Marcel, displays the same ruthless lucidity, and appears equally bizarre.

In one passage, Amiel asks himself whether he should not have chosen psychology as his profession (August 20, 1860). And indeed, had he lived today, one could well imagine him being deeply interested in the discoveries of modern psychology. He divined the immense power of the unconscious :

"For me, it is evident that the nocturnal side of consciousness, the occult part of the psyche, the mystic life of the soul is as certainly real as the other. The origins and the keys are there. Everything comes out of the darkness, the unknown, the mystery. The difficulty is to penetrate into these divine shades with the lamp of science, not with the will o' the wisp of imagination. To introduce some method into this semi-madness,

that is the point. It is easier to explore the bottom of the ocean"
(January 3, 1871).

He also thought a great deal about dreams, "the inner cross-
roads where all the agitations of life reverberate", and suggested
a classification of them into dreams of the body, of the heart, of
the soul and of the mind (September 3, 1880).

Above all, he excels in observing some strange phenomena in
his own psyche and expressing them in the most vivid way. This
is how he describes the lack of unity and cohesion in his psyche
which results in his having not one ego, but many :

"I am a changeable, fluctuating, dispersed being; I have infinite
trouble in keeping my molecules together, I am continually
escaping from myself, in spite of my daily meditations and my
Journal ... It is clear that I am many, not one. My name is
Legion, Proteus, Anarchy" (November 12, 1866).

Particularly in the presence of others, he is able momentarily to
lose his own identity and to absorb theirs through sympathetic
intuition :

"When I think of the many and diverse intuitions I have had
since my adolescence, it seems to me that I have lived dozens,
almost hundreds of lives. I have been mother, child, girl, mathe-
matician, musician, monk . . . In these states of universal
sympathy I have even been animal and plant" (March 8, 1868).

Sometimes, he has a rare spiritual experience, akin to those
which poets and mystics have described : divested of his ego,
depersonalized, he enters into communion with the infinite, whose
secrets he understands, and his spirit, in ecstasy, roams the celestial
plains. Here is a remarkable passage : Amiel, whose poetic
language in verse is often so stiff, invents a marvellously fluid
prose to express these reveries :

—Ne retrouverai-je pas quelques-unes de ces rêveries prodigieu-
ses, comme j'en ai eu quelquefois : à l'aube, un jour de mon
adolescence, assis dans les ruines du château de Faucigny; sous le
soleil de midi, une fois dans la montagne, au-dessus de Lavey,
couché au pied d'un arbre et visité par trois papillons; une nuit
sur la grève sablonneuse de la mer du Nord, le dos sur la plage
et le regard errant dans la voie lactée;—de ces rêveries
grandioses, immortelles, cosmogoniques où l'on porte le monde

dans son sein, où l'on possède l'infini? Moments divins, heures d'extase où la pensée vole de monde en monde, pénètre la grande énigme, respire large, tranquille, profonde comme la respiration diurne de l'Océan, sereine et sans limites comme le firmament bleu; visites de la muse Uranie, qui trace autour du front de ceux qu'elle aime le nimbe phosphorescent de la puissance contemplative, et qui verse dans leur coeur l'ivresse tranquille du génie, sinon son autorité, instants d'intuition irrésistible où l'on se sent grand comme l'univers et calme comme un Dieu!—Des sphères célestes jusqu'à la mousse ou au coquillage sur lequel je reposais, la création entière m'était soumise, vivait en moi, et accomplissait son oeuvre éternelle avec la régularité du Destin et l'ardeur passionnée de l'amour. Quelles heures, quels souvenirs! Les débris qui m'en restent suffisent à me remplir de respect et d'enthousiasme, comme des visites du Saint-Esprit. Et retomber de ces cimes aux horizons sans bornes, dans les ornières bourbeuses de la trivialité! Quelle chute! Pauvre Moïse! tu vis aussi onduler dans le lointain les coteaux ravissants de la Terre promise, et tu dus étendre tes os fatigués dans une fosse creusée au désert.—Lequel de nous n'a sa Terre promise, son jour d'extase et sa fin dans l'exil? Que la vie réelle est donc une pâle contrefaçon de la vie entrevue, et combien ces éclairs flamboyants de notre jeunesse prophétique rendent plus terne le crépuscule de notre maussade et monotone virilité! (April 28, 1852).[3]

And here is another contemplation, more reminiscent of Eastern philosophies :

—Je ne trouve aucune voix pour ce que j'éprouve . . . Un recueillement profond se fait en moi, j'entends battre mon coeur et passer ma vie. Il me semble que je suis devenu une statue sur les bords du fleuve du temps, que j'assiste à quelque mystère d'où je vais sortir vieux ou sans âge. Je me sens anonyme, impersonnel, l'oeil fixe comme un mort, l'esprit vague et universel comme le néant ou l'absolu : je suis en suspens, je suis comme n'étant pas. Dans ces moments, il me semble que ma conscience se retire dans son éternité . . . Cet état est contemplation et non stupeur; il n'est ni douloureux, ni joyeux, ni triste; il est en dehors de tout sentiment spécial comme de toute pensée finie. Il est la conscience de l'être et la conscience de l'omnipossibilité latente au fond de cet être. C'est la sensation de l'infini spirituel (August 31, 1856).[4]

But such heightened moments, like Proust's privileged moments, are rare. More often, what presents itself is not a transcendental vision, but an earthly landscape. Amiel responded to the beauty of landscapes, but he saw in them something more than their own beauty : the reflection of the beholder's soul : "Un paysage est un état de l'âme", he wrote (October 31, 1852), and this thought, which would have delighted Baudelaire, is so much quoted that it is often the only Amiel text which a person may know!

Landscapes are evoked by Amiel in a minor key and with a delicate feeling for the "correspondences" between Nature and man :

Aix-les-Bains—Un clair de lune étrange, recueilli, par une brise fraîche et un ciel traversé de nuages, rend à cette heure notre terrasse charmante. Ces rayons doux et pâles laissent tomber du zénith une paix résignée qui pénètre. C'est la joie calme, le sourire pensif de l'expérience, avec une certaine verdeur stoïque. Les étoiles brillent, les feuillages frémissent sous des reflets argentés; pas un bruit de vie dans la campagne, de larges ombres s'engouffrent sous les allées et au tournant des escaliers. Tout est mystérieux, furtif et solennel.

Heure nocturne, heure de silence et de solitude, tu as de la grâce et de la mélancolie, tu attendris et tu consoles; tu nous parles de tout ce qui n'est plus et de tout ce qui doit mourir, mais tu nous dis : Courage! et tu nous promets le repos (September 7, 1851).[5]

But Amiel is not primarily an artist : he is a philosopher and moralist. He often judges books, for example, more from an ethical than a purely aesthetic point of view. Thus, between Balzac and George Sand, he prefers the latter :
                                                    ˙

"Read *Eugénie Grandet* (Balzac). The first impression, after Sand, is disagreeable. It is, stylistically, an anti-climax. One passes from music and poetry to the acid and noisy prose of reality. Balzac is not the one who will keep you in the 'divine sentiment of immortal harmony' of which George Sand writes in *La Mare au Diable*. Balzac writes of woman with enthusiasm and of true love with sensitiveness, but his style always shows some crudity, lacks delicacy, nobility and taste. It does not show beauty and does not make us feel it. It magnifies, analyses and only exaggerates reality. Balzac has a strong relief, enormous creative energy, a violent and striking expression, but little ideal and no peace. With him, temperament dominates soul and conscience. I infinitely prefer George Sand. She respects life, she climbs the high summits : eloquence, contemplation, passion. She consoles, she reassures, she transports and uplifts. Balzac is a talent, George Sand a soul" (July 25, 1861).

As he grows older, his thoughts turn to the eternal problems of life and annihilation, religion and religions. On religion, his opinions have mellowed. Brought up as a rigidly traditional Christian, he comes to accept, partly under the influence of Renan's writings, that Christianity was not founded suddenly and at a single time, but is the confluence of many spiritual currents whose origin is elsewhere, in Asia and Europe, particularly Platonism. Neither its doctrine nor its ethics are new :

"The conversion of ecclesiastical Christianity into historical Christianity is the work of biblical science.

"The conversion of Christianity from the historical to the psychological region is the wish of our time. Comparative history of religions must give Christianity its proper place. Then it will be necessary to distinguish between the religion professed by Jesus and the religion which took Jesus as its object.

"Perhaps, then, the supernatural will give way to the extra-ordinary, and men of genius will be regarded as the messengers of the historical God and as the providential revealers by whom God moves the human mass. What will be abandoned, then, is not the admirable, only the arbitrary, accidental and miraculous" (January 27, 1869).

His liberality extends to nationalities. He, who had persistently criticized the French, wants to do away with the political concept of nations :

"It seems to me that I am no longer very keen on any nation-ality or church; from year to year critical impartiality increases with me, and it is the type of man who is well-rounded, complete, harmonious, superior, true, who is my measure in judging all those caricatures who claim the privilege of being types. I feel neither French nor English, nor Russian, nor Swiss, nor Genevan, nor European, nor Calvanist nor Protestant, I feel a man, and sympathetic to all mankind. I depend only on ideal. The prejudices of religion, language, nationality, of social class, party, coterie do not hold me imprisoned : I judge them, they are inferior to me and indifferent to me" (January 3, 1876).

If, turning away from the philosopher and moralist, we consider Amiel as a writer, we come up against this question : Is Amiel a Swiss writer with marked Swiss characteristics, or a French writer who happens to have been born in Geneva, as Rousseau before him? I incline towards the second of these views. Switzerland is present in Amiel's work as an ever-inspiring landscape, but culturally, his roots are in France. In spite of his years of study in Germany, he is steeped in French culture, and impatient with German heaviness : "O clarity, lucidity, brevity! Diderot, Voltaire, and even Galiani! A short article by Sainte-Beuve, Scherer, Renan gives one more joy and more food for thought than a thousand of those German pages filled up to the margins and bearing traces of work, not result. The Germans pile up the faggots for the fire, the Frenchmen bring the sparks" (April 9, 1868).

Amiel's own style is always lucid, but except in the heightened passages of reverie or other lyrical passages, seldom personal or distinctive. It is an every day diarist's style, not a writer's style. Amiel's aim is exact analysis and quick notation. He is not really interested in the *art* of writing, and not sufficiently an artist to have a spontaneously striking style.

Is Amiel an "écrivain de toujours"—a writer for all times? Devoted admirers and scholars have, so far, brought out fragments of his *Journal* by stages. Will this process continue? Albert Thibaudet, writing a few years after the first centenary in 1921, anticipated a steady flow of new publications right up to the second centenary in 2021. (A. Thibaudet, *Intérieurs*, p. 194.) I am more sceptical. It is true, as Montaigne said, that every man bears in himself the entire human condition. But there are writers with whom the reader can identify himself more readily than with Amiel. He fascinates as a singular case, but his lack of determination, his incapacity for action are not likely to endear him to a generation who has lived through the Second World War and its sequels and encountered the austere intellectual disciplines of Sartre and Camus.

To reflective readers, however, matured by a long experience of life, Amiel will appear less wanting. "Chacun vit comme il peut", everyone lives as best he can in the inimical circumstances given to him. Amiel lived, as he said, in "fundamental disharmony" with the world around him (July 24, 1876). But he was too lucid to accuse the world only : he laid bare his own deficiencies with utter candour. If he lacked the courage for living, he possessed the courage for self-knowledge in the highest degree. And the vast scope

of his mind, the infinite richness of his *Journal*, the depth and bold-
ness of his psychological explorations, his own unusual personality
will continue to secure him a limited, but steady number of thought-
ful, discerning, or merely curious readers.

TRANSLATIONS

1. *I mused until I fell asleep* became: *I mused with my head in my
hands.*

2. I am writing in my shirt-sleeves near my open window.

3. Shall I not experience again some of those prodigious reveries that
I sometimes used to have: at dawn, one day in my adolescence, seated
in the ruins of the Château of Faucigny; under the noonday sun, once
in the mountains above Lavey, lying at the foot of a tree and visited by
three butterflies; one night on a sandy shore on the North Sea, lying on
the beach, my gaze travelling over the Milky Way—those grandiose,
immortal, cosmogonic reveries in which one carries the whole world in
one's breast, reaches the stars and possesses the infinite? Divine moments,
hours of ecstasy when thought flies from world to world, fathoms the
great enigma, breathes deeply and quietly, deep as the daily rise and
fall of the ocean, serene and boundless as the blue firmament; visits from
the Muse, Urania, who draws the phosphorescent halo of contemplative
power round the brows of those she loves, who pours into their hearts
the calm intoxication of genius, if not its authority, moments of irresist-
ible intuition, when one feels as vast as the universe and as calm as a
God! From the celestial spheres down to the moss or shells on which I
lay, all creation was under my sway, lived in me and accomplished its
eternal task with the regularity of Fate and the passionate ardour of
love. What hours, what memories! What is left to me of them is enough
to fill me with respect and enthusiasm, like visits from the Holy Ghost.
And to fall from these heights with limitless horizons into the muddy
ruts of triviality! What a fall! Poor Moses! You too saw in the distance
the rolling hills of the Promised Land, and you had to lay your weary
bones in a grave dug in the desert. Who among us has not his Promised
Land, his day of ecstasy and his end in exile? What a poor counterpart
of the life glimpsed at is real life! And how much more dreary those
fiery flashes of our prophetic youth make the twilight of our gloomy
and monotonous virility! (April, 28, 1852).

4. I find no voice for that which I am experiencing . . . A deep quiet
invades me; I hear my heart beating and my life slipping by. It seems to
me that I have become a statue on the banks of the river of time, that I
am witnessing some mystery from which I shall return old or ageless. I
feel myself anonymous, gazing like a dead man, my mind vague and

..

universal, like nothingness or the absolute: I am in suspense, I am as if I were not. In these moments, it seems to me that consciousness withdraws into its eternity . . . This state is one of contemplation, not stupor: it is not painful, nor joyful, nor sad. It is beyond all special feeling and all finite thought. It is the consciousness of being and the consciousness of the omnipossibility latent in this being. It is the sensation of spiritual infinite (August 31, 1856).

5. *Aix-les-Bains.*—A strange, calm moonlight, with a fresh breeze and a sky crossed by clouds, makes our balcony enchanting at this hour. These soft pale rays let fall from the heights a resigned, penetrating peace. It is calm joy, the pensive smile of experience with a certain stoical vigour. The stars shine, the leaves rustle in the silvery beams, no sound of life in the countryside; broad shadows sweep along the garden-paths and around the stone steps. All is mysterious, furtive and solemn.

Hour of night, hour of silence and solitude, you have grace and melancholy, you soften and console; you speak to us of all that is no more and of all that must die, but you say to us: Courage! and you promise us repose (September 7, 1851).

BIBLIOGRAPHY

Editions of the Journal intime
Fragments d'un Journal intime, précédés d'une étude par Edmond Scherer, 2 vols., Georg, Genève, 1883-4.
Fragments d'un Journal intime, précédés d'une étude par Bernard Bouvier, 3 vols., Georg, Genève, 1922.
Philine: Fragments inédits du Journal intime publiés par Bernard Bouvier, introduction par Edmond Jaloux, J. Schiffrin, Paris, 1927.
Journal intime, Introduction et notes de Léon Bopp, 3 vols., Pierre Cailler, Genève, 1948, 1953, 1958.
Journal intime de l'année 1866. Texte intégral publié avec une introduction et des notes par Léon Bopp, Gallimard, Paris 1959.
Journal intime. L'année 1857. Editée et présentée par Georges Poulet, Union générale d'éditions, Paris, 1965.

Letters

H.-F. Amiel, *La jeunesse d'Henri-Frédéric Amiel*: Lettres à sa famille, ses amis, ses amies, pour servir d'introduction au *Journal intime.* Publiées, avec une préface et des notes, par Bernard Bouvier, Delamain et Boutelleau, Paris, 1935.

Commentaries

Léon Bopp, *H.-F. Amiel: essai sur sa pensée et son caractère.* Alcan, Paris, 1926. Nouvelle éd. 1931.

Paul Bourget, *Nouveaux essais de psychologie contemporaine,* Paris, 1886.

Auguste Bouvier, *La religion de Henri-Frédéric Amiel.* Fischbacher, Paris, et Cherbuliez, Genève, 1893.

Elme-Marie Caro, *Mélanges et portraits,* T.2. "La maladie de l'idéal ... les dernières années d'un rêveur". Hachette, Paris, 1886.

Bernard Halda, *Amiel et les femmes.* E. Vitte, Lyon, 1963.

Gregorio Marañon, *Amiel. Une étude sur la timidité,* trad. de l'espagnol par Louis Parrot. Gallimard, Paris, 1938.

Gaston Monteil, *La religion d'Amiel.* Dujarric, Paris, 1907.

Albert Thibaudet, *Intérieurs: Baudelaire, Fromentin, Amiel.* Plon-Nourrit, Paris, 1924.

Albert Thibaudet, *Amiel, ou la part du rêve.* Hachette, Paris, 1929.

English Translations and Commentaries

H. F. Amiel, *Journal intime,* transl. with an introduction and notes by Mrs. Humphry Ward, London and New York, 1890. This is a translation of the Scherer edition.

H. F. Amiel, *The Private Journal,* transl. by Van Wyck Brooks and Charles Van Wyck Brooks. Introd. by Bernard Bouvier, New York, 1935.

H. F. Amiel, *Philine,* unpublished fragments from the Journal of H. F. Amiel, transl. from the French by Van Wyck Brooks. Constable, London, 1931.

Van Wyck Brooks, *The Malady of the ideal: Obermann, Maurice de Guérin and Amiel.* A. C. Fifield, London, 1913.

Walter Pater, *Essays from the Guardian,* T.2, 1910. "Amiel's Journal intime".

Charles Ferdinand Ramuz and the Way of the Anti-Poet

Charles Ferdinand Ramuz and the Way of the Anti-Poet

by FERNAND AUBERJONOIS

I OFTEN wonder when and in what circumstances the Swiss writer C.-F. Ramuz will establish a firm *rapport* with the English-speaking world. The question remains largely un-answered. He died too early to discover the American cultural elite. English classicism had not left too much of a mark on him.

When death came, in a Lausanne clinic, in 1947, C.-F. Ramuz was sixty-nine. He had enjoyed only a dozen years of genuine, popular recognition in his own land. Some twenty-two novels, five books of poems, twenty essays and numerous articles had been printed. But he had not yet become the national figure the Swiss honour and revere today.

Paris consecrated his talent at a relatively early stage of the author's development. In the eyes of his French admirers, how-ever, he was above all a poet of the *terroir,* soul brother of Henri Pourrat or Jean Giono, a one-dimensional man admired, perhaps, for the wrong reasons.

It would have been difficult if not impossible for Ramuz him-self to cross the threshold of languages into territory peopled by Englishmen or Americans. He did not speak or read English. The America he encountered accidentally, through travellers, was not yet recognizable to him in terms of his own cultural definitions.

Black America was giving Igor Stravinsky a new musical voca-bulary but Ramuz, his collaborator, was more intrigued than attracted.

C.-F. Ramuz was suspicious of nuclear America and of the ocean between the two worlds, new and old. He told me so on my last visit to him, as he lay on his hospital bed, shortly after the operation which he did not survive. There was no convincing him of the extraordinary poetic catalyst available to European sensitivity in America.

And I can hear him say : "You know, it is still in our old

Europe, the one you were born in, that man will do his best work if allowed to do so."

So far, only six Ramuz novels have been translated into English, four of them in Britain, two in the United States. The rest of his work is unexplored and rich in surprises. I wonder if he wasn't saying gravely what St. Exupéry was singing through the lips of the Little Prince. The two minds were on parallel courses, one in semi-darkness, the other in a rainbow.

To know Ramuz you have to learn something of the land and of the society that shaped him. And you have to mention a few people who, lonely like himself, stimulated one another to a remarkable state of creativeness and originality for a short decade or two in the first half of the twentieth century.

The Romand Environment

First the land where he spent all but ten years of his life. The Rhône River, the deep valley and the lake through which it flows South towards the sun, the fifes and the tambourines, these are the frontiers and links separating and binding the French-Swiss and the French. Ramuz considered himself a *Rhodanien*. Like most French-Swiss with strong roots in their native soil he wished to be both there and far away. In his case the call of exotic lands was resisted.

From early childhood he chose to identify with Romandie, a world of beauty, but not always generous to poets and painters.

"Poetry," C.-F. Ramuz has written, "can only be fashioned out of anti-poetic materials." The inhabitants of an area endowed with spectacular scenic grandeur are tempted to seek evasion in contemplation. Unlike most of them, Ramuz fought the temptation. For he knew too well that when Nature competes with the artist, the latter's instinctive reaction is to avoid the confrontation and to let Nature speak for him.

It was natural, therefore, that Ramuz, like his contemporary the painter René Auberjonois, should favour in his environment whatever others found dour, severe, forbidding, difficult. All other paths could have led to the facile.

The urban middle class of "Romandie" of which Ramuz was a product presented little of interest and, in turn, ignored him for some years. His style was brought into derision. Now the writer has been canonized.

But the farmer and the mountain villager spoke the language he wished to use as an artist. A language where asperities and tenderness blend. From the land he drew his inspiration, avoiding the quaint and the picturesque. He wrote as a painter paints. From this search for a *genre* came some of his most poignant parables.

The Romand is no simple animal. He has a biblical turn of mind, a tendency to judge others as severely as he judges himself, a way of speaking which reveals his need to keep all options open, a language deformed or reshaped by the erosion of time and of obsolete dialects. Afraid of giving, he may, all of a sudden, decide to squander. Rooted to his land he dies on it, often too young, fighting it, taking his own life when despair strikes.

His is a harmonious but not always cheerful community. Sentiment overshadows sensitivity. But man loves his work, his fields, his little acre, his one big river, his vineyards terraced after the fashion of Japan's hillside farms.

In the Valais the very geography of Switzerland creates unholy alliances and antagonisms. Life in the hamlets which attracted C.-F. Ramuz was brutally demanding. Mountains rise so as to make the sun's swift passage across the narrow sky as uncomfortable as possible. Here again, in places and in peoples, you find the harshness, the mythical nakedness poets and painters look for.

The plateau lying between Lake Geneva and the Jura mountains was Ramuz' cradle. Most of the characters in his novels come from there. It was—still is—mostly farmland. The truly representative Vaudois is connected with agriculture in some way or other. The lake moulds the moods of the *riverains*; but the seasons dictate the tempo of life. This is still, in many respects, Puritan country, sectarian too. There is a kinship with New England. Beyond the rolling hills the Jura frowns like a long, black eyebrow. And one morning a hand has laid upon it a thin, sharp blade of snow : one more sword of Damocles for the Romands.

Much has changed in the farms since Ramuz, since Stravinsky's *Soldier's Tale* whose improbable setting was the well-ploughed *Gros de Vaud* where a Russian Satan was let loose (accidentally or not) under the walnut trees and among slow-tolling cowbells.

But the occupants of these farms have remained much the same. Their accent doesn't change. Sin is still the single greatest enemy, unless it is venial sin in which case it can be tamed and trained to sleep at the master's heel.

And so it is quite as it should be that *Aline,* the heroine of Ramuz' first novel, lived and died her short and sad life in a Vaudois village where she killed herself rather than raise a fatherless child. His first novel, and, in the opinion of many, his best, because it is fresh, spontaneous, generous and dictated by a deep sense of pity and justice. Poetic effect is achieved with the least effort by anti-poetic means of expression.

At once a minority in Switzerland acclaimed talent and a promise of rare gifts. But a number of critics refused to consider the local idiom as a legitimate tool in the process of artistic creation. And the critics persist for some years, even when the writer, in his thirty-first year, gives them his third novel, *Jean-Luc Persécuté* (1909) which prompts a reviewer to comment :

> "Because I so warmly admire his talent, I would like Mr. C.-F. Ramuz to leave aside for awhile these cases of primitive humanity and devote his penetrating gifts as an observer and painter to human beings closer to us in terms of intellectual complexity and emotional anxiety."

Although Ramuz established himself from the start as a writer who saw through the eyes of a painter, he himself never attempted to draw or paint. But his descriptions are the work of a man for whom colour and shape are essential. The patience and insistence with which he sets a stage, visually, before letting any of his characters speak, has made Ramuz an easy target for satire. But, to him, the total kinship and association between man and Nature (or, conversely, their close combat) require such a treatment. The result is impressionism, writing from extremely accurate notes, writing, one might say, with consistent brush strokes, building up the picture, never neglecting a single relevant observation. At times, progress is painstakingly slow, as is illustrated by this quote from *Aline* :

> They set up the coffin near the bed, then they placed Aline in it with the infant in her arms. She looked as if she had fallen asleep while rocking the child, and he too seemed to be sleeping. They put down the lid to see if it was a good fit, but the child took very little space; all one had to do now was wait for the bearers.
>
> There was a storm that night, the first storm of the year. Silence then a sound like a cart rolling on, and green lightning against the window panes. After a while the clouds burst and tumbled down in the branches. And then the lightning and the thunder faded; the heavy downpour became a soft shower, sprinkling everything everywhere, and the roof gutters sang

under the rainfall. In the morning the wind scattered the clouds; the sky had been lowered upon the lanes shining in blue wash.

Sin, absolution, purity, Golgatha, the wrath of God against man, the peace following a storm. Always Nature is close by, as the Greek choir follows and accompanies tragedy, as the deity hovers behind the tribal sorcerer.

At other times Ramuz takes the reader along in a few giant strides as in the case of *Aimé Pache, peintre vaudois* (1911) rediscovering his *raison d'être*, the land about him :

The voice said "Look"; and then he was able to see at last. Evening strode uphill from the hollows and on the Jura the sun was coming down, nearly touching the mountain tops : it was that time of day when the shadows reach their maximum length. They could be seen lengthening still, from the foot of the trees, a black line with a black ball at the end of it : the trunk and crown : but the broadest and the swiftest shadow of all was that of the mountain, with the sun diving behind it, and darkness spreading like a tide across the vast landscape, all of vales and hills, with a foam of forests topping the hills. Darkness was growing eastward, and the more it grew the lower the sun sank; the shadows came upon Aimé, and it came upon the village, and then the sun was no more. Whereupon a new peace stretched over the world, a coolness in the air, a surrender, an overwhelming peace : and Aimé could feel that peace flow into him.

C.-F. Ramuz and Paris

As one of Ramuz' most conscientious analysts, Prof. Gilbert Guisan, observes in a book on Ramuz the poet, the Swiss writer was close to the land and the good earth, yet he lived in a city, Lausanne, where he was born in 1878, and it was normal that another, much bigger city, should attract him during his formative years, from 1902 to 1914 : "I sought refuge among ten beautiful centuries of history and civilization."

In *Paris, Notes d'un Vaudois* (1938), Ramuz explains how a Swiss student determined to write had to go to Paris to find his cultural centre of gravity. Besides, "when the young Vaudois in question attended school, most of his textbooks came from Paris. He was learning *good* French, meaning literary French."

The pilgrimage to Paris was as important to the Swiss intellectual as the *Grand Tour* to the Englishman. In Ramuz' case, the pilgrim did at once, resolutely, consciously adopt solitude as a constant companion. As he wrote in his *Journal* (1941) : "There is within me a weight which causes me to sink more and more into solitude. I have never sought solitude. It has come to me very early. I gave in without thinking, in spite of myself, and I surrender more easily each day, for such is my fate."

Was Ramuz ever young? A drawing dated 1914 shows him very much as he looked for the next thirty years with his wing of heavy hair brushed diagonally across a wrinkled forehead, his deeply lined face, his strong nose and thick moustache. The eyes were the same, the eyes of a kindly hypnotist. A curious mask, containing intensity and warmth as a dam contains water.

Paris, for Ramuz, didn't mean freedom. It was foreign, too big, too noisy even in the days of horse-drawn vehicles. His very first visit in 1901 was brief; the excuse : research for a Doctor's degree (never finished) prior to embarking upon a teacher's career (never begun) : "Some go to Paris to learn, others go to Paris to absorb Paris."

Then a second try—very soon afterwards—twelve years in the course of which C.-F. Ramuz "absorbed" the best the capital had to offer. Much later he would write in his book-length essay *René Auberjonois* :

> You led a solitary life, Auberjonois, and so did I, but not a lonely one, nor did I. Everywhere in Paris are those we love. Often at first we must look for them elsewhere than in our daily life—I mean in museums and in books; but what a wealth of discoveries and how alive they remain, these friends, or how alive they soon become . . . there is no longer a contradiction between the street and the libraries . . . Paris is "contemporary". Paris gathers along its streets houses of different ages; and there they live in good harmony, XVIIth and XVIIIth Centuries side by side, no transition between the street of the Revolutionary era and the Second Empire Boulevard. In the same way Poussin and Chardin are found living, breathing freely in the form of a beautiful colonnade, a noble setting of trees or, singly, the face of a child.

But it was not about Paris that the young Vaudois was writing. Every one of his books during that period deals with a village, a mountain, a lake—things Swiss, etched in his memory all the deeper since distance has, somehow, made them seem more vivid and necessary.

The Mountain

A lowlander, C.-F. Ramuz climbed heights because they were there—the classical explanation of the mountaineer's fanaticism—but he stopped at the tree line, at the last village. His understanding of mountain folks began during visits to the large hamlet of Lens, in the Valais, a spot protected from progress by poor communications.

On these summer holidays away from Paris, Ramuz becomes familiar with the gnarled chalets blackened by the years and with the villagers, at first undecipherable, later friendly. Here he collects material for *Jean-Luc Persécuté, Le Règne de l'Esprit Malin* (1917), *La Grande Peur dans la Montagne* (1926), *Derborence* (1934).

Rugged, primitive Catholicism draws the Protestant writer like a magnet. The Valais, more than Vaud, is a world of sharp contrasts, violent and warm, silent and passionate, Alpine and Mediterranean. And between these mountains flows the Rhône: "Everything is ageless here, and all is new because nothing is spoiled and something has yet to be said."

Not far from Lens, nearer the Italian border, another village captures another poet now buried there, in Rarogne: Rainer Maria Rilke. At different times of their very separate lives they worked in the same room of the medieval tower, Le Muzot, near Sierre, but they didn't meet.

Those who accuse Ramuz of having used the Valais as a stage prop and backdrop to characters who never quite come to life, forget that the people who live in the forbidding environment of the last inhabited acres remain for ever displaced persons, easily shaken in their simple beliefs, superstitious, slow moving, ready to stumble or soar. Man is dwarfed by Nature and acts accordingly. And the dwarf turns into a giant at a moment's notice.

Ramuz also knew, as do all who understand mountains, how few painters succeed in reproducing what stares them in the face, how they succumb to the lure of the *pittoresque,* or else create works of stark immobility.

As a geology student at university, I often discussed with C.-F. Ramuz the problems arising out of the need to draw what is there in the complex architecture of a rock formation. It pleased him no end to hear that the best results were obtained by the scrupulous geological draughtsman, without a thought to artistic effect. Then the outcome was art. But any oversimplification by the sentimentalist armed with a brush turned an alp into a bad imitation of itself.

Among his greatest and fondest admirers, Ramuz counted an exceedingly intelligent, fiercely cross-eyed Professor of Paleontology, Elie Gagnebin, selected by Stravinsky to play the part of the Narrator in *L'Histoire du Soldat* at its first and only performance of the year 1918. Geologists, to Ramuz, were people who held keys he needed in order to understand what this earth is about. He always asked questions about fundamentals. Searching questions. As a metaphysician first, as a poet sometimes.

With the poet, Ramuz feigned amusement at such miracles as fossils. One year Jean Cocteau, short of breath and stimulants, was hoisted to the high reaches of a Swiss Alp and enthused at the sight of elegant ammonites in perfect state of preservation. He never doubted Ramuz' word when told: "these are the animals who drivelled the mountains".

There is much above the tree-line of the world that is inanimate yet not insensate. In *Questions* (1935) Ramuz replied to critics: "I have been accused of loving what is inert, but, precisely, I like objects that live. For a living being nothing is ever deprived of life."

This takes us back, of course, to the theme of poetic work born of anti-poetry. We follow Ramuz the word painter into the Blakist world of rockfalls, into the twilight of glaciers, we share his Apocalyptic vision of man alone before his God. But, for safety's sake, the reader must first rope himself to the nearest climber.

The Native's Return

In 1914 the war disperses the small group of Swiss writers and painters living in Paris. Ramuz settles in an apartment on Lake Geneva, between Lausanne and Vevey. The house is wedged against the Paris-Milan railroad line, at the foot of the wine-bearing hills of Lavaux.

He, with others, starts the *Cahiers Vaudois,* a collection of large-size paperbacks, beautifully printed, where the best literary output of French-Swiss writers found its way. The *Cahiers* were a fine showcase and offered contributors an opportunity to remain independent from the Paris coteries.

The most significant works of C.-F. Ramuz during the First World War were *La Règne de l'Esprit Malin, La Guérison des Maladies* (1917) *and Les Signes Parmi Nous* (1919).

The Reign of the Evil One has been translated into English. Perhaps it shouldn't have. It is not translatable. And yet many regard it as the author's masterpiece. It is the story of the village cobbler whose malefic influence on the community never ceases to grow until a child breaks the spell. The cobbler is Satan. Evil doesn't triumph but it corrupts and harms those who come within reach.

In *La Guérison des Maladies* the struggle is between a woman with the gift of healing and the ever-spreading ailments attacking the population of a peaceful provincial town. The confrontation takes place in an unlikely setting, the sort of place tourists take snapshots of from the deck of the lake steamer, enviously remarking that this is the world's safest retreat because "It Can't Happen Here". Ramuz turns a smiling market place into the arena for the big fight between Good and Evil. Unlike many of his compatriots he doesn't allow beauty to coddle him and put him to sleep. He gives it a part in the tragedy—not *the* main part.

Finally, in *Les Signes Parmi Nous,* Ramuz again succeeds in blending myth, banality and poetry to achieve mystery.

But even more mysterious than this alchemy is Igor Stravinsky's arrival in the lakeside province of Vaud. He went there because, in 1915, there was no other place to go, and for health reasons. He settled first near Montreux, then in Morges. Like the cobbler in *The Reign* or the healer in *La Guérison* he was about to change the order of things. Witnesses of his relatively short stay agree that after his departure his friends were never the same again.

Ernest Ansermet, the conductor who introduced Stravinsky to his first audiences outside Russia, brought the young composer to Ramuz' apartment.

"We became friends," Ramuz wrote, "through the good offices of objects, of things. I don't remember at all what we talked about. What I do recall vividly is this complete and immediate agreement on the importance of bread and wine. Thus I saw right away, Stravinsky, that like myself, you liked bread when bread was good, and wine when wine was good, bread and wine together, one meant for the other." (*Souvenirs Sur Igor Stravinsky (1929)*).

In those days, even in wartime, Swiss bakers still made this grey, tightly knit "housewife's bread", keeping the white for Sunday. As for the wine, in Romandie, it has remained the same— light, dry, playful as soon as a ray of sun appears. It is still served as it was then, in straight, unadorned carafes with a thin neck that makes pouring easy.

Igor Stravinsky had come to Switzerland with a big family and very limited funds. His new friends in Geneva and Lausanne were poor too. Poverty was one of the factors in the decision to create a mini-opera to be performed on a midget mobile stage.

The Soldier's Tale

In 1918 it seemed the war would never end. The Swiss, untouched but engulfed, were not worrying unduly about outlets for writers, composers and painters. To achieve a momentary and modest breakthrough, Ramuz, Stravinsky, Ansermet and Auberjonois conceived a sure way to make money, a low overhead enterprise. Why not write a work for a handful of performers and actors and send it on the road, to villages and towns, as was the custom in the old days? The play needed a minimum of props and instruments. The composer would leave the writer free to do what he wanted, and the painter was to display equal contempt for coordination and planning. From the clash of three very different personalities might result fantasy.

One of my early childhood recollections is an evening or late afternoon reading of *l'Histoire du Soldat,* with Stravinsky piledriving our upright piano on top of which his glass of Scotch was gliding closer and closer to the edge of the precipice. I was seven years old. The room had all but disappeared in clouds of *Caporal Ordinaire*. I lay on a sofa turned against the wall as an improvised playpen or cage. From there I observed the adults at play and fancied myself a deadly tiger.

The *Soldier's Tale* turned out to be a fantastic headache for its creators. It gave them an amazing amount of work. It cost them money. Nothing, it seemed ever worked out right. Ramuz took infinite pains to revive the flagging zeal of the cast which included the charming George and Ludmilla Pitoeff. Ramuz was infinitely precise in his instructions to Auberjonois about masks :

> The more abstract the mask, the stronger the impact. We rehearsed yesterday with a plain, unpainted mask—no details or features. I wonder whether this is not what we need. It looks like a void—truly Satanic.

The generosity of Werner Reinhart, a Winterthur textile tycoon, made it possible for the *première* to be performed in Lausanne in September 1918. It was also a *dernière*. Influenza, then known as Spanish grippe, put a full stop to this effort. The audience never quite understood what was happening on stage. The reviewers went berserk. A chapter closed. But something had happened. This particular section of Switzerland had undergone a profound transformation. The late Paul Budry wrote about the "Russification" of Stravinsky's Vaudois friends :

> Stravinsky talked endlessly, at the top of his voice, chewing bits of food. Wherever he happened to be, others vanished and lost all meaning. He taught his Vaudois comrades this rude but satisfying manner of loud speech, this assertion of authority, the constant interrupting of others, this refusal to listen. He was extremely fond of *pêle-mêle sonore,* and he has filled his music with it.

Stravinsky's stay in Romandie lasted a bare three or four years, but he was influenced by it, for awhile, and those who worked with him bore the indelible imprint. He is said to have been impressed by the heavy breathing of brass bands found in every Swiss village. Friends also note that a chorus at the end of "Noces" came to Stravinsky on a mountain train between Montreux and Château-d'Oex where he sat transfixed, with Ansermet, eavesdropping on a couple of drunken Bernese farmers who, mixing alcohol and lyricism, intoned a frightening duet interrupted by loud hiccups.

Ramuz' testimonial to Stravinsky, in *Souvenirs,* is that "You have freed me of my doubts and scruples; by being yourself, you taught me how to become myself. You showed me how to be spontaneous, what we Romands need above all . . . in a country where the individual is so tempted to pass judgment on himself, to confront himself, thus ceasing to act or even to react."

Stravinsky gone, the period immediately following the war is one of agonizing reappraisal for Ramuz and, to a lesser extent, other members of the Russian Mafia. Naturally C.-F. Ramuz doesn't stop writing. But he senses the limits he himself sets to the symbolic novel. Monotony and repetition threaten. He explores variations on the original theme, not always successfully. He tries the chopped-up approach of movie documentaries, something not unlike John Dos Passos' "camera eye", but it doesn't work out. The language restrictions, the corset of classicism are painfully present. There is a no man's land extending from 1920 to 1929, with the brilliant flash of lightning of *La Grande Peur dans la Montagne* (1926). Other titles : *Présence de la Mort* (1922), *L'Amour du Monde* (1925), *La Beauté sur la Terre* (1927), may well be forgotten by chroniclers. And yet two of these novels were translated (*The Triumph of Death*, George Routledge & Sons, Ltd., London; *Beauty on Earth*, G. P. Putnam's Sons, London) when they hardly deserved the honour. In an interesting study of English-language Ramuziana, Miss Marilyn Yalom commented in *Adam*, an international review of repute, "*Beauty on Earth* . . . could not have won for Ramuz an English audience, as there remains little trace of his original poetic style." It suggests "the atmosphere of a tidy English town, rather than that of Swiss peasant terrain".

Aujourd'hui

The twenty volumes of C.-F. Ramuz' complete works, now found on the library shelves of many a Swiss home, were published by Henri-Louis Mermod who devoted half his life to the arts at a time and in a place where benefactors were scarce. Officialdom paid lip service to culture, the academic world brought its spoonful worth of water to the millwheel, but the man willing to encourage talent with hard cash wasn't around.

But Henri-Louis Mermod, legal adviser and director of an important aluminium firm, became attached to a growing number of Swiss artists who, without him, might never have been published. This is certainly the case of C. A. Cingria, the itinerant genius whose prose is so condensed and crystallized that it should be read through a spectroscope.

Mermod had never had training or experience in publishing, printing, editing. Taste and instinct were his sure guides. His home and his garden in Ouchy—a safe distance from hotels inhabited by the *malades imaginaires* of international café society —became the meeting place of artists, but it was never a *salon*. Quite naturally, Picasso, Gide, Claudel, Giraudoux, Valery found their way to *Fantaisie*.

Among H. L. Mermod's more daring efforts was the founding of a weekly journal printed on gloriously expensive paper, a platform for the most alert minds of Romandie. There soon occurred a shortage of material, but the reason was not necessarily dearth of talent or industry, the élite was small, busy earning a living.

For two years, Ramuz edited *Aujourd'hui* and wrote for it about topics he might otherwise have neglected altogether. In retrospect, his most penetrating essays are those dealing with the future of

US-USSR relations, with the role of man in a technological society, with gold, with the slow decline of peasantry.

Once a week, every Monday, assisted by the poet Gustave Roud, Ramuz put together the periodical; the manuscripts and proofs were spread on the highly polished table of Mermod's board room. *Aujourd'hui* lasted three years (1929–31) and the issues are now collectors' items. It was unpretentious even though its columns were open to "men of letters". That it survived as long as it did is a singular tribute to the tenacity of the publisher and editors. Ramuz himself nearly gave up after three issues. He begged Roud to "devise a *modus vivendi* or let the thing perish . . . for I can no longer manufacture this weekly all by myself".

Aujourd'hui was not a paying proposition. It was money well spent, however. The back numbers constitute a worthwhile record of the preoccupations of thinking men, between two wars, in a country where intellectuals were forever asking questions and receiving few answers.

For these were the days of incomplete communication, before TV round tables, when *conférenciers* held forth in theatres, judged on the basis of style and delivery, by audiences too polite to query and too disciplined to cough. *Aujourd'hui* is the nearest thing to a dialogue in print in the Switzerland of the late twenties.

In his essays about man and the land, C.-F. Ramuz examined the *valeurs paysannes,* spoke of writers with whom he felt deep affinities (Claudel, Pégny, Alain Fournier) because they represented a "green France", not provincial but eternal, mystical. He speaks of man face to face with Nature :

Man working and living under such conditions that he finds himself alone or nearly alone in the furrow, under the sky, Above him the unfolding of vast celestial phenomena, their unpredictable influence on harvests because of flood, draught, hail, frost, cold and heat. The awareness of day from dawn till long after sunset. Such is the condition of the farmer . . . as the Germans say, his *Weltanschauung.*

Many before Ramuz have exploited the theme of man under the total influence of the elements. Few have believed so completely in the superiority of "natural beings" and in their kinship with the poet. Today this concept may be challenged or accepted. But the man on his land is moving away from Nature. Ramuz' question, if he were here to put it, would be whether the values of our society are being transformed to such an extent that mysticism is fading away. Would he have been satisfied with the testimony of astronauts who are witnesses to the new dimensions of Nature? Perhaps, but he would have been a rabid questioner.

In *Questions About Gold* (*Aujourd'hui,* October 15, 1931), Ramuz shows premature concern for a subject destined to become headline material. "What is Gold? This is, indeed, a fascinating question, one which addresses itself not only to our curiosity and imagination and our senses, but to our entire self . . ."

And Ramuz calls upon the economists to come forward with a philosophical explanation (they fail to do so) as to what Gold is, why it remains pure, why its value is constant, what a man's conscience weighs in terms of the value of gold, what is the meaning of confidence? Can a nation which has become the master of the oceans and of maritime commerce set the definitive value of Gold?

In a few short sentences we catch a glimpse of Ramuz the questioner, the perpetual inquisitor, who greeted all comers with queries.

Elsewhere in this collection of semi-tropical writings the Editor wishes the sociologist to come clean on a very simple point : "Why does man work?" And he rejects easy answers, noting that, in his opinion, sociologists oversimplify when they assure us that work is an obligation or that work is "given" :

> So does Stalin who proclaims that work is enthusiasm, thus managing, for the moment, to organize work against a backdrop of negativism, in producing a kind of Labour Festival.

More Queries

Between the wars the renown of C.-F. Ramuz becomes more firmly established in Paris. This helps him in his homeland. His works are published by Grasset, praised and attacked in literary journals abroad. The prestigious *Nouvelle Revue Française* welcomes him. But as a poet he is searching for new means of expression. And the big wide world beyond the dark forests and lush fields of his Romandie attract him more and more.

In 1926 *La Grande Peur dans la Montagne* (translated some forty years later as *Terror on the Mountain,* Harcourt, Brace & World, Inc. New York) concludes the series of symbolic novels. Once more, a mythological drama is enacted in the sombre setting of cruel mountains. Again, man and evil, hope and despair play hide-and-seek while Nature condescends to be the moody referee.

For Ramuz the twenties are years of self-questioning. The poet, he argues, must keep asking all the questions side-stepped by the "specialists". One of these questions, "absurd but inescapable" as he puts it, is "Who is man? Where does he come from? Where is he going?"

"We envy the mind insensitive to this query—well-informed, delicate, cultured minds, analytical above all, whose only fault is that they tackle problems, one might say, from their extremities."

Long before Gertrude Stein on her death bed Ramuz was replying to those who asked "What is the answer?", with his own "What is the question?"

We then come to *Taille de l'Homme* (1933), in many ways his most prophetic work, inspired by the trials and tribulations of capitalism and by the inhuman, implacable hammering away of the Soviets at the Russian anvil.

Taille de l'Homme brought Ramuz and André Gide together—somewhat reluctantly since both suspected a vague kinship and wished to avoid the encounter. Mermod has left us an account of the meeting in this recollection addressed to Ramuz :

> Shunning banalities and preambles, you exchanged views on life and death. Original sin, you told Gide, seemed to you to be the very explanation of the world. Gide did not believe in life after death; he felt he had had his full share. Then I recalled how my own grandfather lay dying, surrounded by relatives in tears; how severe he sounded as he said · "For seventy years I have been waiting to meet my Maker. I am going to see him at last, and you are crying." Gide grabbed my arm and exclaimed : "How beautiful !"

Later, Gide and Ramuz kept their distances; they admired each other but preferred to explore different sides of a same summit.

Taille de l'Homme shows Ramuz expressing a measure of sympathy for the lack of sophistication of early Communism :

> What is exciting about Communism is that it is the first establishment attempting openly to organize man's existence on a single level, the earthly plane, while destroying all his reasons for hope . . . The Russian Communist simply claims that Mystery does not exist.

As he prospects for modern humanism, Ramuz foresees much of what is in store. But he does not foresee space travel; nor does he visualize the effects of planned parenthood and "the Pill" against which he might have taken a strong stand judging from

108164

his attacks on "Russia's ferocious offensive against the very source of life", and on abortions "resorted to openly, officially, hygienically".

He foresees the slow eclipse of a race of men who, in his estimation, are the only guarantors of social unity, the farmers. "Man," Ramuz holds, "has stature only to the extent that he can still believe in himself : and he can only believe in himself if he has faith in something greater than himself."

One need not look very far for the reason for the return of Ramuz' works, as paperbacks, to bookstores of the Paris Left Bank. Students have been groping, sometimes noisily, for some fundamental answers. And yet the works of C.-F. Ramuz are not selling well in France. And a Swiss professor who, for the past ten years, has left his students free to choose the books they wish to discusss in the classroom, had only two requests for Ramuz novels, against ten for Malraux, eight for Mauriac, seven for Gide, six for Camus and for Sartre.

As World War II draws near, Ramuz finds countless new subjects of inquiry. After *Taille de l'Homme,* he writes *Questions* (1935), *Besoin de Grandeur* (1937), *Découverte du Monde* (1939). In between there is another alpine novel, *Derborence* (1934), translated in 1949 under the title *When the Mountain Fell* (Eyre & Spottiswoode, London), the story of a shepherd buried in a chalet under a giant rockfall, surviving on cheese and water and finding his way back to the village where no one expects the ghostlike figure.

The Last Years

How can one do justice to Ramuz in an assessment as general as this? The purpose of any bird's eye-view study is only to draw attention to the man, to his labours, and to some of his collaborators. Searching essays and dissertations abound in Switzerland, the most revealing and painstaking work being the collection of letters, *C.-F. Ramuz, Ses Amis et Son Temps,* begun in 1967 by Prof. Gilbert Guisan and published by *La Bibliothèque des Arts,* Lausanne-Paris.

C.-F. Ramuz received his first official award, the Prix Schiller, ten years before his death. He was then living in a spacious and slightly cavernous sandstone house, *La Muette,* in the village of Pully now chained to Lausanne by suburban links. There his archives are still kept. There he spent most of his time in his study, going out to the garden for brief walks, to look at plum trees, privet hedges, a newly grafted espalier or the baby fox abandoned at the foot of a wall by a vixen who either trusted or feared poets.

Ramuz' health was declining and he no longer felt the urge to produce full-length fiction : "I can only manage short stories now" (*Journal*). But these short stories contain some of his best pages.

Unavoidably, as is the case with most Romands, Ramuz began to look back and to doubt. His *Journal* is the last repository of these literary qualms. But he also tells us of the immense joy he derived from the company of a six year-old grandson whom he called Monsieur Paul.

For those who did not know how close the writer was to the end of his long journey, and how depressed the quest had made him, the *Journal* should have served as a warning.

January 8, 1947: I have burned all that needed burning this morning. Relief ! Had another operation in November. And so much unfinished work; All these miserable abortive attempts bearing witness to my efforts to renew myself. In the end I had to accept the evidence of failure. And so the witnesses had to be disposed of for they could only have testified to my disgrace. Start again from zero now. Nothing ahead but a hypothetical future.

The Romand obsessed with the notion of the unattainable goal where others would not care or would ignore the gap between now and death. The Romand walking backwards steadily, resolutely into his own last chapter, blind only in this particular instance to impressive accomplishments.

And yet I have changed. I am a new man (very weak), a new person drained off by two years of medical treatment and operations. A new being aware of improvements in his critical faculties (and perhaps not in other faculties). A new man who reacts violently and instantly to everything that comes within his field of vision or understanding (faces, events, books), but, alas ! so far in a negative way. I see better past mistakes than past opportunities. A tendency to destroy, and above all a habit of self-destruction. For this harshness of judgment, this severity I display toward others is nothing at all compared to my intolerance toward myself. I cannot write a sentence without saying to myself "This is worthless. I have flunked again !"

I would like to put to good use this negative force, for it is a force, isn't it? How can the impulse drive forward? How can it "do" rather than "undo"? How should I deal with this? Should I wait? But I have been waiting so long!

February 25: Even in the worst moments I never stopped loving life with a passion. I try to prove to myself that I exist.

In May of that year he went back to the clinic for another operation. Less than two weeks later he was dead.

On May 8 I paid him a short visit, between two planes. He wore a net over his hair. There was a book on the bedside table and a pack of *Gauloises* like the kind he used to go to the grocer to buy up the steep lane in Pully. He said :

"I am an old wreck. They are opening me up tomorrow. Well, at least I shall know whether I can live without pain. Or croak."

"Are you afraid?"

"One is always afraid."

"Is it dangerous surgery?"

"It works or it fails. Often it fails."

"Does it prey on your mind?"

"In hospital you have to think of illness. At home it is different. But the doctors give me things to make me sleep."

And then he thought of the ordeal ahead. Thought aloud, very much the way he would have written about it :

"It is strange to think that tomorrow morning the doctor will come in his car. He will be right on time. He is always punctual. He will shut the car door, remove his gloves; just as though he were going to the office. He will say Good Morning to the nurse. Maybe he will say Good Morning to me as well. It must be a queer feeling to go to work that way. Well, I must run the risk."

Ten years later, also in a clinic, René Auberjonois, aged eighty-five, was waiting for the end. Another Romand searching his past for failures. But his way of showing disapproval was different. With a shaky hand but a sure pencil he would draw over reproductions of his own drawings, correcting the movement of an arm, erasing the head of a circus rider and replacing it with one that looked sideways, transforming a Swiss army recruit into a Kibbutz fighter, putting a shaggy dog under Milady's dressing table. Not a single work left uncorrected. He could not get his hands on the originals.

In his *René Auberjonois* (Editions Mermod), C.-F. Ramuz reproved the painter for excessive refinement and sophistication. But he said, also :

Where you and I agree completely is when we speak of what is primitive, noble, unadorned, devoid of complexities and of the conventions mediocracy now wallows in."

In the early years the painter had scandalized his compatriots with a still-life of red cabbages in a field, if anything still rooted in the soil can be called still-live or still-born.

His friend the poet was not making himself better understood when he summed up his approach to art in this short policy statement :

Antipoétique

"Only from antipoetry is a true poem fashioned.

Only from antimusic comes music at its best.

Our true friends are the craftsmen, not those called artists.

'Art', we know what that is : it is grafting on ancient graft.

And as all growers know you can only graft on wild stock.

Only wild stock produces new life—and that is our way of
doing it."

BIBLIOGRAPHY

"Pour ou contre Ramuz". *Cahiers de la Quinzaine* (Ed. du Siècle, Paris), 1926.

Adam, international review. Nos. 319–321. London, 1967.

Emmanuel Buenzod, *C.-F. Ramuz* (Ed. des Lettres de Lausanne), 1928.

Pierre Kohler, *L'Art de Ramuz* (Ed. de l'Anglore, Genève), 1929.

André Tissot, *C.-F. Ramuz ou le drame de la poésie* (Ed. de la Baconnière, Neuchatel), 1947.

Maurice Zermatten, *Connaissance de Ramuz* (Ed. Rouge, Lausanne), 1947.

Maxence Dichamp, *Ramuz ou le gout de l'authentique* (Ed. de la Nouvelle Edition, Paris), 1948.

Bernard Voyenne, *C.-F. Ramuz ou la sainteté de la terre* (Ed. Julliard, Paris), 1948.

Albert Béguin, *Patience de Ramuz* (Ed. de la Baconnière, Neuchatel), 1949.

Robert Marclay, *C.-F. Ramuz et le Valais* (Ed. Payot, Lausanne), 1950.

Gilbert Guisan, *C.-F. Ramuz ou le génie de la patience* (Ed. Droz, Genève), 1958.

Yvonne Guers-Villate, *C.-F. Ramuz* (Ed. Buchet-Chastel, Paris), 1966.

Marguerite Nicod, *Du réalisme à la réalité*. Evolution artistique et itinéraire spirituel de Ramuz (Ed. Droz, Genève), 1966.

D. R. Haggis, *C.-F. Ramuz, ouvrier du langage* (Ed. Minard, Paris), 1968.

*The Literature of French-speaking Switzerland
in the Twentieth Century*

The Literature of French-speaking Switzerland in the Twentieth Century

by CHARLY GUYOT

I T seems that a brief introduction to the topic I intend to enlarge upon is necessary, especially as the following essay is meant for readers outside French-speaking Switzerland. I think two points must be considered.

1. Diversity and unity

Just over a century ago Amiel, the philosopher from Geneva, pondered the reality of French-speaking Switzerland. Three French-speaking cantons—Geneva, Vaud and Neuchâtel—together with the linguistically French parts of the cantons of Fribourg, Valais and Bern (Bernese Jura)—did this heterogeneous collection add up to a single unit? Amiel concluded that French-speaking Switzerland was "a body in search of a soul".

On a territory of modest size and in a population barely reaching one million even now, what strikes one at first is the diversity of French-speaking Switzerland. Geographical diversity indeed, for alpine, rural, wine-growing districts contrast with important industrial and commercial urban centres. There contact with the soil is expressed together with an age-old fidelity to one's "native backwater", whereas here it is the opening on to the world and the call of distant lands. To go from the international town of Geneva to the small villages of the high Valais valleys is to discover two utterly different civilizations and completely renew one's mental landscape. Diversity of historical traditions too, for Fribourg is a Swiss canton already at the close of the fifteenth century, whereas Vaud will stay under the authority of Bern until just after the French Revolution. Freeing itself from the sway of its bishops and of the dukes of Savoy, the proud republic of Geneva became the European centre of the Calvinist reform in the sixteenth century. Under its counts then its princes of France or Prussia, Neuchâtel never ceased to defend and increase its franchises, and like Geneva erected in the face of catholicism one of the strong-

holds of the protestant faith. Until 1815 when it was attached to
the canton of Bern, the Bernese Jura was a territory held by the
diocese of Basle. As for the Valais, long a prey to internal strife
and ruled over by the Bishops of Sion, it only reached its political
independence belatedly. Whereas Vaud entered the Confederation
in 1803, the Valais became a member in September 1814 together
with Neuchâtel and Geneva.

This diversity of geographical position and historical eventuality
explains why regional peculiarities have survived so long in French-
speaking Switzerland. From this our literature still bears deep
traces, for the better sometimes—as in the case of Ramuz—but
often also for the worse. Many French-speaking writers, in the
nineteenth century especially, could not free themselves from the
stifling hold of a narrow and over-conformist environment. Their
fidelity to their land and to its traditions was less devotion than
crippling bondage.

Shall we aver that this French Swiss "soul" exists today? How
different men from Vaud, Geneva or Neuchâtel! And catholic
Fribourg on the linguistic border as well as the Bas-Valais from
Sierre to St. Maurice are little worlds of their own. What is more,
inside a canton the turn of mind varies according to the district.
The peasant from Gruyère is different from the Fribourg town-
dweller; the Jura man from the Joux valley is not much like the
wine-grower of Lavaux; and the "Montagnons", whose inventive
minds J–J. Rousseau spoke about, often found it difficult to agree
with the men from "lower" Neuchâtel, that is from the edge of the
lake. No doubt over the whole of the French-speaking area the
sharing of a language is a principle of unity. But the use of the
same language does not imply in the least that there is a shared
"soul". Am I wrong in stating that the "French Swiss soul" has
gradually revealed itself as the link between each of our French-
speaking cantons and the Confederation became stronger? The
people from Neuchâtel, Fribourg, Valais, Vaud, Geneva and
Bernese Jura too—despite what some may think—have felt and
proved themselves "French Swiss" as they became more completely
Swiss. Not at all as a reaction to German Switzerland—and I
hope my meaning is clear. I know such a reaction exists and the
"Welsche" is sometimes thought of as a poor Confederate. But the
awareness of a French Swiss spiritual unity is only very superficially linked to the expressions of that deplorable attitude. Our
feeling of being Swiss has had to define itself more clearly for a
"French-speaking soul" to flare up and develop beyond the "souls"

of Geneva, Vaud, Fribourg, Neuchâtel and so on without taking away any of their lustre.

2. *Major themes in French Swiss literature*

If as Taine thought the literary work is conditioned partly at least by the geographical, ethnic and social environment in which it is born, and if on the other hand the writer, placed as he is at one stage in historical time, seems dependent on a tradition, then our French Swiss literature must present certain characteristics that make it differ from French literature at certain points. Let us mention here briefly the principal feelings that often nourish and enliven the favourite themes of our poets, novelists and essay-writers.

First the feeling for nature—though it is not missing in trans-Jura literature. But nobody will deny that our "nature" is not the smiling and temperate nature celebrated by the lyric poets of the French Renaissance and La Fontaine in his *Fables*. And when our writers describe the rough toils of the peasant, they know all too well in opposition to Mme de Sévigné's opinion that tedding is not "frolicking in a meadow and turning hay over". Rousseau was the first to set the example. And from *La Nouvelle Héloïse* to Ramuz the theme of free nature has found constant repetitions and variants in our literature.

Public spiritedness also appears as one of the constant elements in our French Swiss mind, for there we are clearly different from the French and unite with our Italian or German-speaking confederates. For the writers who have not shown their interest in public affairs for this or that issue are few indeed. And surely it is significant that the solitary and hopelessly idealistic Amiel should be the author of "Roulez Tambours!", one of our most popular patriotic songs.

Our literature allows also a broad scope for religious feeling. The Calvinist reformation has deeply influenced the French Swiss mind. It may be responsible for the taboos which long held our literary production in thrall. And nineteenth century morality could not free us from it. Gaspard Vallette exclaimed one day: "What a chapter could be written on the following theme: 'On the boring genre and the French Swiss writers who excelled in it'." For we have our dull patches though they are less obscure nowadays. But on the other hand it would be unjust not to admit that concern for religious and moral problems gave us also works of no uncertain worth when this went together with a real care for style.

We must consider yet another feeling still persisting in our literature. If some French Swiss writers hardly did or do not look outside the limits of our little land, others appreciate the gusts blowing from the wide outside world and see in our country the favoured spot for intellectual exchanges between the various European cultures. In Coppet Mme de Staël set the example for such cosmopolitan curiosity, and the literature of Geneva is peculiarly influenced by it. For such cosmopolitan men Switzerland stands as a mooring post. But for others the call of the deep has been heard so loud that they have pursued their careers abroad. Guy de Pourtalès, Cingria, Blaise Cendrars for instance. The cosmopolitan feeling of Cendrars for example will be satisfied only with "the whole world"—such is the title of his most famous book of poems—and Denis de Rougemont goes along the same line when he requests us to develop a "planetary consciousness".

This brief introduction over, I now start on the precise subject I was offered, that is French Swiss literature in our twentieth century. As far as literature is concerned, does the century actually begin in 1900? I would myself tend to make it really start in 1914 and consider the 1900–14 period as a transitional one.

During these years there are signs heralding a new but still uncertain turn in our letters. The advice given by the Vaud writer Juste Olivier who died in 1876 : "We must live out our own life" is still followed, but there is a keener preoccupation for a truly artistic expression of the "spirit of the place" which he praised. Undoubtedly the voice of the historian of literature and literary critic Philippe Godet will be to the end that of the late nineteenth century. Godet never stopped praising with much talent his fidelity to the past and to tradition. Until his death in 1922 he deplored the tentative novelties of the new French Swiss generation : "What is left", he sighed, "in our intellectual youth of the influence of a Vinet, an Olivier, a Rambert?" The young looked towards France more and more. They were "hypnotized by the Parisian periodicals", and the critic cried out : "Rid yourselves of all these literary cliques and these periodicals written for an élite ! Live out your own life !" And that our art should then remain "stubbornly national and moral !"

This aesthetic attitude was clearly no longer tenable. What then does a "national" French Swiss literature mean? A work of art from our land, Swiss in a geographical, social, moral, patriotic way, can only be French in a "literary" sense. Our interest in French literature is not that of outsiders but that of people who through the human brotherhood of the language own it as much as the French do. In 1913 Edmond Gilliard from Vaud, taking over from Philippe Godet his column in the *Bibliothèque universelle,* commented in his turn on Olivier's phrase only to add immediately : "Yes but we must also live through our language". And in the following year he went on in one of the first *Cahiers Vaudois* : "We French Swiss shall never have any Swiss creative strength unless we have a French creative strength." The problem was at last clearly set. The essential novelty of today's French-speaking Swiss literature lies then in the feeling that a particular style is absolutely necessary.

We must admit that in the last years of the nineteenth century a few writers had felt such a demand. Among them were some poets who like Edouard Tavan appreciated the austere art of the Parnassiens, or like Louis Duchosal and Henri Warnery the freer forms of Verlaine and the similes of the symbolist movement. A William Ritter, the enfant terrible who shocked Neuchâtel, went like Blaise Cendrars at a later time along "the highway of the world". But those who stayed at home and kept true to their own—a Gaspard Vallette, a Philippe Monnier—expressed in their prose an interest for artistic expression keener than the one shown by the previous generation. Philippe Monnier above all, so near to his elder Godet on some points, yet gave at least partly the lie to the aesthetics of the latter. He was indeed from Geneva as much as one could be, "national" if you like, "moral" without sermonizing, and on the one hand expressed enthusiasm for the *Quattrocento* and *Venise au XVIIIème siècle,* while on the other hand he sang the praises of his old school in Geneva in his *Le Livre de Blaise* or in *Mon Village* those of Cartigny peopled with his fondest family memories.

From 1904 onwards the new tendency in our letters began to find its new way. *La Voile latine* set off carrying on board some young writers concerned with an artistic renewal—among them C.-F. Ramuz, G. de Reynold, H. Spiess, R. de Traz and the Cingria brothers. The wind set fair for some years until the day when diversities in doctrine brought down on their heads the storm which sank their bark. *La Voile latine* had been launched to defend as Reynold wrote both "the idea of art and federalism". As early as 1914 the *Cahiers Vaudois* were to stress even more clearly the same artistic concern, while their uncompromising federalism was to repudiate any compromise with the "Helvetianism" dear to the author of *Cités et Pays suisses*. But such takings up of fixed attitudes were finally not essential. Talented men were what mattered, and we cannot but rejoice when we see our twentieth century literature enriched with the works of Reynold together with those of Ramuz. The first, in poems and even more in a series of outstanding works in the history of literature and history proper, never stopped singing in praise of Switzerland and stressing what unites us. The second, setting firmly his characters in the high Valais pastures or on the banks of Lake Geneva, revealed under the deceptive guise of the regional novelist his constant interest in what is universal. His ambition was "to last through passing things, and himself subject to death to prevent them from dying".

At the start when he published *Aline* (1905), *Les Circonstances de la vie* (1907), *Jean-Luc Persécuté* (1909) and even in the two parallel works of *Aimé Pache, peintre vaudois* (1911) and *Vie de Samuel Belet* (1913), the world of Ramuz was governed by the feeling of loneliness. Thus Aline the servant-girl discovers love followed by deceit. The hero of *Circonstances de la vie* is also deceived by his beloved who is at the same time his housekeeper and mistress. But as misfortunes shower on him he feels he undergoes punishment, and peace gradually descends on him. He asks : " 'Aren't there some unavoidable things?' He did not know—one could not understand. One can only say : that's alright." *Jean-Luc Persécuté* unfolds again the tragedy of betrayed love, a heart compelled to be lonely through the wickedness of men. The hero escapes into madness, but his insanity is for him a gift of God, and the last pages of the novel express the yearnings of a soul set free at last. In *Aimé Pache* and *Vie de Samuel Belet* Ramuz finally shakes off the spectre of solitude and separation. After breaking away from society his heroes make their peace with others. After his years in Paris Aimé Pache comes back home to belong again in the community of the living and the dead, among his people, in his village, there in between the lake and the sky. As an artist he retains from now on the necessary agreement between him and things. *La Vie de Samuel Belet* introduces us to similar experiences. At the end of a life punctuated by unhappiness and failure Samuel has become a poor fisherman on the banks of the lake. Through renouncing himself completely he has reached the deepest love which is communion, all personal demand being forsaken. Death may come, for it is normal and expected : "The earth has left me, together with anything petty", he asserts. "I leave behind what alters for what will not alter."

The works I have just mentioned all belong to the Parisian time (1902–14) of Ramuz, a time when gradually he became conscious of his raison d'être. Solitude in the midst of the great city, the friendship of a few artists especially that of Auberjonois from Vaud like himself, the support given by Edouard Rod another from Vaud, all that gave him the opportunity to find out his true self. The experience he lived through and which is not without analogy to that of Gottfried Keller and his *Grüne Heinrich* remains exemplary. To every French Swiss artist it shows that one can only master oneself after long patient effort, painful renunciation and the gradual acquisition of a technique. All our present day French-speaking Swiss writers, however different from Ramuz himself they may be, owe him this lesson to some degree, even though they may not be aware of it. Since Ramuz's experiences, since the stout battle fought by the *Cahiers vaudois* from 1914 to 1919, such works that may still be the product of that amateurism all too frequent in the nineteenth century—for I dare not say this has disappeared—and which it still managed to produce are immediately disqualified through the criticism of artists. I do not think it too much to assert that with *La Voile latine* and the *Cahiers vaudois,* with Reynold and Ramuz together with his friends Gilliard, Budry, Chavannes, Morax, Cingria and even musicians like Stravinsky and Ansermet a true renaissance has taken place in French Swiss belles lettres. The sources of inspiration may of course differ and the intentions diverge, but from now on the freedom of creation is guaranteed. Fetters are snapped. It is no longer a question of "art and motherland" but art alone, the motherland being honoured all the more as art is better served.

Back in his country on the eve of the war Ramuz published two short but important books : *Raison d'être* and *Adieu à beaucoup de personnages.* In the first he examined his position, looked back on the road covered and formulated for himself the rules of his art. He must find an adequate form for the object he intends to portray. In the language of the Vaud people there is an "accent" which must be transferred through the works of the writer. "What does fluency matter", he exclaims, "if what I have to convey is clumsiness?" In *Adieu à beaucoup de personnages* Ramuz takes leave of Aline, Jean-Luc, Aimé, Samuel. He goes forward to face up to new tastes. The tragic incident of the war and then in 1917 the echoing in him of the Russian revolution—the revolution alluded to in *Le grand printemps*—both shatter his thought to its foundations. Everything is brought into question. War and revolution show Ramuz how powerful unanimous noble feelings are. From now on the poet must "accept everything"; only then will he be able to sing the finest song—the song of "altogether now". No realist art is sufficient for it only catches outward appearances. The vision alone reaches the inward reality. The visionary and unanimist Ramuz is born. The poet sees "signs" everywhere. How is it that men no longer own these prodigies? The task of the writer is now to try and make visible the action of the cosmic powers not only on an individual set apart at the centre of the fiction, but on the masses too. Hence the three "visionary" masterpieces: *Le Règne de l'Esprit malin* (1917), *La Guérison des maladies* (1917) and *Les signes parmi nous* (1919) followed also by *Terre du Ciel* (1921) *and Présence de la Mort* (1922).

With the end of the first world war a new stage in the spiritual evolution of Ramuz seems about to take place. Gradually the writer recaptures his love for simple earthly realities. He is appeased and accepts our condition. Read for example the pages which are true poems of *Salutation paysanne* (1921) or *Chant de notre Rhône* (1920). But we must admit this optimistic song will not last. Moreover it could not be the only theme for works that in spite of their substructure are intended as "novels". Once again, in his fifties, Ramuz will express his tragic interpretation of life with the mastery and control—issue of his previous successful works, though the evolution I underline here took place gradually. In 1925 for example *L'amour du monde* still places its trust in passion. But more and more in the following works the vision of the artist becomes dramatic and pessimistic. The novelist's inspiration proceeds from two antagonistic feelings though in some ways they complement each other—that is death and a mysterious "elsewhere". With the former feeling is associated the prophetic vision of strange disasters descending on men and beasts, geological or cosmic cataclysms. The latter is expressed in symbols such as the fun-fair, an urge to escape everyday life, or by the part given by the poet to woman, who becomes the promise of a love which is fulfilment once the shackles of our earthly prison are broken loose. Of these two groups of works the first reveals an epic imagination and the second a lyric movement. And true to one of the constants of his poetic creation Ramuz sets the characters of his epic in an alpine landscape : *La grande peur dans la montagne* (1926), *Farinet ou la fausse monnaie* (1932), *Derborence* (1934), *Si le soleil ne revenait pas* (1937), whereas the setting for his lyric effusion is always the landscape of the lake reflecting the sky, the hill-sides with vineyards, the small village or the drowsy town : *La beauté sur la terre* (1927), *Adam et Eve* (1932), *Le Garçon savoyard* (1936). I cannot analyze every one. I shall only point out that, among the novels in which obsession, imminence or the horrifying reality of the cataclysm predominate, *Derborence* is without any doubt the outstanding one. As for the dream of a paradise regained after an earthly exile, Ramuz may have given it its most powerful expression in *Adam et Eve*. In all the fiction of the writer I do not know of another work expressing more forcibly than this novel the tragedy of being parted and the eagerness of a heart yearning for unity.

In ending this brief survey of the creative evolution of Ramuz I shall be content to state, together with the outstanding essay-writer Marcel Raymond, that Ramuz is the greatest writer born in French-speaking Switzerland since J-J. Rousseau, "the greatest writer", Raymond claims, "I mean the greatest poet, that is creator".

With Ramuz so deeply rooted in his French-speaking Switzerland let us now contrast three writers, important in their own right too, who yielded to what I have already called "the call of the deep"—I mean Guy de Pourtalès, Charles-Albert Cingria and Blaise Cendrars.

One day when he was inscribing one of his books, Guy de Pourtalès (1881–1941) called himself "A man from Neuchâtel, Geneva, Vaud and France". He was from Vaud only by virtue of his frequent stays on Lake Geneva. He could say more accurately that he was from Geneva on his mother's side. He became French officially when he was naturalized shortly before 1914. Without any doubt he was from Neuchâtel, his surname being that of an aristocratic family who settled there as early as the late seventeenth century. Guy de Pourtalès loved Neuchâtel where he studied for a time. In *Marins d'eau douce* he recalls with delicate tones the charming little town, and Neuchâtel too is the setting for the plot of *La Pêche miraculeuse,* a novel published in 1937. But I must hurry to say that obviously Pourtalès cannot be reduced to the humble title of "writer from Neuchâtel". We shall not make ourselves ridiculous by entrenching this European within the narrow

limits of a small Swiss canton. Enough to read the novel entitled
Monclar (1927), or think of the work of the essayist Pourtalès with
a passionate interest in music, to find out that other environments,
other landscapes, other experiences occupy in the oeuvre of this
writer as much room if not more than his childhood and youthful
memories.

As for Charles-Albert Cingria (1883–1954), his position in French-
speaking Swiss literature is difficult to determine. First, what was
his real nationality? On his father's side he was descended from
a family of Ragusa who had settled in central Turkey, and on his
mother's side from a Polish family who had settled in Geneva. His
father had obtained Swiss nationality in 1870. Cingria called himself at first a man from Geneva, not Switzerland, later he called
himself a Turk, a Ragusan, an Italo-Franc Levantine. Later again
he will maintain : "I have not a single drop of Swiss blood in my
veins . . . I loathe being called a Swiss and above all a 'Swiss figure
of whimsy' as is done ad nauseam in what is still called public
opinion in Paris". He started with Ramuz by giving a few
pages first to *Pénates d'argile* (1904), then to *La Voile latine*. But
very soon he only remained in Switzerland for short stays. He had
a pied-à-terre in Paris but very often too he was seen in Rome,
Spain, Constantinople or North Africa. Cocteau defined him as a
"will-o'-the-wisp, a luminescent dancing elf", and Claudel called
him "an elusive goblin". Yet this figure of whimsy, who could not
tie himself down to live in Switzerland, had an interest in artistic
Switzerland as well as in its history. Enough to recall his outstanding essay on *La civilisation de Saint-Gall* (1929), his *Musiques de
Fribourg* (1945), *La Reine Berthe et sa famille* (1947), *Notre terre
et ses gens* (1937), or again *Impressions d'un passant à Lausanne*
(1932), *Pendeloques alpestres* (1928), *Stalactites* (1941), *Parcours
du Haut-Rhône* (1949) and *Florides helvètes* (1944). The main
body of his work, it is clear, consists above all in essays which are
both well informed and full of dazzling flights of imagination. Of
course he wrote a few stories such as *Les Autobiographies de
Bruno Pomposo* (1928), but one could hardly take him for a
novelist. For he always rejects the demands of a well-built plot and
a logical unfolding of it. For he wants to be free as an artist as
well as in life. Hence what is in a way so elusive about him, yet
also his charm which no other twentieth century French Swiss
writer can offer us to the same extent.

To speak now of Blaise Cendrars I cannot trace here in detail
the various stages of his life in which adventure loomed larger than

literature, the latter being finally only a new kind of adventure and experience passionately lived out though transferred to the realm of his imagination. His pseudonym—Blaise Cendrars—hides his real name of Frédéric-Louis Sauser, born in 1887 at La Chaux-de-Fonds in the Neuchâtel canton. On his father's side they were German Swiss as the family came from Sigriswil. As a child the future writer was shuttled back and forth according to the changing homes of his father—Paris? Egypt? Naples? The track is uncertain already, for Cendrars claimed he was born in Paris! From La Chaux-de-Fonds his family moved to Neuchâtel where Frédéric-Louis attended the College of Commerce. In a delightful little book called *Vol à voile* Cendrars narrated how he escaped, or so he said, from his father's house when he was fifteen, that is in 1902, and started then on a life of adventure which led him to Russia, China, the Balkans, Italy, Canada and goodness knows where else! We think we must take it with a pinch of salt, for in 1903 the young man was still in Neuchâtel. And on reliable authority we may take it that he stayed in Switzerland as late as 1907. However, we cannot contest his journey to Russia probably as a commercial traveller. But it is very unlikely that he should have travelled so extensively throughout the world before his twentieth birthday and have gone through all the adventures he claimed. A critic has spoken of the "prodigious" memory of Cendrars. Even more than "prodigious" I should like to call it "fabulous" or rather "creative of fables".

In 1911—this time we have proof of it—Cendrars was in New York. His first poetic work *Les Pâques à New York* is dated from this town in "April 1912". It was published in Paris where the young writer settled as early as this same year 1912, and where he was admitted into the company of the most "modern" poets and artists: Apollinaire, Max Jacob, Modigliani, Chagall, Picasso, Léger. Before the first world war too (1913) he published *La Prose du Transsibérien et de la petite Jeanne de France*. A volunteer in the Foreign Legion in 1914, he was wounded in the following year and lost his right arm. After the end of the war he produced *Le Panama ou les aventures de mes sept oncles* (1918). A year later his first three great poems were gathered in the collection *Du monde entier,* and in the same year his *Dix-neuf poèmes élastiques* appeared. In 1924 *Kodak* was also to follow. So Cendrars started as a poet, and perhaps *Les Pâques à New York* is his most successful poetic achievement. The novelty of the poem deeply struck Apollinaire who was about to publish *Alcools*. He must then have been writing *Zône,* the poem with which he opened the collection, where some lines very much recall the *Pâques* of Cendrars. Where then is the essential poetic novelty in Cendrars? As Ramuz wrote : "Anti-poetry is the only source of poetry." In his way Cendrars said nothing else when he maintained : "Everything is poetry." Poetic creation in his case seems to spring from the bare fact. And he has every right to declare in *L'Homme foudroyé* : "I do not dip my pen into an ink-well, but into life itself."

In 1924 he answered the call of adventure. It led him to Brazil, the Argentine and Chile. Then he settled once more in Paris. During the second world war the downfall of France made him cast an anchor in Provence for a few years. The war over he returned to Paris where he ended his turbulent life. In January 1961 the City of Paris awarded him its literary Grand Prix. Four days after this official acknowledgement, the writer died. In the second half of his career, he was known mainly through his novels : *L'Or* (1925), *Moravagine* (1926), *Dan Yack* (1929). And his not easily justifiable *Emmène-moi au bout du monde* (1956) belongs to his latter years. To his works of fiction let us add the works of Cendrars the writer of memoirs : *L'Homme foudroyé, La main coupée, Bourlinguer, Le Lotissement du ciel,* all of them written between 1944 and 1949.

The style of living belonging to Cendrars found in his novels a verbal expression of great variety and authenticity. Man's adventure becomes the adventure of words. *L'Or* is the story of Suter a man from Basle founding an agricultural colony in California. Fortune smiles on him until the gold rush, which means utter ruin for his plantations, and he dies completely destitute in 1880. Delteil wrote about it : "In it facts have a poetry of their own, a poetry of the finest." After *L'Or* came *Moravagine* perhaps the most perfect of Cendrar's works of fiction. The novel is built on three levels. A fellow-adventurer of Moravagine is supposed to write the biography of a mysterious character "the only genuine heir to the last king of Hungary". So the first level is the adventures of Moravagine, the second that of the narrator, and the third one that of the author who comments on the story and even intervenes towards the end under the guise of one of the characters. *Dan Yack* does not reveal less about the most secret part of Cendrars, and is as much of a novelty as *Moravagine.* It can be read as a novel of adventure, but beyond the "tangible" adventure it is that of a great spiritual one. The hero escapes into solitude, frees himself from time and all bondage, then comes back to live among men. He settles in Paris where, a solitary man once more, he exclaims : "Today I look into myself. There is nothing, nothing anymore. It is the end of me." Perhaps there is no text in the whole of Cendrars' works better than *Dan Yack* to lead us to the heart of the personal tragedy played out by its author.

Charly Clerc, who was so outstandingly well-versed in the knowledge of French Swiss literature, when he gave his inaugural lecture in 1933 at the Federal Polytechnical School remarked : "In the period between 1900 and 1930 something happened indeed . . . Whereas at the beginning of the century French Swiss literature was only on the edge of France, inward-looking, tied to the tradition of the nineteenth century, since then it has tended to become an integral part, a more or less original chapter in French literature." This evolution is undoubtedly real. As soon as the first world war was over intellectual and literary contacts between French Switzerland and France increased considerably. For a few years the *Revue de Genève* following on our venerable *Bibliothèque universelle* was a rallying-point for many European writers. French periodicals went out of their way to welcome our best writers. And French Swiss works are now frequently brought out by Parisian publishers though that was previously unusual. Ramuz himself is indebted to Grasset and the acknowledgement of Paris for finally being accepted by his compatriots. In the buffetings of 1940, during the years when literature in France was silenced by her occupiers, she asked our publishers to let her voice be heard. A mournful opportunity for new contacts in which closer links were forged; and these links have not since been broken, so that nowadays there is nothing in the way of French Swiss poets, novelists or essaywriters—provided they shake off all conformism —if they want to make their career with chances equal to those of many of their colleagues in France.

During the last fifty years many have been the French Swiss poets who could rival the poets of trans-Jura without fear of inferiority. So to the front we find Edmond Gilliard who has just died, Pierre-Louis Matthey, Gustave Roud. Gilliard (1875–1969) who belonged to the *Cahiers vaudois* team is the author of poetic prose written in an admirable and esoteric manner, centred on what he called *La dramatique du moi* and the searching study of the mystery of the union, of *La Passion* also *de la Mère et du Fils*. The source of inspiration of Pierre-Louis Matthey (born in 1893) is opaque too, transferring to the myth the experience of human passions. From the poems of his youth *Seize à vingt* to his most recent works *Alcyonée à Pallène, Aux Jardins du père,* he has gone on aiming at an exacting form which owes its high-mindedness partly to its self-inflicted restrictions. And we must mention here his exemplary verse translations of poems by Shakespeare, Blake and Keats. As for Gustave Roud (born in 1897) in the lonely village in the Vaud canton where he has chosen to settle, he has developed an intense and often disconsolate meditation throughout his work. We should note that he is also the author of outstanding French renderings of Novalis, Hölderlin and Rilke. A contemporary of Roud and his fellow citizen from Vaud, Edmond-Henri Crisinel (1897–1948) expresses in his work, brought to a sudden end by a tragic death, his longing for an impossible happiness. The bulk of his poems expresses with pathos the cruel struggle of this artist against relentless fate. To the same dramatic experience of an existence felt to be unbearable we owe the poetic work of another man from Vaud Jean-Pierre Schlunegger who took his life in 1964 when he was thirty-nine. Among the poets of the Vaud region we must give a prominent place for the standard of their writing as well as for the authentic quality of their inspiration to Philippe Jaccottet, whose name often appears in the summary of the *Nouvelle Revue Française,* to Jacques Chessex, Mme. Anne Perrier and Jean Pache, whose *Poèmes de l'autre* bring to life so well the atmosphere in which the poetry of Vaud thrives. In the Valais the poetic "climate" becomes harsher. All its wildness is felt in the works of Maurice Chappaz, especially in his *Testament du Haut-Rhône* (1953). As for Fribourg, it now seems devoid of poets except perhaps for the retiring melody of Henri Fragnière in his *Poèmes du temps perdu,* whereas the Bernese Jura reckons several gifted poets. For example Jean Cuttat in his *Chansons du mal au coeur* combines delightful fancy with outstanding formal invention. For his *Signes de soie* (1951) Robert Simon received a Prix de la Société des Poètes français. Let us also mention the other Jura men : Luc Vuagnat and Jacques-René Fiechter. In the last half-century the Neuchâtel canton can congratulate itself on its contribution to poetry. In the front row are Jean-Paul Zimmermann, Edmond Jeanneret, Marc Eigeldinger. The first has sung his longing for *Départs,* but equally the *Cantique de notre terre.* Edmond Jeanneret tells of the agony and sufferings of the creature estranged from God and condemned to death, but at the same time he states the promise of resurrection. This work, renewing in French Switzerland the tradition of religious poetry, is akin to that of the great protestant lyric poets of the sixteenth century, and at the same time some tender chords, the light and innocence of *Matin du monde,* remind us of Supervielle. As for Marc Eigeldinger, his inspiration owes much to the esoteric secrets and the admiration the young poet has always expressed for Breton. Less demanding and artistic than the three writers I have just mentioned there appear in the poetry of Neuchâtel Jules Baillods (1889–1952), André Pierrehumbert (born in 1884) a Lamartinian elegiac poet, or again the foreign-legion poet Arthur Nicolet, bard of his native Jura and the turmoils of an adventurous life. In the canton of Geneva the poets are numerous too. Let us recall first the names of a few of those who made themselves heard between the wars : Mme. Cuchet-Albaret, Albert Rheinwald, Ami Chantre, François Franzoni. The literary group "La Violette" gathered for many a year several poets from Geneva—several times they published a joint collection of prose and poetry : *Le Livre des Dix.* Beside the name of Jean Violette, the probable originator of this venture, we find that of Charles d'Eternod and above all René-Louis Piachaud. Towards the end of the inter-war period a new generation takes over. No doubt Gilbert Trolliet, with his abundant and varied production, may be considered as the leader of the young singers. Among them enough to mention Claude Aubert, Jean Hercourt, Georges Haldas, Jean-G. Lossier. Let us also mention the highly refined contribution Mme. Edith Boissonnas brings to the treasure of our present day French Swiss literature from Paris where she has settled.

As with poetry, the present day French Swiss novel testifies to a gradual emancipation from the limitations and taboos in which the nineteenth century held it. All the application of our best novelists—I am not speaking again of those who "took to the high seas"—aims in the first place at an artistically sound expression whatever the themes chosen. A production like that of Benjamin Vallotton hardly appeals any more; but the Vaud region offers the sturdy talent of C.-F. Landry, the bubbling spirit of Paul Budry, the wit and classical writing of Savary and delicate psychological analysis together with a keen sense of poetry in Emmanuel Buenzod and Jacques Mercanton. And many are the admirers of Mme. Violette Martin's prose or the rather ornate works of Mme. Catherine Colomb. In the Valais three gifted novelists : Mme. Corinna Bille, Maurice Zermatten and Maurice Chappaz give in all their writings a large part to their wine-growing and mountainous district, although nothing in them allows us to apply the limiting epithet of "regionalist writers". In their probing analysis of character and the innermost secrets of the heart, or else like Chappaz joyfully letting loose his wild fancy, they reach a higher and more widely human truth. As for the Bernese Jura, it too has given us some novelists of real merit. We name Mme. Clarisse Francillon, settled in Paris, Werner Renfer, departed too early, who left in *Hannebarde* (1933) the testimony of a deep spiritual search and an art both original and disciplined. Also Jura writers like Lucien Marsaux (the pseudonym of Marcel Hofer), Jean-Pierre Monnier and Roger-Louis Junod, all three of them settled in Neuchâtel. Among the Neuchâtel novelists we must mention first the attractive personalities of Mme. Monique Saint-Hélier (pseudonym of Bertha Briod) and Cilette Ofaire (pseudonym of Cécile Houriet). Both their careers as writers have been run almost entirely outside our little country. But Mme. Dorette Berthoud, Jean-Paul Zimmermann (already mentioned as a poet) and Jacques Edouard Chable are writers belonging in every sense to Neuchâtel. Two "young ones" have recently come to the fore : Georges Piroué, settled in Paris, and Yves Velan, from Vaud but teaching in La Chaux-de-Fonds, whose first novel *Je* was enthusiastically praised by French critics. As for the imaginative literary output from Geneva during the last fifty years, it has been faithful for the most part to the traditional analytical novel. Robert de Traz, Jacques Chenevière, Bernard Barbey, Henri de Ziegler, each in his own way a talented writer, testify to this constant aspect of the Geneva novel. For Pierre Girard, the analysis has a touch of irony, and though it never disappears, it draws back before a delightful taste for whimsy. With Jean Marteau and Léon Bopp, the former from Neuchâtel and settled in Geneva, the novel presents other aspects. Jean Marteau with *La Main morte* establishes it in a soil lit up by lurid flashes. As for Léon Bopp, who has written an essay on the novel, he is an enthusiast of "catalogism", and devotes himself to writing large frescoes such as *Liaisons du monde* and *Ciel de terre*. Three women novelists have also proved outstandingly talented : Mme. Alice Rivaz, Mme. Pernette Chaponnière and Mlle. Yvette Z'Graggen. I cannot go on enumerating as it would become tedious, but enough to say that among the "young" novelists of Geneva many are they who are unquestionably gifted.

I shall also dwell briefly only on drama in French Switzerland. It suffers obviously from the difficulties undergone and lived through by the companies that could perform the works of local playwrights. During the last fifty years the best of our drama production has doubtless been the contribution of René Morax in the Théâtre du Jorat at Mézières, that of Ramuz' composition *Histoire du Soldat* with music by Stravinsky, and that of Ferdinand Chavannes—another of the *Cahiers vaudois* team, who in his *Mystère d'Abraham* renewed a tradition originating in protestant soil with the *Abraham sacrifiant* of Théodore de Bèze. Also with *Guillaume le Fou* Chavannes gave new life to the legend and figure of the national hero William Tell. Between 1930 and 1950 Charly Clerc wrote a series of "mysteries", while J-P. Zimmermann endowed our theatre with two dramas : *Les Vieux-Prés* and *Le Retour*. In Geneva some authors were instrumental in keeping alive a taste for comedy and vaudeville. Enough to mention Alfred Gehri, Georges Oltramare, Rhodo Mahert and Jean Bard. Today there are more and more attempts made to renovate drama in French Switzerland. There is a French-speaking drama centre, a French-speaking popular theatre, and everywhere non-professional companies are springing up, who we must admit play Beckett and Ionesco more often than the works of our own playwrights. French Switzerland is still waiting for its own Dürrenmatt.

Let us end by alluding briefly to the French-speaking Swiss essayists. It is not too much to say that their contribution to the history of literature and present day French literary criticism is large and very often outstanding. Enough to think of Albert Béguin, Denis de Rougemont and Marcel Raymond ! And it would be most unjust not to acknowledge the importance of the production of Charly Clerc, Pierre Kohler, André Bonnard, Auguste Viatte, or among the younger generation P-O. Walzer, Jean Starobinski and Jean Rousset.

I do not think it necessary to give this essay—which some may find too lengthy already—a conclusion that would lengthen it even more. What has been read allows one to conclude that the writers of French Switzerland have now earned their freedom. May they go on showing this freedom, and by so doing increase with works in every genre—apart from the "boring genre"—the common heritage of Swiss letters !

(*Translated from the French by Anne-Marie Keith-Smith and Brian Keith-Smith.*)

BIBLIOGRAPHICAL NOTE

The standard work on twentieth century French Swiss literature is: Alfred Berchtold *La Suisse romande au cap du XXème siècle*. Payot, Lausanne 1963. Nearly 1,000 pages in octavo it includes an abundant bibliography.

Useful also is the *Dictionnnaire des littératures*. Presses Universitaires de France, Paris 1968 in 3 volumes. The articles on Swiss French writers and in particular a long note on *Suisse française* are by me. Various parts of these have been taken over into this study.

Finally may I draw attention to a collection of selected texts *Ecrivains de Suisse française* which was published by me in the Francke Verlag, Bern in 1961.

Italian Switzerland and National Literature

Italian Switzerland and National Literature

by GUIDO CALGARI

"Italian Switzerland"

ACCORDING to the 1960 census there are in Switzerland 198,278 citizens with Italian as their mother tongue—inhabitants of the Ticino and the southern valleys of the Grisons.

The political history of Italian Switzerland gives the clue to its economic structure, which in turn throws light on the ethnic composition of the area, the ever-decreasing influence of Lombardy and the problem of "Italianità" which occupies both Ticinese intellectuals and the best minds in the Swiss Confederation. Political, economic and ethnic developments provide the best yardstick with which to measure the intellectual vitality of Italian Switzerland—a vitality which manifests itself in many ways : in religion and a sense of tradition, in cultural life and ancient customs, in patriotism and an open-mindedness towards other peoples. Nature recognizes no political frontiers or customs barriers, thus from a purely geographical point of view the Ticino forms the northern tip of Lombardy. It is here that the Lombardian Plain merges into the Lower Alps to come up against the mountain frontiers of German and Rhaeto-Romanic Switzerland. The mountain passes—the Lukmanier, the San Bernardino, the San Giocomo and, above all, the St. Gotthard—have had a far-reaching effect on the political fate of Italian Switzerland. But for this fact—and the impact of certain intellectual movements—the Ticino and the Grisons would have remained a small group of unknown and unimportant territories, despite their immense wealth of natural beauty. The history of the area has been, one may say, that of an often backward and insignificant peasant people whose lives have echoed but briefly the great events, decisions and fierce passions beyond its borders. And yet at times, this people has been characterized by a deeply rooted caution, a manly vigour and a stern sense of responsibility. The Gotthard became accessible at a time when Romanesque churches were springing up on the rocky ledges of the Ticinese valleys, and these became a focal point for the "vici" and the "decaniae", as shepherds and muleteers were joined by every type of trader and Italian refugees driven out by internecine party struggles. It brought the valley of the river Ticino, now a sort of corridor, and its natural gateway, Bellinzona, into great prominence. The Dukes of Milan proceeded to fortify the town, and the Swiss Confederation, which later controlled the area, considered it its bulwark in the South. The Gotthard connected the Po and the Rhine, Italy and Germany, and for centuries men, trade and ideas passed through the Ticino. The Gotthard route was opened furthermore at the time of the Italian Communes, and this brings us to a second important factor in the history of the area: the ideal of Communal liberty. Encouraged and protected by ecclesiastical authority in the shape of the Bishop of Como and the Chapter of Milan Cathedral, the Ticinese rose against the feudal lords and dignitaries of the Holy Roman Empire. After the collapse of the Communal movement—which produced a series of heroic insurrections in the Upper Ticino— four separate political powers cast a covetous eye on the country: to the North, the German Emperor, Henry VII, brought a lawsuit for the possession of the Leventina against the Bishopric of Milan and the young Swiss Confederation, which saw in the acquisition of the Ticino an opportunity of making the South strategically secure; to the South there were the Lords Spiritual, the original feudal rulers who had brought civilization to the Ticino, and the Dukes of Milan, first the Visconti, later the Sforzas. The final battles for control over the area were fought near Arbedo and Giornico between the Confederation and the Duchy of Milan.

When the Swiss marched south at the beginning of the sixteenth century to fight on the side of the Sforzas and Pope Julius II against the French, they seized Locarno and Lugano, and by the terms of the Perpetual Peace, concluded in 1516 at Freiburg between François I and the Confederation, the Ticino came under the latter's direct rule. Each Canton sent in rotation a High Bailiff to administer the transalpine territories. Historians on either side of the border have held differing opinions on the three hundred years of Swiss rule, but at any rate it brought three centuries of peace during which the growth of a certain loyalty to the Confederation is clearly discernible.

Later, inspired by the 1798 French Revolution and the foundation on their borders of the Cisalpine Republic, the Ticinese rose again and declared their intention of living as free men, but at the same time maintaining the link with their former masters: "Liberi e Svizzeri". In 1803, thanks to Napoleon's Act of Mediation— Bonaparte did not wish to dismember the famous Confederation from which he was expecting substantial military support—the Ticino was raised to the status of an autonomous Cantonal Republic.[1] After three hundred years of dependence the Canton set about constructing a modern state from scratch. In exemplary fashion work began on roads and bridges, agriculture and trade, the budget and the educational system. Indeed, the young Canton can look back with great satisfaction on the achievements of the last hundred and fifty years. However, the Canton's history owes its intellectual splendour and nobility, above all, to the successes of its emigrants and its contribution to the Italian Risorgimento. Emigration had two distinct causes—artistic and economic. Every country in Europe received its quota of Ticinese craftsmen, including master-builders, architects and artists of genius, who left splendid and famous buildings behind them wherever they went— from Russia to Spain, from Scandinavia to Sicily and Constantinople. Solari, Maderno, Fontana, Borromini, Longhena, Seròdine, Gaggini, Trezzini, Carloni, Raggi and Albertolli, among others, were all natives of the Ticino. Economically motivated emigration —which goes back to the Middle Ages—also bears witness to the vitality of the Ticinese people and its capacity to withstand the greatest hardships, for example, in nineteenth century California, Australia, South America and Africa. A few outstanding pioneer-settlers like Mosè Bertoni enjoyed great fame, as did such industrialists as Delmonico, Gatti, Maraini, Tognazzini and Perazzini, or politicians like G. Guggiani and A. Demarchi. Nor should one forget the Argentine's finest poetess Alfonsina Storni, who was a descendant of Ticinese emigrants from Lugaggia near Lugano.

The tiny, free Ticinese Republic placed weapons, money and printing presses at the disposal of the Italian Risorgimento, and extended hospitality and shelter to large numbers of political refugees. It never wavered in support of its brothers across the border, and this policy exposed the Canton to constant threats and persecution from Austria.

In the Italian-speaking Grisons, too, life in the Middle Ages had its peculiar regional character, revolving round the Alpine passes (the San Bernardino, Maloja, Bernina), the ideal of Communal liberty, the market co-operatives and the monasteries. In contrast to the Ticino, however, the Grisons valleys possess an unbroken tradition of freedom and political solidarity with the Confederation, which has been cemented by many common struggles. It is a tradition of which they are very proud. These valleys have never been subject to the Confederation, but always its allies. Moreover, attached as they were to the Three Leagues, they themselves had for centuries governed other southern territories (e.g. the Valtellina) and provided the country with army commanders and statesmen. In a few areas, especially in the Valle Bregaglia, the Reformation struck fruitful soil and changed the pattern of religious life.

From a political, economic and ethnic point of view, these valleys present the same general picture today as the Ticino. The expression "Southern Switzerland" binds them to the latter both materially and spiritually; for they are both striving to protect the interests of an economically weak border territory and to defend their common linguistic and cultural heritage.

National Literature?

In the case of German Switzerland one can speak of a Swiss German Literature which, although it can be situated within the mainstream of German cultural life, nevertheless reveals characteristics, developments and achievements peculiar to itself. The German Swiss do not have to look to Germany or Austria for writers who have expressed their deepest feelings and attitude to life—they have Gotthelf and Keller. Furthermore, the proud and affectionate loyalty they show to the local dialects they speak and the reverent care with which they cherish and preserve the remnants of traditional folk-values and customs are unmistakable signs of an individual national character. This character has evolved down the ages out of political, economic and social conditions quite different from those in Germany, and out of the consciousness of numerical strength. On the periphery of literary life in Germany, Swiss German literature has developed its own distinctive tradition, and its history deserves respect and attention. It is true that the German Swiss owe their national epic to a German, Friedrich Schiller, but they can pride themselves with justification on having presented German Literature with a number of outstanding poets.

As for the Romansh-speaking Swiss—whose language has "national" status only in Switzerland—they more than anyone can lay claim to independence. The situation in Italian Switzerland is quite different. A people numbering 200,000 cannot feel as strong as 4,000,000 German Swiss. A sense of grandeur and strength can only be obtained by reference to the great maternal culture of

Italy. The self-confidence of this people, concentrated into the hundred kilometres between Airolo and Chiasso, is not drawn from the dialect it speaks as such, but from the language of Dante and the 50,000,000 Italians of modern Italy. In their education, mentality and sympathies, as well as in their literature, the Ticinese bear all the characteristics of an Italian-speaking, Catholic people of the Lower Alps which has lived for centuries by cattle-breeding, agriculture and crafts, and which—to quote Arminio Janner—possesses "no indigenous culture of its own". The medieval concept of Communal liberty was borrowed from the South—Carducci's "comune rustico" can be found in all Alpine districts—and from the South, too, came civilization, culture and literary inspiration.

Even in political attitudes there is no fundamental distinction from Italy, whereas the long tradition of liberty and liberalism in nineteenth century German Switzerland contrasts sharply with the hierarchic, feudal conditions obtaining in Germany. Liberty in the Ticino is a hundred and fifty years old—that is a mere fifty years older than Italy's. The particular Swiss concept of liberty and democracy, peculiar also to the Ticino, corresponds "to an essentially Italian tradition that has always—but especially in the last few centuries—acknowledged an ideal of open criticism and social equality. For this reason a similar attitude in a Ticinese writer might appear typically Swiss, but in fact only serves to underline a specifically Italian characteristic." (Janner). Take for example Foscolo and Parini, Giusti and Porta, whose works enjoyed great popularity amongst the Ticinese in the nineteenth century. Any exploration of the character of the creative writer in Italian Switzerland will bring to light features he shares with his colleagues in Lombardy. The fact that the Ticino has always been a cultural appendage to Lombardy can be seen in its first humanists down to the clerics of the eighteenth century, in the poetasters of the nineteenth century down to the authors of the present day. For Francesco Chiesa, indeed, there is no higher praise than to be considered one of the great heirs of the "Lombardian" Manzoni.

Mention has already been made of individuals who have decisively influenced the intellectual development of the Ticino—Giuseppe Parini, Carlo Porta and Alessandro Manzoni—to whom should be added the Lombardian Encyclopaedists and Carlo Cattaneo. Another quotation from A. Janner underlines the fact that the Ticino stands in a quite different cultural relationship to Italy than does German Switzerland to Germany or French

Switzerland to France : there is no writer either in French or
German Literature "who so perfectly conveys the sensibility of the
French or German Swiss as Alessandro Manzoni does ours". The
Promessi Sposi demonstrates an attitude to life and a predilection
for philosophical exploration which is common to Lombardy and
Italian Switzerland. The political and social, religious and moral
ideas expressed in this great novel are so anchored in the Ticinese
consciousness that, along with the *Divine Comedy,* it is considered
to be the central pillar of Ticinese literary culture.

It is, of course, obvious that one cannot speak of an Italian
Swiss Literature as such, but at most of a contribution to Italian
Literature as a whole. It should be equally clear that contemporary
writers of the Italian-speaking Grisons and the Ticino, of whatever
stature, receive their creative inspiration from classical and modern
Italy just as their forebears did. Indeed, it is Italy's reputation in
the world at large that substantially determines the evaluation
accorded to the area's language and culture by the rest of
Switzerland.

In their political attitudes the Ticinese are "free and Swiss",
but they are Italian in their intellectual life, traditions and customs.
This is obviously a complex and problematical situation, but one
which the Italian Swiss have so far mastered. The results they
have achieved have been modest, but their good-will and fundamental honesty of purpose are beyond question.

Literature up to Independence

Father Alfonso Oldelli, the historian Emilio Motta and Giuseppe
Zoppi endeavoured to rescue the names of the earliest Ticinese
writers from oblivion. Similar efforts on behalf of the Italian-
speaking Grisons were made by Francesco Dante Vieli and A. M.
Zendralli.[2] Of course, Italian Switzerland abounds, as elsewhere,
with scholars, critics and historians who share the general
characteristics of "l'esprit suisse", and they cannot be dealt with
here. Indeed, it is typical of the literatures of Switzerland that
greater importance is attached to sober experience than to imagination—a fact which explains the great preponderance of historical,
ethical and critical works over lyrical and narrative ones. Referring
to this cool, reflective spirit, André Gide once remarked that
"every Swiss carries his glaciers around within himself".

Two clerics placed their personal stamp on the eighteenth
century : Giampietro Riva and Francesco Soave, both from
Lugano and members of the Somask Congregation, which main-

tained a college and a grammar school in the town. Among the pupils who attended the school during the tolerant headship of Francesco Soave was the young Alessandro Manzoni.

Although in the fifty years after Soave's death the Ticino gave moral, financial and even military support to the Italian people, this mutual sympathy was not particularly noticeable in literature.[3] On the contrary, the recognition of the Ticino and the Italian-speaking Grisons as autonomous Cantons within the Confederation brought about a loosening of the personal ties writers had with the literary circles of Italy and an interruption in the natural emigration of our people to the schools and colleges, academies and literary societies of the peninsula, which had been common practice in the eighteenth century when there were no political frontiers.

Their newly won Cantonal sovereignty forced the Ticino and the Grisons to concentrate on their own affairs and to build up the institutions of their tiny republics. Thus whilst the eighteenth century saw Giampietro Riva introduce the Arcadian poetry of Italy to Lugano, Francesco Soave join forces with the Encyclo-paedists of Lombardy and the young Franscini receive decisive and lasting inspiration from Milan, no Ticinese personality came forward in the nineteenth century to champion Romanticism or, however modestly, to join Carducci's vigorous counter-movement with its commitment to classical models. Nor did anyone come under the influence of Vergas' naturalism. The effects of these literary movements were not seen until well into the twentieth century, if indeed they have been seen at all. Angelo Nessi, it is true, managed to link up with the "Scapigliatura milanese" and thus with Italian Literature, but we have to wait for a poet of our own time, Francesco Chiesa, to win for Ticinese Literature the unreserved recognition of both artistic and literary circles in Italy.

By turning its back on the great writers and poets of Italy, the nineteenth century fell into a way of thinking and writing which, if not exactly trivial, was an undeniable pointer to an atrophied literary life. Writers wrote for a very limited readership and turned the Ticino into a provincial back-water. Moreover, the conscious cultivation of the language passed from men of letters to politicians, from literature to parliament and the law courts. It is here that Chiesa has an additional merit that no one has ever commented on, but which seems to me of fundamental significance : it was Chiesa who rescued the language from political speech-makers and clerics and restored it to writers and poets with their profounder and more sensitive concerns.

The poets, novella writers and dramatists of the nineteenth century are almost exclusively colourless individuals. The politicians and statesmen, on the other hand, show more vitality, from Franscini to Battaglini, Romeo Manzoni and Alfredo Pioda, from Vincenzo d'Alberti to G. Respini, G. Cattori, Brenno Bertoni and Giuseppe Motta. The Italian-speaking Grisons possessed one great scholar in G. A. Scartazzini who dedicated his life's work to Dante research. The poverty shown in poetry is all the more painful to contemplate when one looks at the incredible vitality which the Romansh-speaking Swiss—the smallest linguistic minority in the country—developed in this field during the second half of the nineteenth century.

In the midst of the powerful, undisputed supremacy enjoyed by political writers, with their abstruse arguments and civic preoccupations which threatened to turn culture into the monoply of statesmen and journalists, we come across one genuine "man of letters" at the turn of the century who deserves attention for several reasons. Firstly, his cultural background and mentality were genuinely Lombardian, untouched by tendentiousness and Helvetic politics. Secondly, he felt an inner identification with a quite specific phase in the development of Italian Literature—the Lombardian and Piedmontese "Scapigliatura", that short-lived period of Bohemian anarchy and melancholy scepticism, of revolt against a decaying bourgeoisie, which also heralded the advent of socialism as a positive influence. This was the heyday of the late Romantic pseudo-rebels who posed as "crepuscolari" ("Bards of Twilight") or "poètes maudits", yet were themselves incurably bourgeois, equipped merely with an exaggerated and lachrymose sentimentality. Thirdly, this writer gave a fascinating, formal brilliance to his exclusively literary intentions. His name was ANGELO NESSI (1873–1932). Born in Locarno, he spent most of his life in Milan where he composed innumerable operatic libretti, several dialect comedies and contributed articles of a mainly humorous character to newspapers and magazines. He was a "Signore"—a man of the world, elegant, decadent and prematurely exhausted by work, social life and the pressures of an alert, but excessively delicate sensibility. Outwardly inclined to banter and witty argumentativeness, he gave an impression—even on his death-bed—of cynicism and lack of scruple. But in reality he was a man of enthusiasm, warm-hearted, magnanimous and filled with an inner disquiet. As a last representative of the "Scapigliatura milanese", he possessed its typical characteristics : sensitivity, irony, fantasy and a use of language that was at times fastidious, at others negligent.

But Nessi marks a turning point, the start of a new development in Ticinese Literature. Superficially his descriptions of the country-side and people of Lombardy take us back a century to a time when an interest in state affairs, history and politics had not yet been aroused. In fact, they bring us a long way forward, for they transport us to the regions inhabited by genuine poets. Nessi signals the transition to an intellectual renaissance in Italian Switzerland which begins with Francesco Chiesa.

FRANCESCO CHIESA, *the "indefatigable craftsman"*

In 1969 FRANCESCO CHIESA celebrated his ninety-eighth birthday. Thanks to an iron constitution, he still goes for long walks, smokes his "toscano", works in his garden and prunes his trees. His mind, too, remains unclouded and alert. Above the gaunt, sun-tanned face with the clear, bright eyes, alternately pensive and ironic, his thick silver hair gleams and increases the impression of serene dignity and vitality. He published his first book in 1897, and for over seventy years, without a sign of fatigue or doubt, he has devoted himself to literature and Ticinese "Italianità", his artistic and intellectual heritage. Chiesa's life and work represents one of the most important phenomena in the cultural life of a region, which as an intellectual concept knows no frontiers, and which in the Ticino and Italy is called Lombardy. His life is somewhat bare of external events. For forty-six years Chiesa taught Italian Litera-ture and the History of Art at the "Liceo" in Lugano, where he was Headmaster for thirty years. He was not overburdened with teaching duties (although he proved a serious and strict school-master), and the demands made upon him were kept to an absolute minimum so that he could concentrate on his literary activities. Although he was master of his own time by virtue of the tiny republic's generosity—a debt he acknowledged with gratitude —he took the duties of his innumerable official positions very seriously. He did not find writing easy, but he always possessed a unique ability to exploit every free moment; after a lesson, a committee meeting or the inspection of some ancient moment, he would return like a good craftsman to the tools and materials of his beloved trade and re-immerse himself in his creative work, conjuring up once more the images and characters he had been forced temporarily to suppress. His life is an example of the strength of purpose which lies behind rich creativeness. It demonstrates the self-discipline of the patient, conscientious craftsman who can only smile at today's loudly proclaimed theories of improvisation and poetic intuition, which are supposed to produce instant illumination without the artist's active intervention.

There is however, one surprising aspect of this man whom life has brought few painful experiences and much happiness and satisfaction : his solitariness. For many years Chiesa kept himself aloof, and only age has mellowed him. It is true that many young people have been inspired to write by his example, with the result that one can go so far as to speak of a "literary renaissance in Italian Switzerland". But he has founded no school; no writer or poet has received more than superficial encouragement and advice from him or been in close, personal contact with him. Chiesa was eighty-five before he was induced to make his first, comprehensive personal statements. Only then did he open out and become a freer, friendlier, warmer person. For decades the poet had surrounded himself with a protective wall of austere reserve, so that the question was often asked : what is the man really like? Diffident? Taciturn? Courageous? Egocentric? Perhaps the latter; egocentricity may be essential for Chiesa's peace of mind and to safe-guard his work from distraction. This is by no means an idle question, for it is clearly related to another which concerns his creative work : what is Chiesa's attitude to, and knowledge of, his fellow human beings and their fundamental relationships? This question touches on the psychological aspect of his stories, especially his novels, the success and limitations of his work and the spiritual stand-point of the writer. Perhaps Chiesa's apparent naïveté has obscured his obstinacy and pride. Perhaps behind the cool, reserved courteousness is to be found the egoism of a man who does not wish to waste his time on other people. This attitude is easily understandable and even justifiable, but it occupies us again and again when we try to penetrate the innermost nature of the writer. Chiesa as man and artist is clearly influenced by a basic mistrust of his fellow men and a certain scepticism towards physical action and "epoch-making" ideas. From this stems his inability to emerge from his shell, to get himself imaginatively inside another's personality, to perceive via the characters in his novels and stories the unique quality of individual human beings and their experience. This, it seems to me, is the explanation of Chiesa's solitariness, but also of the unmistakeable note of lyricism that pervades all his stories. If it is not possible to speak of intense passions in a man of such harmonious moderation and with such a delicate sense of discretion, what things, at least, hold a place in his affections?

First and foremost, not surprisingly, Chiesa loves his freedom as a creative writer, and secondly his native land. The latter does not simply mean for him the hills around Lugano, the enchanting doorway to the Val Solda, which have prevented him moving to Locarno, Zürich or an Italian university town. His native land is the whole Ticino with its history, cultural monuments and its famous tradition of the "Maestri Comacini"—a bustling land inhabited by a touchy people who are easily offended by lack of sympathy or encroachment on their rights. But patriotism has never led Chiesa to dreams of grandeur—that moral grandeur which fascinated politicians like Giuseppe Motta and Giuseppe Cattori—but has awakened in him the need for clarity and honesty. There has been no greater or more stubborn opponent than he of the "Repubblica dell'iperbole" which at times seems to lose all sense of moderation and dignity. His patriotism has also moved him to describe the work of Ticinese artists of earlier times, to protect and restore cultural monuments and to safe-guard the countryside against the disfigurements of unscrupulous architects, speculators and advertising men. As chairman of select committees and advisor to the Cantonal government on the restoration of churches and important houses, he has drawn up petitions against the vandalism of ultra-modern architects and drafted precise legislation against the use of foreign languages in inscriptions and to protect indigenous alpine flora. It is, however, the language that lies closest to Chiesa's heart. And it is not by chance that Chiesa has initiated a genuine Ticinese Literature alive to its task of protecting the language he has rescued from the dead hand of bureaucracy. Even if a small, but vigorous group of writers had not been inspired by his example, his services to "Italianità" would still have been considerable. He brings to the language that exclusive, stubborn affection which is typical of writers living in border districts, and which has coloured, for example, the work of Niccolò Tommaseo and Umberto Saba in Italy. The proximity of the border gives the writer a sense of imminent danger and dissolution; it gives him a genuine concern for an unfalsified, natural idiom. For more than seventy years Chiesa has urged his country: "Honour your language!"

Nevertheless, in Chiesa's view "the defence of our 'Italianità' must not limit itself to language and culture, but must be interpreted in a wider sense : we must try to maintain friendly relations not only with the Italy of books and the arts, but also with the Italy of today . . . whose people are swayed at certain periods by violent passions we cannot share." It was for this reason that he wished to preserve his "love and loyalty for the country regardless of its political complexion, be it red, black or any other colour". To some these words may seem a superficial justification, but for Chiesa they represent an attitude which is undoubtedly both honest and consistent.

In the sphere of Italian culture Chiesa loves and admires above all Dante. In addition, he is greatly interested in the plastic arts and, especially, architecture. Nor must one forget his love of the soil. Work on the land, as it has evolved among unpretentious country folk, can still offer the contemporary poet—as it once did Virgil—the most profound consolation and a never-failing source of joyful sensations and tranquility. Chiesa has remarked himself that the discovery of this aspect of Nature "was for me a wonderful surprise, an effective antidote for all sorrow which helped me to sweat out literary poisons; it clarified my mind and provided me with an example of a healthier and more natural activity as a counter-balance to my intellectual work".

Today it is a trite commonplace to remark that Chiesa's art has developed from the abstract to the concrete, from the complex to the simple, from remoteness—whether in a world of legend or intellectualism—to a direct contact with life. Even his style, which originally seemed laborious and mechanical (Emilio Cecchi describes it as "arrovellarsi" to indicate a certain quality of deliberate, harsh awkwardness), has gradually achieved a genial and balanced serenity. At the age of fifty Chiesa entered a new phase which was to produce the *Racconti puerili, Tempo di marzo, Racconti del mio orto, Scoperti nel mio mondo* and *Ricordi dell'età minore*.

The writer himself has admitted that the *Racconti puerili* struck him at first as all too thin and lacking in content; he did not feel he had written a work of originality. It is also known that *Tempo di marzo* was not originally conceived as a novel but as a sequel to the successful *Racconti puerili*. But in any case it is beyond question that these two books won suddenly for Chiesa a wide readership in Italy. Chiesa had created an unmistakable and inimitable prose style. It asserted itself successfully against the almost pagan, domineering splendour of D'Annunzio, against the desperate bitterness of Pirandello's dialectics, against the precise, fantastical but very literary style of Bontempelli and Palazzechi, and against the charming irony and ambiguous playfulness of Panzini. For it was original, skilful, free of bombast and, in its sly humour, close to the Lombardian tradition and the wisdom of Manzoni. At the same time—and here lies its modernity—it reflected the author's moods and day-dreams, his joy in creativity.

We can therefore mark two equally productive periods in Chiesa's work. "Culture" defines the first, "Nature" the second. In the former Chiesa attempted a history of man and Culture; he wrote fairy tales, myths and legends, and together they offer a concentrated interpretation of the world which contains insights that are often original and always ingenious. He also took up themes that led to timeless allegories in the manner of Pascoli. Through them he was able to formulate moral truths and to admonish and encourage his readers. At all times Chiesa's aim was to demonstrate the poetry inherent in every aspect of life. He wanted to explore the full range of human experience with all its complex contradictions and ambiguities. This he accomplished by virtue of a pronounced sense for intrinsic values, a strong literary consciousness, a versatile imagination and an uncommon gift for seizing life's phenomena—Nature, historical events, intellectual developments— and transforming them all into a single, exciting vision. Even abstract themes, such as the search for God, moral responsibility, the birth of Freedom and the victory of the egalitarian ideal, take on in his hands a visible, tangible form. Cultural and literary preoccupations, therefore, determine the quality of Chiesa's prose in this first period. Clearly an end in itself, it glitters like marble, multi-coloured and at times, perhaps, all too smooth.

In his second period, on the other hand, Chiesa has attempted to capture the specific quality of his country and his experiences, and the atmosphere of an enchanted, happy childhood. He has discovered in his childhood memories, in the soil and in Nature— explored with growing admiration and emotion—themes whose magic and creative possibilities surpass those he found in literature, legends and fairy tales. In a series of fresh, warm-hearted books he has given us a timeless, uncomplicated image of a landscape and people, seen and experienced through an artist's perception. His style, too, has matched this change; it has become spontaneous and supple, and with expressions borrowed from the dialect of Lombardy it demonstrates an unaffectedness and diversity that few twentieth-century writers have achieved.

Chiesa is above all else a poet, and therefore, whether he is concerned with culture, history or the nature of man, he is initially inclined to detached contemplation, to a careful exploration of the secret nature of life and to a subtle perception of myriad details. He allows impressions to work on his mind and assume plastic shapes. He collects his thoughts in tranquility, and in the process often attains that serene recognition of the moral law of one who has achieved sufficient objectivity to weigh problems and passions soberly. At other times he has produced intelligent meditations on life and its contradictions that are full of charm and humour.

This I take to be the creative process in the writer Chiesa, who is not only the greatest poet of Italian Switzerland, but is one of the most significant figures in contemporary Italian Literature. Chiesa's work, his contemporaneity, his influence as an educator and citizen aware of his political responsibilities, and finally his campaign for "Italianità" represent the most valuable contribution that the Canton of Ticino can bring both to Italy and to Switzerland.

In the footsteps of Chiesa

Although, as we have seen, Chiesa has founded no school, he has nevertheless given a decisive stimulus to literary creativeness. A reawakened literary consciousness has exercised a positive influence on a world of provincial narrow-mindedness. Chiesa's example has had a lasting effect on a number of writers, many of whom are teachers who help to maintain a vigorous intellectual life in the country. These men and women publish their work— often at great personal expense—in their tiny homeland, and sometimes they, too, manage to establish a link with Italian Literature and get their work published in Milan or Florence, thus attracting the attention of literary critics in Italy.

To begin chronologically with the poets, we come first to VALERIO ABBONDIO (1891–1958). He turned relatively late to poetry, and in all his work he displayed a remarkable care and deliberation. A few slim volumes appeared at long, but regular intervals: "Betulla", "L'Eterna Veglia", "Campànule", "Silenze", "Cerchi d'argento". Abbòndio's art suggests the graceful birch, the silvery shimmer of its bark and the trembling of its delicate leaves in sunlight. In "Cerchi d'argento" he takes up a broader theme with great clarity of vocabulary and rhythm : only a slight resonance remains of the pensive fondness for earthly things seen in his earlier work; Woman disappears—at least as a physical presence— and a new longing grows from page to page, a longing for transcendance and a striving for the Absolute.

In strong contrast to Abbòndio's work, "Parabola" and other

poems by FELICE MENGHINI (born 1909) stand out. Menghini was Provost in Poschiavo and died very young in a mountain accident. If one looks to the theatre for a comparison, "Parabola" recalls in some ways Roberto Bracco's play *Piccolo Santo* in its mixture of tormented, uncontrolled lyricism and rich verbal textures which convey a sense of danger permanently threatening to erupt.

GIORGIO ORELLI (born 1921) is a representative of a very modern poetic development which strips form to its basic essentials. This tendency was already discernible in his book *Né bianco né viola*, published in 1944, which won the "Premio Lugano". After two further collections—*Prima dell'anno nuovo* and *Poesie*, published in Milan in 1952—he set to work on a series of translations of Goethe's poems. Orelli is, unmistakeably, a gifted poet familiar not only with contemporary Italian, French and Spanish poetry, but also with such classics as Leopardi, and poets of antiquity such as Lucretius and Catullus. In the peripheral, backward world of the provinces his is the first attempt to continue the values of Ungaretti's poetry and even those of Futurism: the rejection of traditional prosody, a preference for the fragment, the epigram and the startling image, the struggle for a pure, intact language which will give to the word a passionate intensity and to tranquility a lasting magic.

Amongst poets and writers a special place is held by GIUSEPPE ZOPPI. He taught Italian language and literature at the "Eidgenössische Technische Hochschule" in Zürich until his death in 1952 at the early age of fifty-six. It is not easy to formulate a general judgment on his work as a whole. It is perhaps wisest to keep the various aspects of his writing separate and to decide scrupulously which elements of his work have lasting quality. As man, teacher and citizen he is sure of our admiration, and as a poet he deserves appreciation. As a literary critic, however, and compiler of anthologies, he is not altogether convincing. His fiction, too, inclines one to scepticism.

His "Libro dell'Alpe" set Zoppi on an enviable path through life that brought him success after success and largely spared him quarrels and personal animosity. In his poetry he always concentrated on the beautiful and innocent aspects of experience. He sought clarity in subject matter and integrity in creative activity. When he describes the wild panic of cattle caught in a storm or the terrible fate that can befall men in the mountains, one feels in the simple naïveté of the language a profound desire to escape the spell of terror and return to a friendlier environment where he can rediscover the delights of a sentimental idyll and the joyful richness of natural phenomena. This professed attitude and the lyricism in which he takes refuge constitute, in fact, the essential elements of his art. Poetry and freshness permeate the "Libro dell'Alpe". Zoppi's work leaves in the reader an impression of spring-like enchantment, and the clear music of his beautiful verse and poetic prose will keep his memory alive for generations to come.

In PIERO BIANCONI (born 1899 in Locarno) Italian Switzerland possesses a genuinely original writer. His restrained fervour and rich, supple language bring him sometimes—on a purely formal level—close to Chiesa. But he lacks the latter's deep humanity. Bianconi is the typical man of letters whose refinement often degenerates into empty formalism. He is a writer who is constantly stimulated by his imagination, literary reminiscences and aesthetic day-dreaming—in fact, by sheer joy in the creative process. At times he recalls the most skilful modern prose stylists—the famous Italian, Emilio Cecchi, for example, whose intellectual development, however, he has not matched, and from whom he is further differentiated by his deep loyalty to his roots in the Ticino.

The colourful, vivid prose of "Ritagli", "Croci e rascane", "Il Cavallo Leopoldo", "Cappelle del Ticino", "Ossi da mòrdere" and "Gocce sui fili" demonstrates Bianconi's masterly command of the interplay of nuance and striking effect. His style is polished and modern in its vocabulary and sentence structure. Modelled on the Italian "frammentisti", his is the most modern prose being written in the Ticino today, and it deserves the admiration of the most fastidious stylists. "Gocce sui fili" points to a new and more humane Bianconi who at times reveals a surprising facility to understand the everyday worries and problems that beset other people. Naturally, his prose style has benefited, too, from this transformation.

Another excellent writer is Bianconi's favourite pupil, MARIO AGLIATI (born 1922). Indeed, in the treatment of his preferred themes dealing with his homeland, Agliati's work frequently possesses a more attractive quality than his master's. There is hardly anyone who knows more about life in nineteenth-century Ticino, and Lugano in particular. In those days Lugano was still a large, peaceful market town with little guest-houses, coaches and fine arcades with romantic names. *Lugano del buon tempo* has the charm and gentle atmosphere of certain pages of Samuel Butler. Agliati possesses a marvellous knack of bringing the very stones of Lugano to life. He describes the doings of every family, discusses the history of the ancient palaces and churches and gives the reader, in all, a graphic picture of life in every quarter of the town.

A stylist, but of a very different character, is the Bernese ADOLFO JENNI (born 1911). He has published a variety of critical studies, particularly on Dante and Manzoni, numerous volumes of poetry and "prose di romanzo". Jenni considers his prose works as a special genre occupying a position somewhere between literary criticism and fiction, diary entries and free invention, psychology and naturalism. To be sure, these "prose di romanzo", as the author calls them, have a hard time of it in these days of neo-realism and "littérature engagée". What is remarkable is that Jenni has stuck faithfully and consistently to the form he has chosen.

From the Grisons comes RETO ROEDEL (born 1898 in Casale Monferrato). He took his doctorate in Turin and was until quite recently Professor of Italian Literature at the "Handelshochschule" of St. Gallen. He is an essayist and the author of fiction and a number of plays. His encyclopaedic knowledge and taste is illustrated by a volume of critical studies *Con noi e coi nostri classici* (1946), which contains, besides essays on Dürer, G. A. Scartazzini, Leonardo da Vinci, Giovanni Segantini and *Baroque Poetry in the 17th Century* (written in German), his brilliant interpretation, *Individuo e comunità nella Divina Commedia*. This list alone is sufficient proof of Roedel's many-faceted, eclectic mind. His predilection for the psychological aspects of his favourite "classical" writers is accurately reflected in his own critical writing and fiction : *Terra e gente elvetica, Le cose, Lo spinarello e i miti dell'uomo* (Turin 1957). The latter book, up to now his most engaging work, fuses cultural, fictive, mythical and fantastical elements into one unified whole.

The remaining writers of fiction can be roughly categorized on the basis of their techniques and their intellectual preoccupations. Piero Scanziani, Elena Bonzanigo and Carlo Castelli keep to certain rules of traditional fiction, whilst Felice Filippini and Giovanni Bonalumi depart from them, although each in a different direction.

PIERO SCANZIANI (born 1908) comes from the Ticino, but lives today in Rome, where he enjoys a high reputation as an author and journalist. He appealed to a wide readership with his *Bericht* : *L'Avventura dell'uomo,* published in twenty instalments in the Milanese weekly, *Tempo.* His other interests find expression in the popular medium of sophisticated journalism. These include the world religions, animal psychology and, especially, dog-breeding, in which field Scanziani has founded and edits several specialist journals. He is a man of the world, a "Roman" with international tastes, but yet a writer who has remained close to his roots among the sensitive people of the Mendrisiotto.

His most important works have been translated into German, French and Spanish. Two main features characterize his literary output : on the one hand, his original, fertile imagination, and on the other, the sweeping, comprehensive scale of his narrative technique. Scanziani's originality is apparent in his choice of subject matter, behind which there usually lies a philosophic concept or a symbolic significance of general validity. In addition, his characters are frequently used to embody whole cultures and contrasting philosophies, and to illustrate the distinctive features of different races and peoples.

Though perhaps Scanziani may simply dazzle us with his formal brilliance and ultimately remain unconvincing, his unusual delineation of every problem he faces is impressive and reveals new relationships between men and their environment. This formal brilliance is evident not only in his skilful technique of fading one scene into another and linking stories together within a single framework, but also in the diversity achieved through a unified sensibility. Each of his works pours forth an incredible profusion of tonal qualities which collide, attract each other and fuse into a powerful surge of human emotion. It is neither easy nor comfortable to be in command of so many registers, to produce so many motifs and master and organize them all into a precise theme.

ELENA BONZANIGO, born in Bellinzona, comes from a wealthy, industrious emigrant family, and her first published work was a collection of childhood stories set in London and the Ticino. Next came two historical novels *Serena Seròdine* and *Oltre le Mura* (Lugano). At the centre of this cycle (which is to be completed with a third volume) stands the gentle Serena, scion of an old-established Ascona family which has produced, among other personalities, the important Ticinese painter of the seventeenth century, Giovanni Seròdine. The action is set in seventeenth-century Rome and in Locarno, bustling with Swiss mercenaries. The book depicts the encounters and conflicts between various races and mentalities, the quiet heroism of a woman and the astonished curiosity of the inhabitants of Locarno and Bellinzona, who came into contact with a vast cross-section of people in those turbulent and adventurous times. *Viaggio di notte* is a charming short story set in our own day which chronicles a night journey by train from the Ticino to Rome. It begins with a description of the travellers : an immediate tension is created which leads directly into the plot. The novel *La Conchiglia,* however, marks a return to Elena Bonzanigo's favourite historical themes. The book, which was awarded the Prize of the Swiss Lyceum Club, tells of an old lady from Lombardy who, as the wife of a Ticinese statesman in Bellinzona, witnesses the fierce conflicts of 1890 in her adopted country.

The stories of the Lugano author CARLO CASTELLI (born 1909), collected in the volumes *Saturnino e le ombre, Gli uomini sono tristi* and *Storie d'amore* (Locarno), deal with painful psychological conflicts and are overshadowed by a bitter, devastating pessimism. Yet they shine with human truth and are written with a conscious heightening of effects. However, Castelli's talents have found their best expression in drama; his radio plays and works for the stage mark a solid achievement. For the *Ballata per Tim, pescatore di trote* he received the Prix Italia of the "Unione radiofonica internazionale". His moving work *L'altra vita* had previously won a literary prize in the Ticino. Various of his radio plays have been translated into other languages, including Japanese.

Felice Filippini and Giovanni Bonalumi, who are both still comparatively young, rebel against traditional prose rather as Oldelli has done against traditional poetry. The means they choose are different : Filippini sees a way forward via a revolutionary handling of vocabulary and syntax; Bonalumi, on the other hand, belongs to the experimental movement begun by Cesare Pavese.

FELICE FILIPPINI was born in 1917 in Arbedo, a village set amidst valleys, rocks and rivers. He lives in Lugano and runs the Talks Department of Radio Monteceneri. This position has brought him many friends and useful contacts in literary circles. Filippini is a self-educated man of unflagging energy, and moreover, an eccentric. His writing employs every possible mode of expression— critical essay, fantastical fragment, short story, poem, novel, meditation, radio play. Literature, however, is not enough : he not only sculpts, paints frescoes and pictures in oils and tempera, produces etchings, lithographs and pen-and-ink drawings, but he also composes music. The multiplicity of his gifts is astonishing. His skill in a variety of artistic media has brought him a number of prizes in art and literary competitions.

In his first creative period his work was dominated by an almost obsessive excitement, by distorted images perched on the edge of caricature or madness and by strange, confused gestures of despair. Gradually he discovered a more temperate mode of expression, subdued his emotions and began to organize his imagery and books more consciously. Rebellious restlessness has not entirely disappeared from his work, it is true, but it has been extenuated by the joyful sounds and voices of one of Filippini's favourite themes : the country festival. In this constantly recurring motif the poet and painter gives full scope to his artistic skill and limitless fantasy. Drawing on the inexhaustible richness of his imagination, he depicts Nature and men relaxing in boisterous festivity. Amidst the general gaiety Filippini inserts brief scenes that are moving and painful, but often comic, too. Against this backcloth his fellow countrymen reveal themselves as genuine human beings full of emotional warmth, and the "génie du lieu" of the Lombardian-Baroque Ticino stands out in its purest form. Motifs from everyday life are not, however, lacking—stonemasons hew granite, traders extol their wares in the market place—and even misfortune and death are briefly hinted at. But in the foreground stand the people, gesticulating, quarrelling and forgiving, dancing and drinking in the cool shade of thick-foliaged trees. We meet this country festival atmosphere, however paradoxical it may sound, in Filippini's very first book, *Signore dei poveri morti* (Florence and Bellinzona).

A similar impression of rich tonal diversity is conveyed in his second novel *Ragno di sera* (Milan and Bellinzona) which is the story of a village threatened by avalanche. This is a catalogue of human types, workers and peasants, practical, vigorous families and families whose health is undermined by diseases brought home by returning emigrants. The unique, elemental quality of the language, sometimes shading into dialect, corresponds to Filippini's inner vehemence. His fragmented, arbitrary sentence structure and unrestrained vocabulary, combined with sudden irruptions of light, flashes of graphic imagery and ever-recurring motifs and tone-colours, create a stifling atmosphere. This extravagant language, born as it were out of the soil, rocks and mountain torrents, possesses a sombre beauty.

To a certain extent the novel *Gli ostaggi* by the Locarno author GIOVANNI BONALUMI strikes one as equally modern. A line from Gerard Manley Hopkins, which stands as a motto at the beginning of the book, indicates that the "hostages" are the boys preparing for the priesthood who, untouched by the worldly spirit, are dedicated to Christ in the flower of their youth. The book touches on the theme of religious doubt endemic in contemporary literature. The action is set in a seminary. A crisis brings to a young seminarist the decisive perception that isolation is harmful and that open relationships with other men can only be beneficial. Bonalumi has also written critical studies on *Dino Campana* (Florence), the stylistic development of satire in Parini and the genesis and poetic values of Tasso's "Aminta". In his capacity of Professor in the University of Basle he has published a selection of philological studies and lectures under the title *Il libro di Miranda*. His literary output shows throughout a refined taste and a modern sensibility, although he is less convincing as a stylist— for his prose contains, despite qualities of discernment and perception, elements of a whimsical sentimentality.

Even a small country will support the literary arts once it grasps that literature can give a richer, more dignified meaning to its people's lives in just the same way that prudent legislation or economic prosperity can and does. One thing above all should not be forgotten : the security that a vigorous literary tradition offers to a country which is ethnically threatened, whose language and culture are endangered and which urgently needs new writers and poets.

NOTES

1. Recent historical research has shown that, although the Canton's liberty won in 1789 was no longer in jeopardy, the affiliation to Switzerland hung in the balance until the defeat of Napoleon in the Russian Campaign in 1812. Two years previously the Canton had been occupied by French troops, under the command of General Fontanelli, in the service of the first King of Italy, Eugène de Beauharnais.

2. Oldelli is the author of the *Dizionario storico-ragionato degli uomini del Canton Ticino* which has not always been favourably reviewed, as we shall see. Mention should be made of E. Motta's excellent research work published in the *Bollettino storico della Svizzera italiana*. For Giuseppe Zoppi, F.D. Vieli and A. M. Zendralli, who has published an anthology of writing from the Italian-speaking Grisons, v. Bibliography. (*Scrittori della Svizzera italiana*).

3. Stefano Franscini remarks in his *Annali* (Bellinzona, 1953) on the "parochialism" of the Franciscan G. A. Oldelli's *Guide to Famous Men of the Ticino*, published in 1807, in which "utter mediocrities are showered with inordinate praise". The statesman speaks emphatically of

the "extreme poverty of the literature produced by our Canton", and concludes, not without a trace of bitterness: "The book might have merit if it led to an examination of why, with so large a number of students, we have contributed so little to the literary fame of Italy." In a brief footnote he sketches the introduction to such an enquiry, which was never carried out: "Why? Suggested causes: studies uncompleted, idleness, lack of libraries and competitive spirit, indifference to the country's history on behalf of the reading public, and so on." The unmistakable voice of Franscini!

(Translated by Michael Butler.)

BIBLIOGRAPHY, *see* p. 287

Rhaeto-Romanic Literature

Rhaeto-Romanic Literature

by ANDRI PEER

The Rhaeto-Romance Language

RHAETO-ROMANCE, or Romansch, is the language spoken in three areas of the Canton of Grisons; the valleys of the Rhine, Engadine and the Val Müstair. In early times, up to the invasion of the region by the Alamanni and Baiuwarii, it was spoken throughout Raetia Prima and over large areas of Raetia Secunda. Other Romance languages related to the Romansch of the Grisons are the so-called Ladin, spoken in certain high valleys in the Dolomites by a population of approximately 20,000 and the language spoken in Friuli, the area between the Tagliamento, the Carnic Alps and the Yugoslavian border, which has a population of 450,000.

What is the history of the language? Before the conquest of Raetia by Drusus and Tiberius in 15 B.C. the language of the Raeti was spoken in these mountains. Very little is known about this language. Ancient accounts describe it as a variety of Etruscan, but this can only have been true of the language spoken at the southern foot of the Alps, an area to which many Etruscans had fled, following the invasion of their lands by Gaulish tribes (*circa* 400 B.C.).

Another theory, no longer tenable, held that the Raeti spoke Celtic in pre-Roman times. The present view is that Old Raetian was related to Lepontic and to Veneto-Illyrian, both of which, like Latin and Greek, belong to the Indo-European family of languages but were strongly influenced by Celtic.

Following the subjugation of the warlike Raeti, the vernacular Latin of the conquerors mixed with the partly Celtic Raetian tongue and there developed, under the growing influence of Christianity, a highly distinctive form of vulgar Latin. The colloquial development of this language led to the formation of Romansch. Traces of early Romansch, bearing remarkable similarity to Old French of the same period, are already evident in Latin documents of the late tenth century. Romansch never gained the status of an official language and consequently split into a number of increasingly divergent dialects.

An important factor in this process was the loss to the Romansch speaking area of its focal point, when, in the fifteenth century, the town of Chur went over to German. In the middle of the sixteenth century the need for a written language for use in Church services in Protestant parishes gave the impetus for a written Romansch language. Men of initiative in the different valleys set down versions of the New Testament, the Psalms, morality plays and hymns in their local dialects. The first writings appeared in the Ladin dialect of the Engadine and were followed within a few decades by writings in the Surselvan dialect of the Outer Rhine and in the Middle Grisons dialect of the Inner Rhine and the Albula. Thus the seeds were sown early for the development of Romansch into a number of quite distinct idioms, a process which subsequent attempts at consolidation have failed to arrest.

About a hundred years ago the Italian Romance scholar Graziadio Isaia Ascoli investigated the relationship between the Romansch of the Grisons, Friulian and the Ladin spoken in the Dolomites. He came to the conclusion that these once formed a chain of related languages, a family of a quite unique character, deserving the same independent status accorded to French, Italian and Spanish. Quite a different view was advanced by nationalistically minded Italian scientists and polemists during the First World War and again in the thirties under the Fascist regime. They argued vehemently that Romansch was an offshoot of Italian and must be replaced by Italian in religious, educational and administrative practice if it were not to disappear entirely in the continuing advance of the German language. A succession of philologists, of predominantly Swiss nationality, set out to refute these repeated presumptions by the irredentists.

It was, admittedly, strange to find a language community astride the Alps, extending from the St. Gotthard down to Trieste, but they pointed out that the original Raetian speaking area had lain to the north, extending eastwards from the St. Gotthard to the North Tyrol. The really formative influences had spread from this direction. A powerful influence had also come from the south and left its mark on the language, but had not altered its essential character.

Our country lies in the heart of the Alps, on the watershed between North and South, and inevitably both North and South have played a part in the cultural and linguistic development of its people. As early as pre-Roman and Roman times the North exerted a considerable influence upon life in Raetia, and one which became even stronger with the incorporation of Raetia into the Frankish kingdom, in 537, which led to the Germanization of the northern part of the region and the early removal of the diocese of Chur from the north diocese of Como to that of Mainz. From this time on, in successive waves, large numbers of German words found their way into the Rhaetian language, adding a German flavour to both vocabulary and syntax. On the other hand, in the sixteenth century, after the conquest of the Valtellina by the Grisons, the South gained a more significant influence on the Engadine. Indeed, in the eighteenth century, fostered by emigrants and men of education, theologians and teachers, this influence became a threat to the continued existence of Romansch.

But it would be a mistake to suppose that the language of our mountain homeland was ever a plaything, tossed between its neighbours, as at times, its political existence was. Romansch had become far too deply rooted in the traditional way of life of the Grisons, a people who lived in relatively isolated, fiercely independent communities. It had shown itself capable of so thoroughly absorbing language elements of northern and southern origin, and, in a mysterious way, of making them so unmistakably its own, that the genius and identity of the language could no longer stand in question. Our Swiss Confederates are as convinced of this as we are and it received almost unanimous affirmation in the 1938 referendum, when Romansch gained recognition as the fourth national language, the official language in the Grisons. In this preservation of what is good in the old, and assimilation of the new, we see active forces at work, forces which have always benefited the Neo-Latin peoples.

In the second half of the nineteenth century, dangers threatening the language as a result of neglect, of the at that time fashionable imitation of foreign speech habits and of the lack of concern bred by that age's obsession with "progress", were for the first time consciously recognized and attacked, in a good-humoured but determined spirit, by a whole series of philologists.

Foremost among these was the leading Indo-germanic scholar Robert von Planta, who was joined by other scholars from the Grisons, such as Florian Melcher, Giusep Huonder, Caspar Decurtins, Chasper Pult, Ramun Vieli, followed in the present day by Andrea Schorta, Alexi Decurtins, literary historians such as Reto R. Bezzola and Jon Pult and also by distinguished philologists from the German speaking part of Switzerland, such as Jakob Jud and Karl Jaberg. Through research, through the position they secured for Rhaeto-Romance as a university faculty and through their eloquent championing of the language, both vocally and in print, these men brought it to the position of prestige which it enjoys today. Scholars embarked upon monumental works; the *Raetian Book of Names,* and the *Dicziunari rumantsch grischun* which promises to become a comprehensive, realistic encyclopedia of the Alps. Language societies, established with the aim of protecting the Rhaeto-Romanic heritage, have now joined forces in the *Lia Rumantscha.* At the same time dictionaries, grammars, text-books, song-books, almanacs and reading matter suitable for young people have all been produced.

Belles-Lettres

Somewhat surprisingly, original Romanic literature and poetry did not emerge in the Grisons until the nineteenth century. Legal affairs had been conducted in Romansch since 1550, but during the long development of the language in historical and devotional literature, from the earliest translations of the Bible to the hymns of the Pietist movement, no original epic or lyrical works appeared, with the single exception of the simple, down to earth war-song, written in 1527 by the Zuoz politician Gian Travers. Based upon his experiences in the "War of Musso", this was also the first account of local history to appear in Romansch. But although original works were lacking in these three centuries, translations and versions of the Bible had a seminal influence upon the development of a literary language. "L'g Nuof Sainc Testamaint" of Jachiam Bifrun (1560) and Durich Chiampel's version of the Psalms of David (1562) were as important for the development of the written language in the Engadine as Luther's Bible was in Germany. The writers of this period went beyond mere translation and commentary; the devotional, historical and polemical works they produced abound in examples of a very personal, characteristically Romanic style of expression. There is a quite unmistakable, creative impulse asserting itself in these writings, particularly in those of the sixteenth and seventeenth centuries, in both the Inn and the Rhine valleys. Good examples of this are the brilliant, extended version of "Simler's Hymnal" by the Engadine pastor Jon Martin, in his *Philomela,* and the deeply spiritual hymns of the "Consolaziun da l'olma devoziusa", a collection for use in the

Catholic Mass, many editions of which were printed in the Outer Rhine area.

When, in the nineteenth century, literary forms finally emerged, there was a powerful and living tradition of theological, legal, historiographical and pedagogic literature for writers to draw on, but virtually no original poetic models to imitate. Furthermore, the spread of the written word with the advent of printing and the Reformation had widened the gap between the main dialects of the Grisons. There are today three written Romansch languages in the canton; that of the Engadine and Müstair (rumantsch-ladin in the two versions, spoken in the Upper and Lower Engadine); that of the Outer Rhine, (romantsch-sursilvan); and the slightly differing dialects of the Domleschg, Schams and Oberhalbstein (rumántsch-sutsilvan). Nothing would be gained by trying to force these three idioms into one standard mould, and much would be lost; the linguistic heterogeneity of the Grisons is a positive asset. All three written dialects have writers of their own, writers who, despite basic similarities, are strikingly different in the quality of their expression and the particular awareness they convey.

The writers and poets of the Engadine

Foreign travel gave the original impetus to the belles-lettres. Numerous travellers, returning from Italy, France, Germany and Holland, brought with them the songs of these countries, which were an inspiration to local writers. Conradin de Flugi (1787–1874), an uncle of Guillaume Apollinaire and a man who did much to foster the tourist-trade of St. Moritz, had, as did many other Romanic poets of the period, business interests in Italy and returned to his native Engadine for his holidays and retirement. His "Rimas" in a tone of elation, express a mixture of nostalgia and love of nature. The same mood is expressed in the poems of his contemporaries, sometimes with a playful joie de vivre, often in more wistful tones. Zaccaria Pallioppi (1820–73) a jurist, philologist and editor of a valuable Romansch-German dictionary, tried his hand at a variety of metrical forms, from the classical ode to the sonnet. In lyrical inspiration however, his "Poesias" are rather less impressive than the poetry of Gian Fadri Caderas (1830–91), a poet of fine sensitivity, inspired by melancholy and a delight in the beauty of the countryside, whose finest works were later collected by Peider Lansel, in the anthology Poesias (1930). Simon Caratsch (1826–91) and Giovannes Mathis (1824–1912) bring to life in their writings, the former in innumerable and enchanting occasional verses, the latter in prose, the folklore of the Engadine and the delight of its inhabitants in festive occasions. The Federal judge Andrea Bezzola (1840–97) wrote a number of "Lieder" which the people have taken to their hearts.

This first, modest crop of occasional and travelling poets drew the language and imagery of their songs and poetic miniatures both from the tradition of devotional literature and from that more powerful, unwritten source of folk tradition, contained in fairy-tales, folksongs and proverbs.

Unfortunately the protagonists of the Reformation and Counter-Reformation in the Grisons had not been well-disposed towards folklore and folksongs. The rich oral tradition had existed beneath the surface for centuries, until an age came that was conscious of this invaluable legacy. Scholars and poets now rediscovered folksongs, fairy-tales, proverbs and legends and incorporated them in what they wrote. One piece of good fortune was the preservation of both the text and the melody of the famous medieval *Canzun da Sontga Margriata*. This is the story of a mountain woman with magic powers, half saint, half alpine fairy. Another was the preservation for posterity of the best in both the oral and written traditions in the *Rätoromanische Chrestomathie* (published in Erlangen in twelve volumes between 1896 and 1917), by the far-sighted scholar and one time Rector of the University of Fribourg, Caspar Decurtins. This work bears witness to the desire for synthesis prevalent at the turn of the century.

With the exception of Lansel, the Grisons of the next generation, tending towards Italy, were no great innovators. The verses of Chasper Po (1856–1936) sparkle with a Florentine "arguzia". Gudench Barblan (1860–1916) was a writer of humorous short stories on traditional themes. Balser Puorger (1864–1943) described family life in the Engadine in Dickensian breadth. Clementina Gilli (1864–1943) was important mainly as an influential mediator of German and Italian literature.

Pallid, idyllic and nostalgic verse now gave way to a poetry that was urgently concerned with the genuine, native forms of expression. The face of Ladin had become distorted through the imitation and absorption of foreign speech patterns and the wholesale borrowing of foreign, particularly of Italian words. The pioneer of the reaction of Engadin poets and writers against this state of affairs was Peider Lansel. An educated businessman and self-taught philologist, Lansel dedicated himself to the uphill struggle against the conformism and apathy of his countrymen and taught them self-discipline, loyalty to their inheritance and the preservation in their daily lives of the dignity of their language. Lansel's acute awareness of the values of a well-knit Alpine community also bore poetic fruit. "Il vegl chalamer" established Lansel as the first Romanic author to be a poet in his own right. In his art the mentor of the people gives way to the lover of beauty, assiduously gleaning the best of what tradition has handed down. But, above all, Lansel is a deeply subjective poet, inspired by the twin forces of nature and destiny, whose poetry is a fusion of the tone of the ballad with a refined expressive art, schooled in the greatest works of world literature. Lansel was an inspiration to others, less perhaps through his poetry itself, which only gained a limited popularity, than through the example he set and through his liberation of the hidden resources of an Alpine culture which for so long had misunderstood itself.

Literature now moved towards realism. Writers such as Schimun Vonmoos, Chasper Pult, Gian Gianet Cloetta, Nicolaus Wieser and "Gian Girun" (Ursina Clavuot) present a lively and charming picture of village life, though still with a bias towards folklore and the idyllic. On the whole poetry had been more favoured than fiction in the nineteenth century. Schimun Vonmoos (1868–1940), one of the many pastors to further the Romanic language and literature, started a fruitful development with his *Il corn da puolvra d'Abraham*. From the biblical serenity of this work fiction developed through the tall stories of Men Rauch (1888–1958) and the impressionistic as psychological Novellas of Selina Chönz, to the direct realism of the younger generation, which, in the vivid stories and the historical novel *La müdada* of Cla Biert, returns to the level of everyday life. The dawning of a new, more down to earth realism, emancipating literature from the narrow confines of idyllic and parochial motifs, gave new life to the drama as well. The pioneer of the modern Romanic theatre, at the turn of the century, was Florian Grand (1847–1926) with his play *Adam da Chamues-ch*. Social and political themes were taken up in the plays of Jon Semadeni, who, for instance, showed the undermining of the traditional way of life of the peasant awakening to the attractions of the hotel trade, and in another play brought back to the stage the figure of the bellicose preacher Jürg Jenatsch. A third play, *La S-chürdüm dal sulai* (Eclipse of the Sun) shows how a man can escape from the clutches of absolute powers, the church and totalitarian parties, through self-sacrifice. Gian Belsch (Albert Wihler) and Men Gaudenz revived Biblical drama, the former with *La Festa dals Tabernaculs, Israel* and *David,* the latter with *Giob l'etern.* The Münstertaler Tista Murk turned the Battle of the Calven Gorge, fought in 1499 by the Grisons and Swiss against Maximilian I, into an impressive folk-drama and also dramatized the life of the Rhaetian humanist and poet Simon Lemnius, author of the famous Latin epic, the "Raeteis" who, surprisingly, did not write a single verse of poetry in his mother tongue.

The *Festspiel,* a cross between play and pageant, performed in the open air with the participation of everyone, was well represented by Artur Caflisch with his *Ils duos Travers* and by Men Rauch, whose *Chanzun da la libertà,* performed in Scuol in 1952 on the tercentenary of the Unterengadine becoming independent of the Tyrol in 1662, was a clear demonstration of how well suited this dramatic form is to our modern conditions. A more recent development has been the radio play. Witty satire is well represented by Reto Caratsch. His wildly extravagant story *La Renaschentscha dals Patagons* and his *Commissari da la cravatta verda* castigate, in a Rabelaisian spirit, the excesses of cultural over-organization in the Grisons and the ruthless exploitation of hydro-electric power in the valleys of the Alps.

Several poets have contributed to the development of lyrical verse. Jon Guidon (1892–1966) with his mood-lyricism; Jachen Luzzi (1880–1949) especially as a translator of poetry and drama; Artur Caflisch with his mordant satirical verses; Chatrina Bott-Filli in naive, poignant verses, and Tista Murk in a romantic vein. Luisa Famos is an impressive writer of delicate lyrics. Duri Gaudenz writes autobiographical, contemplative poetry.

During the last twenty years the literature of the Engadine has undergone a transformation as a new generation of writers, stimulated by their studies and travels abroad, have turned their back on the aesthetic canons of the twenties and thirties and sought new forms of expression which incorporate elements of important literary movements of the past century; expressionism, symbolism and surrealism.

Now as before many translations of foreign works have been undertaken, including great works of literature, especially plays and works of fiction. There have been translations of T. S. Eliot and Federico García Lorca, literary essays, aphorisms and prose poems. The reading public has viewed this avant-garde with scepticism; only a small proportion of the potential readership of fifty thousand has had any literary education. However, the unadulterated freshness of the Romansch language ensures that even these more daring experiments in modern genres remain firmly rooted in their native soil. The literature now seems to be more broadly based to take its place among the other literatures of Europe.

Poets and Writers of the Surselva

From its beginnings in the middle of the nineteenth century the literary output of the Surselva had a far more patriotic, rhetorical flavour than that of the "pasticcieri" of the Engadine. Right up to the present day a note of pathos echoes like a clarion call among the voices of the Outer Rhine poets. The first important poem of the new era, "Il pur suveran" by the poet Gion Antoni Huonder (1824–67) stands like a monument carved out of the mountain rock, and affirmation of the simple, proudly independent existence of the mountain peasant. Subsequently the Surselvan dialect was less exposed to the undermining effect of the imitation of Italian than was the case with the Engadine dialect. This was due also to the concerted efforts of a number of prominent poets to preserve their literary heritage and the deeply rooted language of the peasantry, which established once and for all the conservative, parochial character of the valley. The epics and ballads of Giachen Caspar Muoth (1844–1906) are the crowning achievement of Sursilvan literature. In sweeping epic cantos he depicts the Romanic history of the past centuries in a modern version of the "chanson de geste". Conservative, deliberately choosing archaic motifs, Muoth surpasses his predecessors in this form in the suppleness and range of his expressive art. He is fond of classical metres such as the hexameter. His poetry is like the Sursilvan language itself; substantial, impressive, impetuous in its rhythms. He sings the praises of a proud peasantry, depicts the events of the peasant's year in vast frescoes, village festivals, village customs, the local parliaments, midsummer on the Alp, the gaiety and bustle of the flaxbreakers and other typical village characters. He revels in humorous descriptions of processions, enormous peasant gatherings; in a wistful tone he praises old customs that a new, hurried age is undermining and he inveighs against the faddishness of modern times. In his ballads, the finest of which is perhaps *La dertgira nauscha de Valendan,* Muoth interprets history freely in celebrating the Grisons' hatred of tyranny and their fight for freedom against the Austrians and the French. And in his short epic *Il Cumin d'Ursera* he shows the grey-bearded abbot of Disentis, Pieder da

Pultengia, as bold as Savanarola and cunning as Machiavelli in his successful defence of Romansch against the influences threatening it from Canton Uri. Muoth's most talented pupil was Flurin Camathias (1871–1946), the widely-travelled translator of Mistral and Verlaine, who drew the inspiration for his cycle *Historias dil Munt Sogn Gieri* from folk legend. In a more romantic vein is the lyrical poetry of Alfons Tuor (1871–1904). Like Leopardi's, his was a passionate spirit in a weakly body. He was fated to live a brief and painful life, which he spent in contemplation, hovering between sad resignation and bitter despair. Inevitably he became the target of sarcastic comment from those who could not understand him. Wasting away in inactivity, he finally found solace in an ardent piety. Sep Modest Nay (1892–1945) and the highly musical poet Gion Cadieli (1876–1947) stay equally close to the domestic sphere. Their favourite themes and forms have been taken up again in more recent times by other Surselvan poets, such as Luis Candinas, Gion Deplazes, Donat Cadruvi and Riget Bertogg; others, such as Flurin Darms, Paul Tumaschett, Ludivic Hendry and especially Hendri Spescha strike out into more modern forms of expression. Maurus Carnot (1865–1935), the amiable Benedictine Father from Samnaun in the Lower Engadine, made the Surselva his new home when he came to the famous monastery of Disentis, the cultural centre of Catholic Surselva, and celebrated the region in both poetical and philosophical works. Narrative fiction appeared earlier in the Surselva than in the Engadine. The vivid descriptions of country life, written by the country doctor and shrewd observer of human nature Gachen Michael Nay (1860–1920), distinguished as they are by their masterly observation and truth to life, form a worthy complement to Muoth's cycles. Indeed, Nay has been compared with Gotthelf and Ramuz. It was left to Gian Fontana (1897–1953), a native of Flims, to inject really modern themes into Sursilvan literature. In his short life he concerned himself with the social and religious predicament of modern man and with the interplay of the various groupings within society, the State, local community and the family, which he deals with penetratingly, in historical and contemporary settings, in his subtle and vivid *Novellas*. For all his resignation, his attitude to life remains that of a Christian. Fontana's greatest work, however, is his poetry, much of which remains unpublished. A mixture of mystical, contemplative verse and nature lyric, it has a richly musical tone and bears the uniquely personal stamp of the best of Lansel's work. Fontana also wrote operettas and satires on the contemporary scene, which provide an intellectual background against which to view his *Novellas*. Another first-class delineator of village life on the Outer Rhine is the social historian Guglielm Gadola (1902–61), for instance in his "Brulf".

What Muoth, Nay and Fontana began is being carried on by younger men. Toni Halter is a prolific dramatist and novelist, writer of the important bronze-age novel *Culan da Crestaulta* and of other tales for young people, plays for the open-air theatre and for the radio. Clemens Pally writes archetypal hunting stories; Leonhard Caduff is an essayist and author of the fiction works *Cronica della Famiglia R.* and *Vacanza ad Uaulverd;* Donat Cadruvi is a critical observer and conscious stylist in his *Tiara e desiert*. Surselvan prose reaches a new level of seriousness in the short novel *Marietta* and the true to life novelle *Igl cavrer de Vigliuz* by Gion Deplazes. Alois Arpagus has written, in *Per rovens e runtgras* charming short stories.

Sursilvan drama is best represented by the historical "Festspiel", for instance by Maurus Carnot's *Clau Maissen,* Toni Halter's *Festival de Porclas* and by the works of the prolific writer Carli Fry (1897–1956), an active man of letters who has been a valuable mediator of German literature. Two more writers to appear are Gian Caduff a discriminating essayist and poet, and Alfons Maissen, a writer of folk tales, translator and writer for the radio.

Modern Literature of the Surmir and Sutselva

It was not until thirty years ago that the Sutsilvan dialect became standardized as a written language. There were some early religious works in the dialect; Daniel Bonifaci's *Catechism in the idiom of the Domleschg* (1601); Adam Nauli's letter attacking the Engadine Steivan Gabriel for preaching the new doctrine on the Outer Rhine; and later, in the Schams valley, the religious and pedagogic works of Mattli Conrad; but in spite of these, the people of the Middle Grisons valleys lost their written language. Until quite recently German, the Sursilvan or the Engadine dialects were the medium of instruction in schools. The Oberhalbstein idiom had, in Father Alexander Lozza O.S.F. (1880–1953) a highly gifted and versatile poet, the equal of Tuor, Fontana and Lansel. Idiosyncratic in his choice of themes, compelling in his imagery, exuberant and full-blooded, at times indulging in biting satire, Lozza, like Lansel before him, modelled himself on the Italians as a young man. Gion Not Spegnas comes close in tone to Lozza's poetry in his "Rosas e Spegnas", but underlines his effects more deliberately,

often becoming rhetorical. The elegance of Leza Uffer's verse attests
to his schooling in the Romance languages and his refined taste.
Uffer did pioneering work as a collector and interpreter of
Rhaeto-Romanic fairy-tales. His sister Margarita Uffer is a gifted
poetess and his father G. M. Uffer (1883–1965) was an original
lyric-poet and prolific author of radio plays. Fiction in the
Oberhalbstein idiom is well-known by the works of Gisep Sigron,
Peder Cadotsch and Gion Peder Thöni. The Domleschg and the
Schams idioms also have their native writers and poets. Outstanding among the latter are Steafen Loringett, whose best lyrical
poetry is published in the collection *Sur punts a pitgognas* and
Curo Mani, the poet of "Stamungias". As well as being the writer
of highly melodious lyrical poetry, Loringett is also one of the foremost protagonists of Sutsilvan in areas where it is threatened with
extinction, and a compiler of folklore. Mani has shown his dramatic
gifts in *Feasta da Schons,* a "Festspiel" in which he commemorates
the liberation from feudal rule of the valley between Rofla and
Viamala. Tumasch Dolf (1889–1963) and Gieri Ragaz both write
charming regional stories. Jonas Barandun and Anna Capadrutt,
one of the last poetesses of the Heinzenberg, which the good Duke
Henri de Rohan was so fond of, are two young writers to swell the
ranks of Sutsilvan poets. Prominent among writers of the new
poetry is Gion Tscharner in his "Tissi ambrosian".

Prospect

In a famous poem Peider Lansel raised the dying pine forest
of "Tamangur", bordering on the Swiss National Park, to a symbol
of the perennial struggle for the preservation of Rhaeto-Romance.
Just as the forest has suffered the inclement forces of nature
and ruinous human exploitation, the Romansch language is
threatened with extinction, if the people do not make of their
mother tongue the undying landscape of their inner world.
Whether, like Lansel, Muoth and Lozza, they make this struggle
the leitmotiv of their work, or share the growing pre-occupation
of modern writers with questions of existence and identity, and
with the public and private sense of alienation which social change
has brought in its wake, Rhaeto-Romanic writers have, in the
language in which they write, an enduring link with their native
soil. Undeterred by the meagre prospects of material rewards
and popularity, these writers recognize, in the fate of the
Romansch-speaking people, their highest source of inspiration, and

continue to probe the hidden resources which have brought into being so many works of lasting beauty.

The present age's growing awareness of common human bonds, transcending the frontiers between cantons, nations and even continents, has brought about great changes in our literature, as in others. The old and the new have come into conflict. The growth of the mass-media has facilitated contact and cross-fertilization between groups of writers who, in the past, existed in relative isolation from one another. This world-wide informedness of what is happening on the literary scene, new techniques, new interests, new styles, is hardly an encouragement to less well established writers, particularly to writers in a small language community such as our own. For socio-linguistic reasons the Romansch-speaking area is already more or less bound to give all possible support to the preservation of its language and culture and to view all modern, international trends with caution and even with suspicion. The inevitable developments of the modern way of life—immigration by non-Romansch speaking people, tourism, communications and the emigration of many young people to the lowlands, all threaten irrevocably to estrange the population from their native culture and tongue. On the other hand, the Grisons have historically always been open to influences from outside, willingly assimilating them into their way of life, and have always shown a lively interest in the cultural life of the West and more recently, as improved communications have brought it closer, of the world at large.

We should beware of the notion, popular with German thinkers, that all change is inevitably for the better. Literature and art are not like telecommunications and motor manufacturing. Development there is, but it does not of necessity beget products of a higher quality. Sappho and Catullus stand head and shoulders above many prominent contemporary poets, which is not, of course, to detract from the efforts of the latter. Homer, Dante and Shakespeare will always represent a standard very hard to surpass. And so we can quite safely continue to admire the standard-bearers of Romanic literature, Muoth, Peider Lansel, Alexander Lozza and Gian Fontana. Our admiration of them can only further the cause of contemporary literature. For literature is a living tradition; to be true to our times is to succeed in making the living forces within the tradition present to our contemporaries in what we write.

The effects of modern trends upon Romanic literature are

perhaps nowhere more evident than in lyrical poetry. Young men of letters, themselves poets and critics, have made the younger generation aware of modern movements in European poetry, symbolism, imagism, expressionism and present, new forms of expression. The most recent world literature is, of course, available to all in anthologies and inexpensive paperback editions, and reaches an even wider audience through the radio. Clearly the time has come both for inwardness, but also for a new outwardness on the part of Romanic poets. For far too long the ideal of Engadine poetry remained the rather mawkish, nostalgic poetry of Caderas and de Flugi; at the same time the Oberland (Surselva) was content to rest on the laurels of Huonder's "Pur suveran" and Muoth's ballads, all courageous ventures in their time, "dadaint e dadour munts" (both in and outside of the mountains). The Rhine area has had its innovators already in Alfons Tuor, more lyrical by temperament than either Muoth or Huonder, and in Gian Fontana, who fused the sensibility of late romanticism with a naturalistic form in "Il Favugn" and "Il luvrer d'uaul". Peider Lansel, in his time, renewed Ladin poetic diction. His strong personality has had a visible influence upon poets of his own and the subsequent generation, although the idiosyncratic rhythm of his verse and his austerely impressive nostalgia (an "increschantüna" with the future in mind, perhaps) defy imitation. Lansel published his two major collections of verse in 1892 and 1912. In the years between then and his death in 1943 a great deal happened in European literature; war and crises, which shook it to its foundations; dadaism and surrealism in France; expressionism in Germany; the grandiose, rhetorical outpourings of the poetry of the Russian revolution; the remarkable revival of Spanish and South American poetry; and the staggering poetic output of Great Britain and America. Clearly we, in our Romansch language-reservation, ran the risk of adopting a single poetic form, exemplary of its kind, and taking it as a model for all future poets to emulate.

This danger is all the greater as our readership is so much more conservative than that of the great, highly civilized nations which surround us. Having, usually rather late in the day, come to accept an aesthetic form as an ideal, it has been very slow to relinquish it and to move on to a new one. Here, where the aim of preserving our language is so often mistakenly thought to imply avoidance of cultural change, the innovator comes up against violent reactions or infuriating indifference and has to fight much longer than elsewhere for a hearing. However, the new poetry need not of necessity be the antithesis of the old. Innovation should be sustained by tradition, by those elements of the tradition which the new poet sees to be valuable and feels bound to preserve in his work.

(Translated by Christopher Blurton)

(Dr. Andri Peer is not only one of the outstanding poets and writers of contemporary Rhaeto-Romanic Literature, but is also regarded to be one of its foremost literary critics. He has half a dozen volumes of poetry, four volumes of collected essays, various collections of short stories and several radio plays at his credit, all written in Rhaeto-Romanic. Ed.)

Jeremias Gotthelf

Jeremias Gotthelf

by J. R. FOSTER

In the first edition of J. G. Robertson's *History of German Literature,* published in 1902 and for many years the standard work on the subject in English, the Swiss novelist Jeremias Gotthelf was dismissed in half a dozen lines. Today it would hardly be an exaggeration to claim—echoing Goethe's famous prophecy about himself—that there is a new science called Gotthelf. The standard edition of his works already extends to forty volumes with four more planned, new books on him are published almost annually (one of the most recent is in Japanese) and in 1967 saw the timely appearance of a "summary of the state of Gotthelf studies".[1] All this is as it should be; Gotthelf is a writer of tremendous force and vitality whose partiality for larding his German with his native Berndeutsch must not be allowed to obscure his essential universality, even if it does erect a barrier—though by no means an insuperable one—to appreciation outside Switzerland and to translation into languages other than German.

The name Jeremias Gotthelf is a literary pseudonym, as is fairly obvious from its prophetic and biblical overtones. The real name of the man who chose to write under it was Albert Bitzius. Although Bitzius lived for most of his life in the country and wrote almost exclusively about country people, the Bitzius's (the name is a corruption of the Christian name Sulpicius) were in fact a patrician family from the city of Berne itself, where under the *ancien régime* they belonged to the circle of families entitled to hold all but the highest offices. Albert Bitzius was born in 1797 in the little country town of Murten, some twenty-five miles west of Berne, on the linguistic frontier between French and German-speaking Switzerland. His father was a pastor in the Bernese Church (a Calvinist Church that shows traces of Zwinglianism) and there never seems to have been any doubt that Albert would follow in his father's footsteps. After learning the elements of Greek and Latin from his own father, he went in 1812 to the "Green School" (the Gymnasium) in Berne, and on from there to the Academy, the forerunner of the University of Berne. He completed his theological studies successfully in 1820 and was appointed curate to his father in the parish of Utzenstorf, whither the latter had moved in 1805 when Murten was allotted by Napoleon's Act of Mediation to the Canton of Freiburg. However, Bitzius's formal education was not yet over, for in 1821 he took leave of absence from his pastoral duties and went off for a year to the University of Göttingen—much favoured at that time by students from Berne—to enlarge his theological and general knowledge. There he attended G. J. Blanck's lectures on theology, read a good deal of Scott and developed an enthusiasm for Schiller, about the only classical German writer whose influence can be clearly traced in his work (in the historical tales). He rounded off his year at Göttingen with a trip to North Germany, penetrating as far north as the island of Rügen and returning home via Berlin, Leipzig, Dresden and Munich. It is worth laying some emphasis on the extent of Bitzius's formal education, for it reminds us that although he was thoroughly familiar with the Bernese farmer's life—the rectory at Utzenstorf had a farm attached to it—and tends to be described as a "novelist of peasant life" (which indeed, among other things, he was), his mental world is basically that of an educated upper-class urban Bernese, not that of a peasant. Similarly, although Bitzius emerged as a writer fairly late in life—he was nearly forty when he wrote his first novel—research has shown that it cannot be asserted, as it once was, that there are no signs of literary interests and activity in earlier years. If little is proved by the fact that in 1816 he won third prize at the Berne Academy for an essay on the subject "Ist sich das Wesen der Poesie der Alten und Neuern gleich? Zeichnet sich die Neuere durch besondere Eigenschaften aus, and welches sind die Ursachen dieser Verschiedenheit?"[2], it is rather more significant that the papers he left behind after his death contained a number of unpublished early essays and reports of considerable interest (especially the *Gespräch der Reformatoren im Himmel* and the *Chronik von Lützelflüh*), that his youthful sermons display an increasing clarity and rhetorical force, and that before he sat down to write his first novel he had contributed some twenty-five articles to the *Berner Volksfreund*, the organ of the moderate Liberals in the canton of Berne. Some of these Frühschriften would repay a good deal more study than they have yet received.

Back in Utzenstorf with his father, Bitzius threw himself with enthusiasm not only into the normal pastoral duties of a curate but also into the educational work that devolved on a country clergy-man in those days (the pastor was directly responsible for primary education in his parish). His father was a keen educationist who had had dealings with Pestalozzi, and his son inherited the interest to a marked degree. In fact, Karl Fehr[3] rightly speaks of Bitzius as possessed by the *furor paedagogicus,* and it is this enthusiasm for education that is the key to the eventual transformation of Albert Bitzius into Jeremias Gotthelf, or at any rate the trigger that started the process. A word is here necessary, if we are to see Bitzius's passionate interest in education in the proper perspective, on the social background to it. Up to 1798 Switzerland had been a loose confederation of independent cantons and subject territories, with full citizenship confined to the patrician oligarchies who ruled the capitals of the cantons; by 1831 not only had the subject territories been raised to the status of independent cantons but all the inhabitants of the individual cantons had full political and legal rights. The trouble was that a large proportion of the population, especially in the country, was not equipped to exercise its new responsibilities. People in Bitzius's position were acutely aware of this gap between duty and capacity, and the desire to fill it was the conscious aim that made Bitzius a writer.

When Bitzius's father died in 1824 his son did not succeed him as pastor of Utzenstorf because he had not yet served the required five years as a curate. Instead he was moved, still a curate, to the big parish of Herzogenbuchsee, in the valley of the Aare, between Solothurn and Langenthal. It is interesting to note that during his early years here Bitzius had his only personal encounter with Pestalozzi. In 1826 Pestalozzi addressed the *Helvetische Gesellschaft* in Langenthal (it was in fact the last public speech he made), and the list of those present includes V(erbi) D(ivini) M(inister) Albert Bitzius.[4]

Bitzius's time at Herzogenbuchsee was on the whole not a success; he clashed with the local *Oberamtmann* or governor, Rudolf Emanuel von Effinger, over a proposal to build a new school (Bitzius was a man who liked his own way), and was dismissed from his post. But for the good offices of a friend in Berne he would have been sent to the lonely parish of Amsoldingen, near Thun; in fact the posting was cancelled and he was appointed instead to the Church of the Holy Spirit in Berne itself, the most important church in the city after the Minster. Bitzius had misgivings about this appointment because he did not possess a very good speaking voice for sermons. His misgivings were justified; the Church

authorities were not satisfied with his efforts in Berne and a year
and a half later, on New Year's Day 1831, he found himself on
his way to the remote country parish of Lützelflüh in the Emme
valley, north-east of Berne, still a curate and in fact by now the
oldest one in the canton. Bitzius was now thirty-three; he was a
man of considerable ambition, as is clear from several passages in
letters he wrote as a young man, and at this point in his life he
could not have felt that he had achieved a great deal or that
his prospects looked particularly encouraging. Nevertheless, it was
in Lützelflüh that Bitzius was to find himself and to end his days.
The rest of the story of the birth of Jeremias Gotthelf cannot be
better told than in the words of a brief autobiography which Bitzius
wrote in 1848 : "After the death of Herr Fasnacht (the pastor of
Lützelflüh) I was elected pastor of the parish. . . . A year later I
married the grand-daughter of my last principal [i.e. Fasnacht],
the daughter of Professor Zeender of Berne, who was famous in
his time.

"At that period the Canton of Berne was the scene of various
struggles, none of which was fought out with more bitterness than
the educational one. As a member of the Cantonal School Board,
as a lecturer at a refresher course [for teachers] which the Education Department arranged in Burgdorf, while Herr Fellenberg held
an opposition course at Hofwyl, and later as a school inspector, I
was to some extent involved in these struggles and broke more than
one lance with Fellenberg.[5] This, and the character of my parish
[the Emmental farmers were proud and reserved, and viewed their
pastor, an 'outsider', with suspicion], which condemned me to a
slow wait, to a kind of passivity, awoke in me more and more
the urge to express myself in writing on matters concerning the
people, although nothing was more contrary to my nature than
sitting down to write. My nature had to submit; in July 1836 the
continually increasing need broke out in the 'Bauernspiegel'. Since
then there is no end to it, so that I am constantly amazed how
a boy who could not keep his feet still could develop into a man
who spends so much time sitting and writing."[6] The end in fact
came some eighteen years after *Der Bauernspiegel*, in 1854, by
which time Bitzius had produced twelve novels and half a
thirteenth, about forty shorter tales and a considerable number of
Kalendergeschichten or anecdotes, not to mention his political
journalism, a fairly voluminous correspondence and the sermons
he preached to his flock every Sunday.

DER BAUERN-SPIEGEL (to give the title its original ortho-graphy) is an Ich-Roman, the autobiography of an orphan to whom Bitzius gave the name that he was to adopt as his permanent pseudonym. It begins with a memorable sentence of remarkable power :

> Ich bin geboren in der Gemeinde Unverstand, in einem Jahre, welches man nicht zählte nach Christus.[7]

The habit of giving characters and places imaginary names indicative of their nature is one which Gotthelf shares with his contemporaries Trollope and Dickens; no doubt the farmers of Unverstand would have gladly supplied a school like Dotheboys Hall with skimmed milk and stale eggs. This first sentence sets the tone of the whole book, which deals almost exclusively with the darker side of rural life, the "Schattenseite", as Gotthelf calls it in his preface. He was writing primarily, as we have seen, to educate his fellow-countrymen, and he had to show them their faults before he dared to dwell on their virtues. Jeremias loses his father, a poverty-stricken tenant-farmer, early in life. The home is sold up and Jeremias is thrown on the parish, who board him out, as was the custom with orphans, with various farmers. Despised and ill-treated by most of them, Jeremias grows up with little faith in God or man. He falls in love with Anneli, a maid on a neigh-bouring farm, visits her in her room one night (in accordance with the custom of the "Kiltgang" frowned upon by Gotthelf) and gets her with child. He determines to marry her, but Anneli dies in child-birth, thanks to the clumsy and brutal ignorance of a country doctor. Sick of life, Jeremias runs away to Paris, where he joins the Swiss guards of Charles X. There he makes friends with Bonjour, a veteran of Napoleon's Russian campaign, who restores his faith in life and makes a true Christian of him. With the fall of the Bourbons in 1830 Jeremias and Bonjour return to Switzerland. Jeremias falls ill, and on his recovery finds that Bonjour is dead and has left him some money. He looks round for some useful job under the new-born democracy, but is advised by a wise friend, a weights-and-measures inspector who is a mouthpiece for Bitzius's own views, that the democracy has not yet found itself and is not ready for the services of honest men. His friend suggests that he should settle down at some decent country inn, do a little unofficial educational work on the regular guests and write his auto-biography. Jeremias follows this advice. He is about to be appointed parish clerk when he falls ill and dies, his book just completed, with visions of Anneli before his eyes. This bare, compressed summary of *Der Bauernspiegel* naturally gives no idea of its power, which proceeds from its manner as much as from its matter. In this first novel Gotthelf's highly individual style is already almost fully developed. Sometimes terse, sometimes leisurely and rhetorical, it is always vivid and trenchant, like the Emmental dialect that it echoes and occasionally introduces word for word, as for example in a class-room scene, where any request for an explanation of the catechism is met with the sharp injunction : "Büb, lern du, das gaht di nüt a !"[8] As Gotthelf remarks, with a touch of the ironical humour that abounds in his novels,

> Das waren noch die guten, alten Zeiten, wo man in der Schule Religion lernte, and nur Religion. . . .[9]

Der Bauernspiegel brings in many themes treated in greater detail in later books : the meanness and avarice of many farmers, the unchristian treatment of the orphaned and the poor, the inadequacy of the primary schools and the superstitious conception of religion too often prevalent in the farm-houses. Indeed, as Carl Manuel first pointed out in his early but still pertinent biography of Bitzius (1861),

> Es [*der Bauernspiegel*] ist das Urbild und Vorbild, wir möchten fast sagen : das Programm aller seiner späteren Schriften. Seine wichtigsten späteren Bücher sind gleichsam schon *in nuce* in diesem ersten enthalten.[10]

Gotthelf's second novel, *Die Leiden und Freuden eines Schulmeisters,* (two volumes, 1938–39), takes up the school question. It describes the struggles of Peter Käser to teach reading, writing and the elements of religion to classes of a hundred or more, and to support a growing family on his miserably inadequate pay. Like *Der Bauernspiegel,* it emphasizes the darker side of Swiss country life. The third novel, *Uli der Knecht* (1841), and its later sequel, *Uli der Pächter* (1848), are more mellow in tone. The indignation that had first driven Gotthelf to write had temporarily exhausted itself, and it is not until the course of political events roused his angry opposition that a note of bitterness again returns to his writing. The two Uli books portray the successful struggle of a farm labourer to improve his position in life. The next novel, *Anna Bäbi Jowäger* (two volumes, 1843–44), deals with the preference of the peasants for consulting quacks rather than qualified doctors, and was written at the request of the Bernese public health committee. A rich and many-stranded book, it contains amongst much else an interesting discussion between a country clergyman and his progressive doctor-nephew on the proper relationship between priest and doctor, and is in many ways the most profound of Gotthelf's novels. The most delicate in psychological analysis is *Geld and Geist* (1843–44), the story of the misery brought on a happy and prosperous family by a quarrel between the farmer and his wife about a sum of money the former loses through negligence. The knot is loosed by the wife's humility and her readiness to cast out the beam in her own eye first. *Geld und Geist* has been described by H. M. Waidson in an interesting comparison as a work of "classical simplicity", possessing "the inwardness and purity of Goethe's *Iphigenie auf Tauris* or *Torquato Tasso*—an action limited to a small number of characters who represent the highest ethical and cultural level attainable by the social group to which they belong".[11] *Jakobs des Handwerksgesellen Wanderungen durch die Schweiz* (1846–47) is the one novel with a theme totally outside Gotthelf's own experience and is less convincing than the rest, though often very entertaining. Like the last two novels, *Zeitgeist und Bernergeist* (1851) and *Die Erlebnisse eines Schuldenbauers* (1854), it reflects Gotthelf's alarm at contemporary political and social trends.

Of the three novels not so far mentioned, *Der Geldstag* (1845), *Käthi die Grossmutter* (1847) and *Die Käserei in der Vehfreude* (1849), the first two date from Gotthelf's mature middle period, while the last may be roughtly described as a "political" novel, though it is a good deal more relaxed in tone than *Zeitgeist und Bernergeist* or *Die Erlebnisse eines Schuldenbauers*. The dates given in brackets after the names of the novels are in all cases those of publication, which usually followed fairly swiftly on composition, except in the case of the unfinished *Der Herr Esau*, written in 1844 but not published until 1922.

The main criticism that can be advanced against Gotthelf's novels is that they are formless. It is true that he is always ready—like many eighteenth- and nineteenth-century novelists—to digress from his narrative in order to discuss, usually in a didactic tone, any subject that arouses his interest or indignation. It has in fact been discovered that, on average, about one-tenth of each novel is taken up by the author's reflections. But Gotthelf's work defies the application of ordinary canons (if such exist in the case of the novel)—he has been described as an "erratic block" in the landscape of German literature—and in most of these digressions the vigour of his language and personality carries off what in a lesser writer might well seem tedious and out-of-place. This formlessness reaches its climax in the huge fragment *Der Herr Esau,* where after 500 pages of rumbustious description of the doings of three separate families—those of a Radical politician, an old-fashioned aristocrat and a prosperous farmer, all three presented almost as caricatures— it is difficult to see where and how (if ever) the novel was going to end. But it is only fair to Gotthelf to remember that he never published *Der Herr Esau.* It would be equally possible, certainly nowadays, to criticize others of the novels as too well made, in so far as they are neatly tied up with happy endings. The fact is that Gotthelf, as with any important writer, a plot is only a peg for the presentation of a view of life. Rudolf Hunziker gets near the heart of the matter when he says in his notes to *Jakobs Wanderungen* :

"Gotthelf's Künsterlernatur (war) nach ethischen, nicht nach ästhetischen Prinzipien orientiert. Ihm bedeutete stets die Sache, die zu sagen das Feuer seines lodernden Temperamentes ihn zwang, das Wesentliche. Hatte er jeweilen den stofflich— ethischen Plan gefasst, so war damit zugleich die Frage nach der Form zu einem guten Teil gelöst. Zu der Lehre, dass die gleich- zeitige Konzeption, die aprioristiche Vermählung von Inhalt und Form die natürliche Vorbedingung für die Entstehung eines Kunstwerks sei, bildet der Fall Gotthelf ein vortreffliches Para- digma."[12]

Gotthelf himself was little concerned with literary artistry as such; he declares in the *Armennot,* a treatise on the problem of poverty published in 1840, that he has found more intellect displayed in a well-laid hedge than in many a book. Nevertheless, some of his short stories do show a good deal of conventional artistry, especially *Die Schwarze Spinne* (1842), a horrifying tale of a pact with the devil, and *Das Erdbeeri Mareili* (1851) the charming little idyll of a poor country girl who finds her niche in life as the lady's maid of a woman whom she worships. It is significant that attempts to trace links between Gotthelf and the literary movements of his time find most of their supporting evidence in these shorter tales (many of them can properly be described as *Novellen*), which meant less to Gotthelf than his novels; he felt that his genius needed a big canvas. There can be no question that the historical tales, the *Bilder und Sagen aus der Schweiz,* are Romantic in inspiration; themes from Scott's novels have been traced in some of them.[13] Attempts, on the other hand, to classify stories like

Das Erdbeeri Mareili as "typically Biedermeier"[14] are less well-conceived; the theme of *Das Erdberri Mareili* may be—coincidentally—Biedermeier, but the language and style as a whole remain pure Gotthelf and highly individual. The same is true of the almanac stories which Gotthelf produced for the *Neuer Berner Kalender* from 1839 to 1844. In editing an almanac Gotthelf was following in the footsteps of Matthias Claudius, Johann Peter Hebel and many other lesser writers too, but again he put his very personal stamp on the whole project. As H. M. Waidson says,[15] the *Neuer Berner Kalender* gives us a picture of Gotthelf's imaginative world in miniature.

The ground-note of all Gotthelf's work is a deeply-felt, undogmatic Christianity expressed in straightforward and traditional terms :

"Es ist und bleibt also das Christentum in vollem Sinne des Wortes der einzige wirksame Balsam für die eiternde Wunde [poverty and social discontent].
Christus ist und bleibt der einzige Heiland für die sieche Welt."[16]

As a young theological student, Gotthelf had given signs of a fairly casual attitude to his chosen profession and shown less interest in the subtleties of theology than in going out into society and meeting people. He says in the short autobiography already mentioned :

"Die Gesellschaft und namentlich die weibliche nahm mich mehr in Anspruch als die Wissenschaft."[17]

Here, by the way, we surely have a glimpse of that side of his nature which made him into a novelist, and one with such sure psychological insight. However, be that as it may, by the time Albert Bitzius decided to turn himself into Jeremias Gotthelf, Christianity had become a tried, tested and all-embracing view of life which was to colour everything he wrote. As K. Guggisberg puts it pregnantly in his introduction to the *Frühschriften,*

"Die reformierte Tradition Zwinglischer Observanz hat sich in ihm mit dem Herderschen Offenbarungsuniversalismus zu einem einheitlichen, Natur, Geschichte und Gegenwart umfassenden Wirklichkeitsverständnis verbunden."[18]

If a certain unresolved tension between an Old Testament and a New Testament conception of God is sometimes apparent, that is perhaps due to the Volksschriftsteller's need to frighten his readers from time to time—for their own good—with a little thunder from Sinai.

For Gotthelf, man is a creature of God, who had defined good and evil in his commandments and revealed himself more fully in the person and teaching of Christ. His presence can also be felt behind the whole visible world :

"Doch noch viele Engel gehen durch die Welt. Die Feuerflammen sind Engel des Herrn und auch die Wasserströme; Bettler sendet der Herr aus und ruft uns durch sie bald zur Weisheit, bald zur Barmherzigkeit. Steine legt uns der Herr in die Wege und lässt den Tau fallen zu unseren Füssen, alle sind Engel Gottes."[19]

Reminiscences of the Bible are common in Gotthelf's language and imagery. The world is "God's immense temple" and what we do in it decides not only our life here and now, but also what will happen to us for all eternity :

"Der Mensch ist nach dem Ebendbild Gottes geschaffen; nach der Herstellung dieses Ebenbildes soll der Christ streben, er soll versuchen, göttlich zu leben im sterblichen Körper, die Erde zu einem Vorhofe des Himmels zu machen."[20]

When Uli realised that he had been living a worthless life,

"Es kam ihm vor, als ob da zwei Mächte sich um seine Seele stritten, fast gleichsam ein guter und ein böser Engel, und jeder ihn haben wollte."[21]

In spite of the "als ob" and "gleichsam"—the fundamentalist bowing to the rationalist— there is no confusion in Gotthelf's world between good and evil, although they may sometimes be closely intertwined and difficult to differentiate. Behind his characters stand heaven, hell and eternity. Good is compliance with God's will, and evil opposition to it. Evil may spring from inside, from man's naturally weak and sinful nature, which Gotthelf strongly emphasises :

"Was ists nun aber, das eine, welches die äusserlich so verschieden gestellten Menschen auf die gleiche Stufe bringt, in ihren Verhältnissen zu ihren Mitmenschen innerlich so gleichmacht? Es ist die Leidenschaft, das Laster, die übermächtig gewordene Sinnlichkeit, der alte Mensch, der jede Hülle abgeworfen, alle Rücksichten überwunden hat. Es ist dieser alte

Mensch, der Gott und Nächsten hasset, untüchtig ist zu allem Guten und geneigt zu allem Bösen."[22]

The novels contain many characters enslaved to these evil instincts : the Dorngrutbauer in *Geld und Geist* more or less selling his daughter to Kellerjoggi, Johannes in *Uli der Pächter* reviling his dead father after bleeding him white while he lived, the lazy inn-keeper Steffen and his wife Eisi in *Der Geldstag* living for nothing but their own comfort. Even those in whom the new man has already stirred may fall back into serious sin; Uli becomes a cheat and perjurer. Not that the tone of the novels is pessimistic; Christ has broken the power of evil. In the last resort, of course, evil always springs from inside the individual, but it can come from outside in the sense of spreading from one set of persons to others. This, Gotthelf felt, was happening in the political life of the Canton of Berne, and of Switzerland as a whole, in his own day. He was no mere reactionary and as an enlightened Liberal had welcomed the "new order" of 1831, but in the rise of Communism, and more urgently Radicalism, he saw the traditional Christian way of life of his countrymen threatened. His attack on Communism is the novel *Jakobs Wanderungen*; his long struggle against the Radical politicians who governed Berne from 1838 to 1850 reaches its climax in *Zeitgeist und Bernergeist*. This unyielding, obsessional opposition to the materialistic tendencies of the time as they appeared in microcosm in Switzerland is one of the things that make Gotthelf a particularly interesting figure. In many respects his attitude was an exaggerated one; but he did point to the dangers to society implicit in Radicalism (Communism, of course, was still in its infancy and at that time a less pressing danger) with prophetic rightness, and studied moderation is not to be expected of prophets. Even Gottfried Keller, who was on the other side of the fence politically (though he was not blind to Gotthelf's purely literary gifts), was prepared to admit by the time he wrote *Martin Salander* that "progress"—a Radical watchword mercilessly guyed by Gotthelf—had its limitations as an ideal.

It has to be remembered that in those days Radicalism signified for contemporaries more or less what Communism signifies for us today. It implied a philosophical as well as a political standpoint, and one that was quite contrary to the traditional Christian view of life. The Liberals of the thirties had put the individual before the State, which, with Montesquieu, they regarded as a necessary evil, whose main function was to protect the liberty and rights of the individual. The Radicals of the forties gave the State a more positive function. Their thinking was largely based on that of Hegel, who regarded history as the progressive self-revelation of the universal spirit and the Prussian State as its most perfect embodiment so far. But the real prop of Radicalism was Hegel's critic Feuerbach, who changed the whole character of his predecessor's system by doing away with God and asserting that the decisive factor in human existence was physical environment. His theory that religions are merely attempts to provide imaginary compensation for real misery was to have a profound effect on Marx, Engels and Lenin. It would be futile to pretend that the reforming spirit of Radicalism produced no beneficent results, but nothing has occurred in the century since Gotthelf's death to prove that he was wrong in opposing its materialism, which he saw, rightly or wrongly, as liable to affect every aspect of life. He says in the preface to the novel *Zeitgeist und Bernergeist* :

> "Wer mit Liebe am Volke hängt, klar in dessen Leben sieht, der muss überall mit der radikalen Politik feindlich zusammen-treffen, denn dieselbe ist eigentlich keine Politik, sondern eine eigene Lebens- und Weltanschauung, die alle Verhältnisse einfasst, der ganzen Menschheit sich bemächtigen will.[23]

Zeitgeist und Bernergeist, perceptively described by H. M. Waidson as "an eschatological novel", may be regarded as Gotthelf's final reckoning with Radicalism. It was written to support the Liberals (who were now in effect the conservative party) in the electoral campaign of 1850, but did not appear until after their victory. Like *Jakobs Wanderungen* (where we never learn what craft it is precisely that James the Journeyman is supposed to ply), it suffers from the schematic construction always liable to spoil tendentious books (usually, once Gotthelf began to write, his joy in creation swamped his conscious aims, so that what was planned as a short story would end as a full-length novel), but remains an impressive summary in plastic form of his beliefs about the nature and purpose of human life. It is the story of two families, those of Ankenbenz and Hunghans. Friends from boyhood, these two are the richest and most respected farmers in the village of Küchliwyl. When the book opens, a shadow is about to cloud the two men's friendship. Hunghans' wife confides to Benz's wife that her husband is neglecting his family and his farm in favour of politics, in which he supports the Radicals. The rest of the book describes how Hans gradually ruins himself by his devotion to Radicalism. Not until his wife has died from worry and his favourite son from a stroke at a drinking-party does he realise the error of his ways and decide to mend them. His old friend Benz, who has quietly remained a staunch Conservative, is only too glad to help him make a fresh start. Only the worst side of Radicalism is shown in the book, and Gotthelf admits as much in the preface, where he declares that he has no quarrel with the honest men in the Radical Party. The politicians who lure Hunghans away from his wife and family are depicted as godless, pleasure-seeking careerists, whose motto is "Look after yourself first". One day Ankenbenz meets Hunghans and his Radical friends at an inn, and one of the politicians describes his conception of religious freedom thus :

"Politische Freiheit ist ein Unding ohne religiöse Freiheit, und die religiöse Freiheit besteht nicht darin, dass jeder glauben kann was er will, sondern darin, dass keiner mehr einen Glauben hat, anders zu handeln als Naturgemäss, keiner mehr an ein zukünftig Leben denkt . . ."[24]

Benz walks home reflecting with horror on the idea of a life without God. The most convincing parts of the book, considered purely as a novel, are the pictures of Benz and his wife and children at home. They form one of those old-established farming families that Gotthelf excelled in portraying.

But before we write off *Zeitgeist und Bernergeist* as, artistically, not a complete success, it is worth pausing to consider just what artistic category Gotthelf fits into, if any. With his scathing denunciations of the times in which he lived and his large output of political journalism, he seems to me to be a figure who can be as well compared with a Juvenal, a Savonarola or a Karl Kraus as with other novelists. In his lighthearted moments (and there are plenty of these) there is almost a touch—ludicrous though it may sound in this context—of Gilbert and Sullivan. In the last analysis he is simply *sui generis*.

Nevertheless, for much of the time he is also a superb novelist who possesses the one gift essential to a novelist—*pace* modern literary theory and champions of the New Novel—that of being able to create convincing characters and to place them in a realistic setting; in other words, the gift of creating a coherent world of his own. Gotthelf possessed this gift in such abundant measure that he was able to sit down some time after completing a story and continue it quite effortlessly, almost, it would seem, *ad infinitum*; he added in this way two further long sections to the original

Gold und Geist and talked at one time of adding a fourth; and *Uli der Pächter*, the sequel to *Uli der Krecht*, was written some seven years after the original novel.

Gotthelf unfolds before us a living panorama of a people whose life he thoroughly understood (he was as good a judge of a horse or a cow as any of his parishioners) and with whose attitude to it he sympathised. It is a picture of a world of farmers and country tradesmen—some poor, some rich—engaged in the essential business of life : working, eating, sleeping, marrying, dying. No romantic halo hovers over the countryman's life; a farmer's prosperity is measured by the size of his manure heap, and on at least two occasions people fall into the ponds of liquid manure that surround the heaps. On the other hand, farming is not regarded as a sordid round of unsatisfying toil; it is a hard but interesting life accepted as a matter of course, the fundamental form of civilised life. The unit is the family, with, in the richer ones, the labourers and maids who live in the farmhouse. This society is not a matriarchy, but the farmer's wife has an important part to play, knows it, and is swift to dominate a shiftless husband. Marriages are arranged preferably for love, but with an eye to convenience. The Emmental farmer's attitude to marriage is amusingly illustrated in the short story *Wie Joggeli eine Frau sucht;* a rich young farmer does his wooing disguised as a tinker, so that he can see the local young ladies at work in their homes. The outward sign that all is well with a family's spiritual condition is attendance at church on Sunday; Anneli, in *Geld and Geist,* is reconciled to her husband after a Sunday sermon. Round this central core of the family farm in the Emmental or Oberaargau stand pictures of the other aspects of country life : the village schoolmaster's home in *Die Leiden und Freuden eines Schulmeisters,* the inn in *Der Geldstag,* the vicarage in *Anne Babi Jowäger,* village life as a whole in *Die Käserei in der Vehfreude,* which describes, with a wealth of expert knowledge, the establishment of a cheese co-operative. The details are filled in by the short stories, which provide vignettes of almost every country trade and delve back as well into the history and legends of this long-established and stable society, a society with which Gotthelf has a sort of love-hate relationship, feeling that it needs reform as well as defence.

For Gotthelf is no mere Heimatkünstler or sentimental chronicler of rural life; these country scenes and country people are simply the particular form of life which he knows best and in which as an artist he therefore necessarily clothes his own enormously powerful vision of life, a vision based on a deep and subtle understanding of human nature.

It is the same with his use of dialect. Gotthelf's Berndeutsch is not something that he introduces into his Hochdeutsch at nicely calculated intervals to add charming touches of verisimilitude; his characters rise up before his eyes speaking as they would in every-day life, and he cannot at these moments do anything but write Berndeutsch. Here again, form and content are one. In so far as dialect invades the narrative as opposed to the dialogue (which occupies, on an average, roughly two-fifths of each novel)[25], it is again because Berndeutsch terms and forms are the most concrete and vigorous means at Gotthelf's disposal for expressing the ideas he has in mind. Gotthelf made the point himself in a letter to I. Gersdorf :

> "Ebenso will ich nie im Dialekt schreiben, und auf den ersten zwanzig Seiten wird man wenig davon merken, nachher werde ich dazu gezwungen, ich mag wollen oder nicht, und vieles lässt sich freilich nur im Dialekt treu geben. Zudem ist unser Dialekt wirklich gar bündig und kräftig, und manches verdiente in den allgemeinen deutschen Sprachschatz aufgenommen zu worden."[26]

He tried at times to produce versions of his work—*Uli der Knecht,* for example—with the Berndeutsch eliminated, for the benefit of the North German public, with whom he scored quite a hit in his lifetime. The result was not a success; most of the speed and vigour has gone. For instance, "Dein Hudeln kömmt mir zu oft wieder" expands into the dull paraphrase, "Deine Nachtschwärmereien und dein Betrinken kommen mir zu oft wieder".[27] Not that Gotthelf is a dialect writer in the normal sense of the term; his language is a Mischsprache that swings constantly between the two poles of Hochdeutsch and Berndeutsch—this is part of its fascination—and is really his own creation. The early twentieth-century French critic Muret saw this :

> "En matière de langage, Gotthelf doit être considéré comme un génie créateur."

Walter Muschg is even more enthusiastic, and more specific :

> "Sein Berndeutsch ist monumental, von einem Riesen geprägt, es setzt sich nur zur Hälfte aus dem mundartlich Geläufigen zusammen. Die anderer, grössere Hälfte war vor ihm und nach

ihm niemals da. Sein Sprachgefühl hat den Dialekt in eine
Sphäre weggehoben, die nur vom Schöpfer her überschaut und
begriffen werden kann.[28]

In this domain it is hardly too much to compare Gotthelf with
Luther, to whom, as Guggisberg has pointed out,[29] he is remark-
ably similar in character and temperament. In the *Gespräch der
Reformatoren im Himmel* it is Luther who gets all the best lines,
like the splendidly Gotthelfian challenge :

"Wisst ihr auch, was Reformation ist? Die endet sich nie."[30]

Of course, Gotthelf's use of dialect does put difficulties in the
way of the non-Swiss reader—what is needed is an edition of the
novels with notes at the foot of each page, so that the reader is not
held up—but it has not prevented him from being translated into
French, Italian, Dutch, Danish, Swedish, Finnish, Norwegian,
Hungarian and English.[31] Most of the English translations date
from the nineteenth century and are a bit heavy-handed, but a
very effective version of *Die schwarze Spinne* appeared only a few
years ago.[32] Dialect presents less of a problem in the shorter
stories because it appears much less frequently than in the novels;
sometimes hardly at all.

Gotthelf has had no real literary progeny because he is quite
literally inimitable, but Strindberg's second novel, *Hemsöborna,*
seems to have been modelled on *Uli der Knecht* (Strindberg came
across Gotthelf's work while living in Switzerland),[33] and Thomas
Mann has described how he read *Uli* and its sequel while writing
Doktor Faustus, "in order to keep in touch with great narrative
literature".[34] In Switzerland Gotthelf has been for many years
now a popular classic, with all kinds of paper-back editions of
individual stories on sale in every bookshop. The centenary of his
death in 1954 provoked a number of radio and film adaptations,
some of them, naturally enough, conveying little more than the plot
of the particular stories on which they were based. As Karl Fehr
says,[35] Gotthelf is a mine of poetic beauty—and of religious,
psychological and ethical wisdom—that is far from being exhausted;
it is the scholar's job, especially as we move further and further
away from Gotthelf's own age, to ensure that the true nature of
his greatness is not lost from sight.

NOTES AND TRANSLATIONS

N.B. SW=Gotthelf's *Sämtliche Werke,* ed. by R. Hunziker and H. Bloesch, 24 volumes and 16 supplementary vols., Zürich, 1911 ff.

1. Karl Fehr *Jeremias Gotthelf (Albert Bitzius),* Sammlung Metzler, J. B. Betzlersche Verlag, Stuttgart, 1967.

2. "Is ancient and modern poetry similar in nature? Is modern poetry distinguished by special characteristics, and what are the reasons for this difference?"

3. K. Fehr, op. cit., p. 38.

4. *Verhandlungen der Helvetischen Gesellschaft zu Langenthal im Jahre 1826,* quoted by Bloesch, *Jeremias Gotthelf. Unbekanntes und Ungedrucktes über Pestalozzi, Fellenberg und die bernische Schule,* Berne, 1938.

5. Philipp Emanuel von Fellenberg (1791–1844): a Swiss educationist with an international reputation at the time. Bitzius disliked the amount of influence he wielded in Berne and considered his rationalist approach harmful to religious life.

6. *Selbstbiographie,* in *Jeremias Gotthelfs Persönlichkeit,* ed. by W. Muschg, Verlag Benno Schwabe & Co., Klosterberg, Bâle, 1944, p. 26. Gotthelf wrote this compressed autobiography at the request of G. L. Meyer von Knonau, archivist of Zürich, for a handbook on Switzerland which was never in fact published.

7. SW, vol. 1, p. 7. Almost untranslatable. "I was born in the parish of No-sense, in a year which was not reckoned as one of our Lord's."

8. SW, vol. 1, p. 79. "You just learn, boy; that doesn't concern you."

9. "It was still the good old days, when one learned religion at school, and only religion . . ."

10. C. Manuel, *Jeremias Gotthelf, sein Leben und seine Schriften,* reprinted by the Eugen Rentsch Verlag, Erlenbach–Zürich, 1922, p. 52. "It is the archetype and prototype, one might almost say the programme of all his later writings. The most important of his later books are already contained *in nuce,* so to speak, in this first one".

11. H. M. Waidson, *Jeremias Gotthelf, An Introduction to the Swiss Novelist,* Oxford, Blackwell, 1953, p. 84.

12. R. Hunziker in SW 9, p. 510: "Gotthelf's artistic nature was guided not by aesthetic but by ethical principles. To him, what his fiery temperament compelled him to say was always the essential thing. Once he had decided on the content and ethical theme [of a story] the question of form was already largely resolved. The case of Gotthelf is an excellent example of the doctrine that simultaneous conception, the *a priori* marriage of content and form, is the natural precondition for the birth of a work of art."

13. T. Salfinger, *Gotthelf und die Romantik,* Bâle, 1945, pp. 123 f.

14. F. Sengle, *Zum Wandel des Gotthelfbildes,* GRM, 1957, p. 248.

15. H. M. Waidson, op. cit., p. 158.

16. SW 15, p. 255 (Addendum to *Die Armennot*): "Christianity in the full sense of the word is and remains the only effective balm for the festering wound. Christ is and remains the only saviour for this sick world."

17. "Society, especially feminine society, made more demands on my time than scholarship."

18. SW, supp. vol. 12, p. 8. A Tacitean summary that almost defies translation. "The tradition of the Reformation in its Zwinglian form united in him with Herder's notion of universal revelation to form a unified view of reality embracing nature, history and the contemporary world."

19. SW, 3, p. 156. "Many angels still walk through the world. Flames are angels of the Lord, and streams, too; the Lord sends out beggars and through them He calls us now to wisdom, now to mercy. The Lord lays stones in our path and drops the dew at our feet; all are angels of the Lord."

20. SW 15, p. 97. "Man is created in God's likeness; the Christian should strive after the restoration of this likeness, he should try to live a godlike life in this mortal body and to make this earth a forecourt to heaven."

21. SW 4, p. 46. "It seemed to him as if two powers were striving for his soul, almost as it were a good and a bad angel, and each wanted to possess him."

22. SW 13, p. 361. "What is it, the one thing that reduces men who are superficially quite different to the same level, and makes them so alike in their relations with their fellow-men? It is passion, vice, sensuality triumphant, the old Adam, who has cast off every veil and conquered every scruple. It is this old Adam that hates God and neighbour, is incapable of any good and inclined to every sort of evil."

23. SW 13, p. 9. "Whoever is fond of the people and sees clearly into its life must clash with Radicalism, for it is not merely a political standpoint, but a whole philosophy of life that effects every human relationship, that wishes to gain control of the whole human race."

24. SW, vol. 13, p. 200. "Political freedom is useless without religious freedom, and religious freedom does not consist in everyone's believing what he likes, but in no one's any longer believing in anything but a natural mode of life without any thought of a life to come . . ."

25. A. Reber, *Stil and Bedeutung des Gesprächs im Werke Jeremias Gotthelfs*, Walter de Gruyter & Co., Berlin, 1967, p. 23.

26. SW, supp. vol. 5, p. 335. "Similarly, I never set out to write in dialect, and in the first twenty pages little of it will be noticed; after that I am compelled to do so whether I want to or not; and certainly many things can only be rendered truly in dialect. Moreover, our dialect is very succinct and forceful, and many expressions would merit being incorporated in the general German vocabulary."

27. *Uli der Knecht*, North German, "bowdlerised" version published by Springer, p. 3. Quoted by A. Reber, op. cit., p. 80.

28. Gabriel Muret, *Jérémie Gotthelf*, Librairie Félix Alcan, Paris, 1913, p. 443; W. Muschg, *Gotthelf. Die Geheimnisse des Erzählers*, C. H. Beck'sche Verlangsbuchhandlung, Munich, 1931, p. 447. "His Berndeutsch is monumental, coined by a giant; it is only half composed of current dialect. The other, greater half never existed before or after him. His feeling for language lifted the dialect into a sphere which can only be surveyed and understood by the creator."

29. K. Guggisberg, *Jeremias Gotthelf. Christentum und Leben*, Max Niehans Verlag, Zürich and Leipzig, 1939, p. 53.

30. SW, supp. vol. 12, p. 186. "Do you really know what reformation is? That is something that never ends."

31. H. M. Waidson, *Jeremias Gotthelf's Reception in Britain and America*, Modern Language Review, vol. 43, Cambridge, 1948; J. R. Foster, *Jeremias Gotthelf's Reputation Outside Switzerland*, German Life and Letters, 1955.

32. The Black Spider, trans. by H. M. Waidson, Calder, London.

33. M. Lamm, *August Strindberg*, Stockholm, 1940, vol. 1, pp. 378 ff.

34. Th. Mann, *Die Entstehung des Doktor Faustus*, Bermann-Fischer Verlag, 1949, p. 60.

35. K. Fehr, op. cit., p. 96.

SELECT BIBLIOGRAPHY

Editions

Sämtliche Werke in 24 Bänden. In Verbindung mit der Familie Bitzius und mit Unterstützung des Kantons Bern, edited by R. Hunziker and H. Bloesch and, since their deaths, by K. Guggisberg and W. Juker. 24 vols. and 16 supplementary vols., with 4 more planned. Eugen Rentsch Verlag, Erlenbach bei Zürich, 1911 ff. The same publishers also produce a cheaper version of the main volumes of this standard edition, with the same text but without the critical apparatus and notes.

Jeremias Gotthelfs Werke in 20 Bänden, ed. by W. Muschg, Verlag Birkhäuser, Bâle, 1948, ff.

Biographies

K. Fehr, *Jeremias Gotthelf*, 1954. Very comprehensive; makes use of newly discovered material.

R. Hunziker, *Jeremias Gotthelf* (Die Schweiz im deutschen Geistesleben, Bd. 50/51), 1927.

W. Muschg (ed.), *Jeremias Gotthelfs Persönlichkeit. Erinnerungen von Zeitgenossen*, Verlag Benno Schwabe & Co., Klosterberg, Bâle, 1944.

General Critical Studies

W. Günther, *Der ewige Gotthelf,* Eugen Rentsch Verlag, Erlenbach-Zürich, 1934; 2nd, revised and enlarged edition, 1954. Very good literary appreciation; corrects the balance disturbed by W. Muschg's largely psycho-analytical study (see below).

G. Muret, *Jérémie Gotthelf. Sa vie et ses oeuvres,* Librairie Félix Alcan, Paris, 1913. An early product of the resurgence of interest in Gotthelf; very thorough and still useful.

W. Muschg, *Gotthelf. Die Geheimnisse des Erzählers,* C. H. Beck'sche Verlagsbuchhandlung, Munich, 1931; 2nd edition, 1967. Profound and illuminating; lays a little too much emphasis on the psycho-analytical approach.

W. Muschg, *Jeremias Gotthelf. Eine Einführung in seine Werke,* A. Francke, (Dalp-Taschenbücher, vol. 303), Berne, 1954; 2nd ed. (Sammlung Dalp. vol. 63), 1960. Mellower and more balanced than Muschg's original study; consists mainly of the prefaces to the 20-volume Birkhäuser Klassiker edition of Gotthelf (see above).

H. M. Waidson, *Jeremias Gotthelf. An Introduction to the Swiss Novelist,* Blackwell, Oxford, 1953. Comprehensive, thorough and balanced; highly esteemed by Swiss Gotthelf scholars.

Gotthelf's Religion and Philosophy

E. Buess, *Jeremias Gotthelf. Sein Gottes- und Menschenverständnis,* Evangelischer Verlag, Zollikon-Zürich, 1948.

K. Guggisberg, *Jeremias Gotthelf. Christentum und Leben,* Max Niehans Verlag, Zürich and Leipzig, 1939.

D. Schmidt, *Der natürliche Mensch. Ein Versuch über Gotthelf,* Giessener Beitr. z. dt. Philologie 76, 1940.

Language and Style

E. Fankhäuser, *Die Flexion des Berner Dialekts nach Jeremias Gotthelf,* Lausanne, 1898.

L. W. Forster, *The Language in German Switzerland,* German Life and Letters, Vol. IV, Oxford, 1939.

F. Hubert-Renfer, *Berndeutsch und Hochdeutsch im Werk Jeremias Gotthelfs,* Berner Zeitschrift für Geschichte und Heimatkunde 17, 1955, No 1.

R. Hunziker, Supplementary essay (on Gotthelf's use of language) in *Jakobs des Handwerksgesellen Wanderungen durch die Schweiz,* SW, vol. 9, pp. 504-533.

A. Reber, *Stil und Bedeutung des Gesprächs im Werke Jeremias Gotthelfs,* Walter de Gruyter & Co., Berlin, 1967.

Miscellaneous

K. Fehr, *Jeremias Gotthelf (Albert Bitzius),* J. B. Metzlersche Verlagsbuchhandlung, Stuttgart, 1967. A concise summary of the present state of Gotthelf studies; good bibliography.

W. Günther, *Neue Gotthelf-Studien,* Francke Verlag, Berne, 1958. Essays on various aspects of Gotthelf's work.

W. Laedrach (ed.), *Führer zu Gotthelf und Gotthelfstätten,* Francke Verlag, Berne, 1954. Essays by various hands.

W. Laedrach, *Jeremias Gotthelf in Lützelfluh,* Verlag Paul Haupt, Berne, Berner Heimatbücher No 9, no date. Brief introduction (including Gotthelf's autobiography) followed by an interesting collection of photographs of places associated with Gotthelf.

Gottfried Keller

Gottfried Keller

by J. M. LINDSAY

I

GOTTFRIED KELLER is the representative author of the German Swiss. In a way that is true of no other Swiss man of letters his fellow-countrymen have taken him to their hearts. Other great Swiss authors, like Jeremias Gotthelf and Conrad Ferdinand Meyer, may excel Keller in particular qualities, and either of those men can be regarded more fully than Keller as the literary embodiment of a particular social group, in Gotthelf's case the rich farmers of Canton Berne, in Meyer's the old Zürich patriciate. But Keller, with his roots in the village of Glattfelden and his life spent in Zürich, with his excursions to Munich, Heidelberg and Berlin and his constant awareness of his cultural dependence on Germany—this contrasting with his political independence —is a more complete and more universal poet and author than those others.

Switzerland has made a distinguished and distinctive contribution to German literature. When Luther with German "Dämonie" was shaking the foundations of Christian spiritual life in Europe, Zwingli, his Swiss counterpart, was making a cool, rational Swiss appraisal of the needs of the reformed church and arriving at equally radical but less stormily expressed convictions. Niklaus Manuel is remembered among early German dramatists for his vigorous and expressive Reformation plays. In days when German literary life was almost at a standstill the great Albrecht von Haller composed notable poetry, but only as a hobby, for Haller was more famous in his profession as anatomist and physiologist. The names of Professors Bodmer and Breitinger of Zürich are familiar to the student of literary history, even if he has never read their works, as the men who discerned which direction German literature needed to take in the 1740s. Salomon Gessner was another talented Züricher of the generation which immediately precedes the great awakening of German literature in the 1770s. Goethe was bound by ties of affection to Switzerland, and one of Schiller's best-known plays has become the Swiss national drama. In the nineteenth century Switzerland contributed quite disproportionately to her size to German literature with the authors already mentioned, to say nothing of the poet Leuthold and the historian of the Renaissance, Jakob Burckhardt. In more recent times the names of Carl Spitteler, Max Frisch and Friedrich Dürrenmatt show that Switzerland's venerable literary tradition is still very much alive.

The individuality of Swiss literature is difficult to convey in a few sentences. While it could clearly enjoy no separate existence apart from German literature it has a strongly characteristic flavour and often reflects attitudes which would be unthinkable in Germany. Swiss political institutions are reflected both directly and indirectly in German Swiss literature, as the reader of Keller's works soon realizes. Certain fundamental human rights have enjoyed continuous recognition in Switzerland for longer than in Germany, and there may be a connection between this and the fact that Swiss literature shows less sign of storm and stress, of Faustian striving for unattainable absolutes, of the Kafkan calling in question of the justice and value of life than that of Germany. Kleist would have been unthinkable in Switzerland; Nietzsche was there only as a foreign professor, he had no organic link with the place.

The most eminent men of letters in Switzerland have firmly and sensibly opposed the idea of a dialect literature; this can only have a limited appeal, and it is preferable to speak in German with Swiss overtones to the whole German-speaking world rather than enjoy the cosy, parochial self-indulgence of talking in accents understood by but a few about things which in any case would not interest the many. Keller always wrote in the standard German language even though this cannot have been easy or natural for him.

II

Gottfried Keller was born in Zürich in 1819. His father, a woodturner, was a person of great energy and very considerable artistic ability. The poet certainly inherited most of his artistic gifts from his father. His mother, the daughter of a country doctor, was a good but very down-to-earth person. Rudolf Keller died when his son was only five, and the widow, being left in fairly straitened circumstances, had to take in lodgers and let off most of her roomy old house in the Zürich *Rindermarkt*. Gottfried was a solitary child, given to brooding and daydreams. His teachers were for the most part rather insensitive and unimaginative, and he did not much enjoy school. But he learned quickly those subjects which interested him, and it must have come as a great shock to his mother when he was expelled from the *Industrieschule* at the age of fifteen; he had taken part in an unpleasant persecution of an unsatisfactory master who had been dismissed, yet it seems improbable that he was the ringleader or merited so severe a punishment.

When the question arose what to do with the boy, Gottfried declared emphatically that he wished to become a landscape painter. His mother tried to talk him out of this, but he was all the more determined to have his own way. After several years of trying to learn at home under unsatisfactory teachers, Keller set off for Munich in 1840, resolved to learn something there about landscape painting. Two and a half years later he returned to Zürich, having spent all his patrimony and made little if any progress as a painter. His sense of failure deepened in the following few years, till suddenly, in the mid-1840s he turned to literature and quickly produced some poems, mainly inspired by the political poets, Grün, Herwegh and Freiligrath. Now Keller was hard put to it to make himself sufficiently master of the technical side of versifying to reduce his abundant poetic material to some kind of order. In 1846 he was able to bring out his first book of poems.

Gradually Keller became known in Zürich as a poet, and in 1848 his native canton gave him the money to enable him to study in Heidelberg. He hoped one day to become a dramatist. In this period falls his acquaintance with Ludwig Feuerbach, the atheistic philosopher, who swept away the last remnants of Keller's inherited religious faith, and for years remained the principal intellectual influence in Keller's life. Keller moved from Heidelberg to Berlin in 1850 and spent several years there. By now he was engaged in writing *Der grüne Heinrich,* the great burden of his Berlin sojourn. The work was not completed till 1855.

Between 1842 and 1855 Keller was in love over and over again with a succession of young women, for the most part tall, handsome Amazons who would certainly never have considered uniting themselves for life with his four foot ten inches. Henriette Keller, Luise Rieter, Marie Melos, Johanna Kapp, Betty Tendering, all, and especially the last two, made a deep impression on him. *Der Landvogt von Greifensee* reflects Keller's constant attempts to achieve a satisfactory relationship with the other sex.

From 1861 till 1876 Keller served as First Secretary of Canton Zürich. This period of official activity made heavy demands on his time and energy, and he took pride in carrying out his duties efficiently. In 1856 he had published the first volume of *Die Leute von Seldwyla,* but no further literary work appeared for many years. By the early 1870s he was beginning to long for his freedom, and the publication of his *Sieben Legenden* in 1872 marks the first re-emergence of the poet and prose-writer from the burdens of office. He continued to serve as *Staatsschreiber* for several more years, but he was by now seriously concerned about the works which he still hoped to write. In 1874, just before his retirement Keller completed Part II of *Die Leute von Seldwyla.*

In the years after 1876 Keller was extremely productive. In 1877 appeared the *Züricher Novellen,* in 1880 he revised and greatly improved *Der grüne Heinrich,* 1883 brought *Das Sinnge-dicht* and the new and augmented edition of his poems, 1886 the novel of his old age, *Martin Salander.*

By 1885 Keller's health had begun to fail, and his sister Regula, who had kept house for him since his mother's death, was now a dying woman. Although he still had faith in the younger generation Keller withdrew more and more from outside contacts. It was widely but falsely believed that he had become sour and mis-anthropic in his old age; though the years had brought him his fair share of disillusionment and disappointment he remained to the end fundamentally a man of good will. Regula died in 1888, and after this his health deteriorated rapidly. Keller was a sick man, quite uninterested in the public celebrations of his seventieth birth-day in July 1889. But although he was clearly incurably ill, death did not claim him till nearly a year later, on July 15, 1890.

III

In later life Keller was proud that it had been "der Ruf der le-bendigen Zeit" which had stirred him into poetic activity in 1844. He was roused by the example of the German political poets into writing his first verses. For the most part these tendentious political poems impress us as rather naive, even ridiculous nowadays. The *Jesuitenzug,* for instance, which is intended to be menacing, even frightening, now seems merely funny. It had been reasonable enough in his father's day for a democrat to have a healthy dislike for aristocrats and priests, but within one generation the situation had become quite different. The nature poetry from Keller's first collection has worn better, and often in only slightly modified form his early nature poems were preserved by the aged poet in his *Gesammelte Gedichte* of 1883. The cycle entitled *Lebendig begraben* was adversely criticized by Varnhagen von Ense, that connoisseur of poetry, who on the whole reacted very favourably to Keller's verse, and the modern reader generally finds these poems in poor taste. However, Keller's genuine feeling for nature, his keen painter's eye, his evident liking for his fellow-men and the plants and animals of the field, and an occasional moment of high poetic inspiration combine to make his verse memorable and important as a personal document of the poet's life.

In the *Gesammelte Gedichte* the *Spielmannslied,* which is the first poem in the collection, characterizes Keller's poetry most effectively; he makes no excessive claims for himself, but he does through the parable of the sower make it clear that he regards himself as a true poet; he would not claim that he has always made the most of himself, that he has never been slack or heedless or missed an opportunity; yet now and again "a hungry little bird" has gathered nourishment from him, he has provided the sustenance that sent the bird soaring heavenwards again, and he has therefore not entirely betrayed his mission.

Unter Sternen, a short poem originally written in 1846, communicates Keller's love of night; this was, of course, a characteristic of much Romantic poetry, in Germany and elsewhere. But Keller's poem appears to be the record of a particular and precious experience; in the evening starlight, he claims :

> "Hier fühl ich Zusammenhang
> Mit dem All' und Einen."[1]

This poem, with its joy in the beauties of creation, places Keller among the true nature poets of Europe, side by side with Goethe or Wordsworth. His famous *Abendlied an die Natur* is a hymn of homage to the benign and refreshing influence of Nature to which he turns for comfort in every difficult situation in life : Nature has given him the only pure pleasures he has ever known with no bad after-taste, no regrets or repentance. When Keller fails to appreciate Nature's benefits, his heart will be sick or corrupted. When his end comes, he is happy to think of reposing under Nature's green grass. He loves and accepts the natural order, which he regards as fundamentally beneficent.

Abend auf Golgatha is the most direct evidence we possess that Keller may have turned away from Feuerbach towards the end of

his life. This is a beautiful and subtle short poem about Christ on
the cross. It is evening, getting dark, and the dew is falling. A large
moth comes and settles for a moment on Jesus' gleaming white
shoulder and then flies off into the darkness. But Christ is not quite
deserted, for His mother, Mary, who is also His creature, embraces
the pillar of the cross. Within these lines Keller uses the words
"der Erlöser" (Redeemer), "des Herrn" (the Lord), "das Kreuz"
(the cross), "der Schöpfer" (Creator), "das Weib, das er zur Mutter
sich schuf" (the woman whom He created for His mother). It is
possible that he wrote the poem only or mainly because of its
admirable pictorial quality, but it seems to me more likely that he
wanted to say those weighty words, of whose truth he was by now
(1881) more than half convinced, in as non-committal a way as
possible. Keller handles the hexameter here with great skill, and
this is undoubtedly one of his best lyrics.

We do not remember Keller primarily as a lyric poet, but in the
poems mentioned and a handful of others he has produced work
which ranks with the best written in the German tongue. His best
known and best loved poem, *Abendlied* (*Augen, meine lieben
Fensterlein*) is the work above all others in which the quintessential
Keller, the man of the seeing eye, who treasures the precious gift of
life, reveals himself. Here Keller achieves that rare synthesis of
thought, emotion and form which constitutes a true work of art.
Winternacht, a delightful poem in which the imprisonment of
natural forces in the winter is symbolized by the nixie's struggle to
emerge from below the ice of a frozen pond, is another poem that
haunts the memory.

IV

Der grüne Heinrich, even in the very imperfect form in which it
first appeared in 1854 and 1855, was recognized as a work of
genius by those most competent to judge. It is the story of Heinrich
Lee, the clever son of a poor widow in Zürich. In the later version
(1880) Heinrich tells his life's story in the first person, from his dim
memories of his father who died when he was quite small to his
withdrawal as a still comparatively young man to a minor
administrative post in a Swiss mountain village. His childhood and
adolescence are recalled in considerable detail, and we soon know
intimately the imaginative child's life in his mother's big, rambling
old house in the centre of a then very much smaller Zürich. With
disarming frankness we are told of the child's first religious doubts,
his difficulty in behaving honestly, the few occasions when he knew

he had done something really shameful to other people without being found out. We learn that Heinrich early makes the discovery that even children can be completely and radically depraved; this is shown by his experiences with a horrible juvenile usurer, Meierlein, who tries to enforce payment of debts by methods which, as Keller points out, would be perfectly legitimate in the adult world, but which no right-thinking person would dream of allowing one child to use against another. Then we hear of Heinrich's expulsion from school and of his fateful decision to become a landscape painter. He is sent to his uncle's house in the country for a time. His adolescence is dominated by the conflict of his two loves, that for the country schoolmaster's delicate daughter, Anna, and that for the handsome young widow, Judith, a living embodiment of the power and abundance of Nature. After various unsuccessful attempts to find a reliable teacher in Zürich Heinrich persuades his guardians to let him have the money left for him by his father, and goes off to Munich to study art. There he is not very successful; he wastes some of his time, he does not have the means to pay a good teacher, and in any case landscape painting has gone out of fashion. So by the time he has been two years there he has spent his all and gained nothing. We hear of his friendships with the other painters Erickson and Lys, who are contrasted as a talented and likeable Philistine and a man of more genuine and problematical genius who has the most sublime disregard for other people's feelings. Keller himself as a young painter in Munich did not have friends like these; the loyal Johann Salomon Hegi was nothing like as accomplished a painter. Heinrich resolutely refuses to do what he would consider inferior work to help to pay for his studies, but in the end he finds himself reduced to painting flagpoles for a royal wedding in order to pay his rent and have something to eat. However, he takes pleasure in his honest labour and its reward. The later part of the book is much inferior. We cannot easily believe in Heinrich's introduction to Count Dietrich's castle and the events that happen to him there—the Count turns out to have bought all Heinrich's paintings and studies from the junk-shop dealer in Munich who had given Heinrich next to nothing for them. The Count's adopted daughter, Dortchen Schönfund, falls in love with Heinrich, does what she reasonably can to encourage him, but he is too slow and cold. In the end Heinrich leaves the castle with the Count's good will, a large sum of money and the uneasy feeling that he could have had Dortchen if he had but tried. The whole castle episode harks rather of a fairytale ending. At home Heinrich is just in time to say farewell to his mother on her deathbed. After a little time he takes a position in a country valley as a minor official; his life is brightened by the return of Judith from America whither she had emigrated. The two do not marry, but take great pleasure in one another's company. Judith dies during a great epidemic while she is nursing sick children; she has become a much more charitable if less passionate person meantime.

Der grüne Heinrich is a great novel in the tradition of the German *Bildungsroman,* which gives the story of a single individual's development from innocence and ignorance to maturity and wisdom. Heinrich Lee is in many ways the most engaging hero of all the German *Bildungsromane.* A clever child with an inquiring mind, he has the modesty and diffidence that prevent him from seeming disagreeably precocious. From a very early age he makes his generally accurate observations about other people; we find his frankness about his early faults of character disarming. The death of Heinrich's father results in a particularly close and affectionate relationship between the boy and his mother. When Heinrich tells lies and steals, what rescues him from his wayward and irresponsible behaviour is more than anything the fear of losing his mother's confidence and causing her serious offence. The story of Heinrich's two loves in his native village is one of the great delights of the book; instead of loving one girl in different ways Heinrich divides his capacity for loving into the spiritual, respectful worship from afar which he bestows on Anna—she cultivates a kind of ideal remoteness, and on the one occasion when Heinrich so far forgets himself as to kiss her, her emotional equilibrium is seriously upset by the incident—and the passionate, sensuous love for the strong, healthy, beautiful Judith. With Judith Heinrich is often tempted almost beyond endurance, but she is considerably older than he and refrains from seducing him. Later in the book after his two brief excursions with Hulda and Dortchen Schönfund, Heinrich sees Judith again, but by now their relationship is quite different, serene, mature, based on the memory of those stormy passions of long ago. They do not marry, and from what we know of Keller's views on marriage and relations between the sexes in general we can be sure that he does not mean us to understand that Heinrich and Judith are ever "lovers".

Der grüne Heinrich has its *longeurs,* of course; most readers find the account of the Munich Carnival tedious in the extreme, and the story of Albert Zwiehans' amours (really introduced to show the dangers of not being able to make up one's mind between two women) tries the reader's patience sorely. The *Meretlein* story, another digression, comes earlier in the book, seems more closely related to the hero's difficulties with his teachers, and is altogether more tolerable. Later on, the whole episode in the Count's castle suggests that Keller was becoming impatient of the book and was prepared to use almost any means to bring it to an end quickly. While the last book of *Der grüne Heinrich* has some good pages one loses that feeling of being in close touch with reality which makes Books I and II so memorable.

The work gained enormously from being re-written in chronological sequence and in the first person throughout in 1880. The original version was much too disjointed, being partly written in the first, partly in the third person. The style of the book was carefully scrutinized, and many improvements of detail were made. But Keller discarded *Judiths Bad,* a most artistically affecting passage in the original book, in the interest of avoiding cheap erotic effects. To Emil Kuh he wrote as early as 1871 that it was "die roheste und trivialste Kunst von der Welt . . . in einem Poem den weiblichen Figuren das Hemd übern Kopf wegzuziehen,"[2] and made it plain that he was no longer prepared to seek popularity by such methods. Most of his readers would be inclined to think that Keller's judgment betrayed him over *Judiths Bad,* even if in principle they sympathized with the attitude that made Keller drop it in 1880.

The first book of *Der grüne Heinrich* rings true on every page. Not only does Heinrich enlist our sympathy, we relive his life with him, step by step, and reflect how much of his experience is universal human experience. There are no boring passages, because every reader is reminded of his own early days and thinks how remarkable it is that Keller should remember his childhood and adolescence so much more distinctly than we ourselves.

The novelty and wonder of the world in childhood are recaptured in all their freshness by this author who retains so much of childlike naïveté in his grown-up character. Then we are delighted by Heinrich's love for Anna; we fear a little for him when he begins to see too much of Judith; it is almost with relief that we learn of her departure for America. But as the book progresses we begin to make reservations about it. The story of Meretlein is still more or less relevant; Heinrich's teachers show little understanding of him, and this cautionary tale of what can happen when a very sensitive child is treated with an exemplary lack of understanding by parents and teachers has a direct bearing on the theme of the book. The long account of Albertus Zwiehans and his amatory vacillations is too much for our patience, even if it may not be completely unrelated to the theme of the book. When we read of Heinrich's first impressions of Munich we are thrilled as the author was evidently thrilled by his first contact with the wealthy Catholic culture of South Germany, but later on we realize that Keller has not been as selective as he might have been; his account of the Munich artists' Carnival celebrations is allowed to run to seed, and even the most indulgent reader finds himself tempted to skip some pages. The fourth book is not as dull as the third, but is full of improbabilities. It is plain that in his anxiety to use to literary advantage as many elements as possible of his real life experience Keller has scarcely maintained a due sense of artistic proportion; the romantic fantasy of Heinrich's chance meeting with Dortchen, his introduction to Count Dietrich and his sojourn at the castle, Dortchen's love for him, his failure to respond, all strike us as far fetched and quite out of keeping with the earlier part of the book. Then at the very end we once more become reconciled to the work; the hero's reunion with Judith and his withdrawal to his modest civil service position seem to us a good and seemly ending.

Der grüne Heinrich is an untidy, sprawling work, measured by the neat, competent standards of today's novelists, but it is the honest record of a well-lived, full life, and has many beautiful pages. If not Keller's most accomplished work it is certainly his richest.

V

The Seldwyla stories (*Die Leute von Seldwyla*), begun while Keller was working on *Der grüne Heinrich*, were published in two parts, in 1856 and 1874 respectively. They demonstrate convincingly that, while Keller might still have a good deal to learn about the novelist's craft, he was capable of a high degree of *expertise* in the handling of the *Novelle* form. The earlier set of five stories shows a somewhat more indulgent attitude towards the shortcomings of his fellow Swiss than the second series, which was the product of his late maturity. Keller may be allowed to speak for himself in the famous words of his introduction to Part I of the book :

"Seldwyla bedeutet nach der älteren Sprache einen wonnigen und sonnigen Ort, und so ist auch in der Tat die kleine Stadt dieses Namens gelegen irgendwo in der Schweiz. Sie steht noch

in den gleichen alten Ringmauern und Türmen wie vor drei-
hundert Jahren und ist also immer das gleiche Nest; die
ursprüngliche tiefe Absicht dieser Anlage wird durch den Um-
stand verhärtet, dass die Gründer der Stadt dieselbe eine gute
halbe Stunde von einem schiffbaren Flusse angepflanzt, zum
deutlichen Zeichen, dass nichts daraus werden solle."[3]

Although the town of Seldwyla serves as the background of
all the stories, most of them are concerned with exceptional people
who happen to have lived there. Thus the first story, *Pankraz der
Schmoller,* deals with a boy, Pankraz, who has close affinities with
Heinrich Lee. Pankraz conquers his serious fault of character and
manages to succeed brilliantly in his chosen military career; a
great disappointment in love and a painful encounter with a hungry lion in the Arabian desert prove to be the means of grace that
enable him to master the negative elements in his own make-up.
Pankraz is really a *Bildungsroman* in miniature, and the reader is
left with the feeling that the theme called for more ample and
leisurely treatment. *Romeo und Julia auf dem Dorfe,* the most
powerful and affecting story in the collection, tells of the quarrel of
two originally good and moderately successful peasants, Manz and
Marti, and of its disastrous consequences for their children Sali
and Vrenchen. Finding it impossible to achieve the natural fulfilment of their love in marriage because of the dispute between their
families, Sali and Vrenchen spend a single gloriously happy day
together, make their nuptial bed on a hay barge and in the grey
light of dawn drop into the water and drown. The newspapers talk
prudishly of the degeneration of morals, but Sali and Vrenchen,
whose love is absolute and all-demanding, find it equally impossible
to separate for ever or to marry; their tragedy has an awful inevitability. Keller's wonderful descriptive powers and his mastery
of colour and symbol are revealed in this story. *Frau Regel Amrain,*
another offshoot of *Der grüne Heinrich,* is concerned with the
education of Fritz Amrain, a young Seldwyler, by his mother, Frau
Regula. Deserted while still a young woman by her improvident
husband, Frau Regel makes it her main task in life to educate her
youngest son to ideal citizenship. She steers him carefully past all
the pitfalls of childhood and adolescence and last of all sends him
to cast his vote when, as a grown man and husband, he is prepared
to neglect his civic duty. No doubt this book is very improving, but
the didactic intention is too obvious, and the British reader rebels
at the idea of a young man remaining quite so closely tied to his

mother's apron strings. *Die drei gerechten Kammacher,* one of the most entertaining stories of the collection, illustrates Keller's thesis that three just men could not live together under the same roof. The three combmakers are all men with a rather wooden idea of justice; essentially mean and grasping, they all hope to buy the same business and to marry the same woman. Keller's gift for caricature and his tendency towards the grotesque find free rein in the *Kammacher.* It was a story which was particularly dear to the author's heart, and he always tended to have a good opinion of people who thought well of this work. Like all the best comedy *Die drei gerechten Kammacher* has tragic overtones. The figure of Züs Bünzlin, that terrible woman whom all the combmakers wish to marry for her money, is a monument to the cautious bachelor's fear of the designing human female. *Spiegel das Kätzchen* is oddly out of place among the other mainly realistic stories, being a fairy-tale with talking animals, a magician, and a witch on a broomstick. It purports to explain the proverb: "Er hat der Katze den Schmer abgekauft," by telling the story of a little cat, Spiegel, who, hungry and neglected, sells himself to Pineiss the magician. The latter wishes to use his fat for nefarious purposes connected with his art. Spiegel contrives to thwart Pineiss and remain alive; the moral of the story is that we should not try to take advantage of the distress of our fellow-creatures. Spiegel, an entertaining fantasy, would certainly make an excellent children's story. The stories of Part II have a single theme in common, the need for a man to be himself, to forget sham and concentrate on living a full and good life within his natural and proper limits. In *Kleider machen Leute* the tailor Strapinsky causes confusion and trouble for himself and others because he has always romanticized himself and assumed clothes which do not befit his station; he does not mean to deceive the world, but when the world shows itself ready to take him for what he is not he makes no effort to put things to rights. *Der Schmied seines Glückes* was a young man who had so little self-respect that he was prepared to pretend to be the illegitimate son of an eccentric, rich relative in return for being made the old man's heir. All might have been well if John Kabys had not been foolish enough to seduce the old man's wife. She became pregnant, and John found that the husband did not take kindly to the suggestion that someone else must have fathered his wife's child. And so very soon John found himself disinherited; the rest of the story tells how he had to resign himself to a modest career as a maker of nails. *Die missbrauchten Liebesbriefe, Dietegen* and *Das verlorene*

Lachen all deal with the same theme of being true to oneself and not poisoning life and confusing human relations by pretence. The first of these contains some entertaining literary satire, the second has a historical background and the last is a short novel of contemporary life about a husband and wife who forsake their true natures for trade and religion respectively, and are restored to one another by natural affection; here again Keller allows Nature to rectify the wrong brought about by a perverted and unhealthy culture. Compared with the first stories of the collection the later five seem a little contrived and doctrinaire; Keller's powers of poetic invention have become relatively restricted, but *Kleider machen Leute* is a true work of art. *Dietegen* bears close affinities to *Ursula*, which was based on the same source book, Melchior Schuler's *Taten und Sitten der alten Eidgenossen* (1839), and *Das verlorene Lachen* anticipates *Martin Salander*.

VI

In his *Sieben Legenden* (1871) Keller uses as his source some legends of the saints as retold by Ludwig Theobul Kosegarten (1758–1818), a Protestant Prussian minister, in a somewhat sentimental and cloying manner. Kosegarten takes the point of view that the desires of the flesh are bound to be sinful, and he sets great store by asceticism and self-denial, in this respect even outdoing his sources. Keller's approach is very different. Although in most instances he adheres fairly closely to the narrative frameworks of his originals he alters the spirit of the Legends completely, and in fact, Keller's legends are tributes to the good, natural life, which must be regulated only by reason and common sense, not impoverished by a damaging asceticism. This asceticism need not be religious in origin; the heroine of the first story, a clever Alexandrian girl, Eugenia, forces herself into an impossible situation through the conceit of the bluestocking. By trying to make her admirer, the Proconsul Aquilinus, meet her on her own terms she alienates his affection; in her unhappiness she assumes men's clothes and takes refuge in a monastery, becomes a monk and then even abbot; only through pure chance is she rescued by Aquilinus from her false situation and restored to her proper sex and surroundings as his wife. Eugenia causes herself and Aquilinus great distress by her attempt to deny her femininity in favour of an unnatural intellectualism, and she is fortunate in being falsely accused of pursuing a lecherous widow who had taken a liking to the personable young abbot. When Proconsul Aquilinus investigates the case and discovers who the abbot is, all is well. Aquilinus and Eugenia marry, and he, too, becomes a Christian. *Die Jungfrau und der Teufel* shows the Virgin Mary in the guise of protectress of her children. Count Gebizo loved to make a parade of his generosity, so that he was prepared to hand over his wife to the devil in return for money. The Virgin changes places with the good and beautiful Bertrade, goes with the devil, and when he is about to make love to her, assumes her true form and puts him to flight. On the way home from handing over Bertrade Gebizo falls down a cliff and perishes. The Virgin now has to find Bertrade a new husband, and *Die Jungfrau als Ritter* tells how she assumed the form of the diffident knight Zendelwald, defeated all comers in the tournament, the winner of which was to marry Bertrade and gracefully withdrew when the young man arrived in time to claim the lovely prize the Virgin had won for him. Zendelwald is one of Keller's delightfully modest self-portraits. *Die Jungfrau und die Nonne* portrays the Virgin in her role of matchmaker and upholder of family life. Beatrix, a young nun, runs away from her cloister, marries a handsome knight and has a family of eight sons. In her absence the Virgin does her duty as sacristan of the nunnery; when her children are grown up Beatrix returns and finds that her absence has not been noticed. At a great festival in the cloister each nun brings a gift to the Virgin. Beatrix, old and worn out by child-bearing and rearing, cannot think what to bring. Then, as the service begins, her husband appears with the eight sons, who kneel before the altar. In symbol of their acceptability as offerings a garland of oak leaves appears on each young head. Beatrix's natural desire to fulfil herself as a woman has not been regarded in heaven as a fault; indeed she is honoured above the other nuns by the Virgin. *Der schlimm-heilige Vitalis* tells of St. Vitalis, who dedicates his life to the reclaiming of prostitutes. An enterprising young woman manages to turn him from his career of self-denial and unnatural well-doing and makes of him a model husband. In *Dorotheas Blumenkörbchen* Keller describes the efforts of a well-favoured girl to elicit a declaration of love from an amorous but diffident and reluctant swain. Dorothea is a Christian, but Theophilus, her lover, is not. They quarrel, and Fabricius, the Roman governor, pursues her. When she will not yield to him, Fabricius has her tried and put to death. From Dorothea an angel comes to Theophilus bearing a heavenly gift of fruit and flowers. He accepts the Christian faith, is put to death by Fabricius, and his

soul is united with Dorothea's in heaven. The last paragraphs of
this beautiful little legend describing the reunion of these two
blessed souls have a Dante-like flavour. *Das Tanzlegendchen* tells
of a maiden named Musa who loves dancing. One day King David
appears to her in a vision and promises her heavenly joys if she
will refrain from dancing on earth. This she agrees to do; she dies
the death of a medieval saint on a bed of moss in her cell, and is
received up into heaven where she immediately joins a dancing
throng. In heaven the Nine Muses have been invited up from the
underworld for a visit that day. Out of gratitude the Muses
rehearse a chorale which they sing in heaven, but its tone is so
nostalgic, it reawakens such tender memories of happy days on
earth for many inhabitants of heaven that the Muses have to be
brought to silence by a heavy peal of celestial thunder and sent
back to hell. There is a division of interest in the *Tanzlegendchen*
between the story of Musa and the fate of the Muses in heaven.
The story is too slight to contain two main themes, and, despite
one or two extremely well written paragraphs, it is the weakest of
Keller's legends. Keller shows in his legends that for men and
women on earth there is no more holy duty than that of living a
good, wholesome and natural life. Any intellectual or religious
exercise which is at variance with this first duty of mankind should
be abandoned. Sometimes life is tragic, as in *Dorotheas Blumenkörbchen*; then it will be a comfort to have lived according to the
best insights of our human nature.

VII

The *Züricher Novellen* (1878) are very different from *Die Leute
von Seldwyla*. The earlier collection of stories was about imaginary
people in an imaginary Swiss town. In the *Züricher Novellen*
Keller is mainly concerned with historical figures in his native city.
This makes these *Novellen* more credible than the earlier collection, but it also cramps the author's style occasionally. One is
sometimes very aware of the trouble Keller took over his historical
backgrounds. At least one of the stories, *Der Narr auf Manegg*
concerns a person in a state of mind quite remote from ordinary
experience; it is the weakest in the collection. *Ursula,* the last
Novelle, though interesting as the document of a collective religious
aberration, is not in Keller's best vein. Keller is again much preoccupied with the question of a good and wholesome development
of the human personality. His characters fail or succeed in life

according to whether they are true to themselves or not. A rather flimsy framework story lends unity to the collection. A young Züricher, Herr Jacques, has harmless adolescent delusions of grandeur. He wants to be an original genius, but his godfather, who cannot envisage him in such a role, relates the five stories to show what constitutes genuine and spurious originality.

Hadlaub, the son of a Swiss peasant living in medieval times, was able by virtue of his exceptional gifts of intellect and imagination to rise from his humble milieu to fame as a *Minnesänger* and win the hand of a noble lady. He was originally commissioned by his aristocratic patron, Rüdiger Manesse, to compile a fine manuscript collection of all examples he could find of the *Minnesang* before they were lost. In the course of conscientiously performing this service Hadlaub discovered his own poetic vein, and found a young lady to adore. She was Fides, the illegitimate daughter of the Lady Abbess of Zürich by the Bishop of Constance. Against the wishes of her family and friends Fides returned Hadlaub's love, and in due course they were married and set up house in Zürich, where their family lived for many generations. Hadlaub had originally aspired to do far less than he was capable of, unlike Herr Jacques, who had imagined himself to be a far more wonderful person than he was. Hadlaub, like Gottfried Keller, was a poet, but unlike his creator Hadlaub found happiness and fulfilment in love. *Hadlaub,* a wish-fulfilment story, is not unlike *Pankraz der Schmoller* in a late medieval setting.

Der Narr auf Manegg warns Jacques of the dangers of trying to seem to be what one is not. Buz Falätscher, an illegitimate descendant of the Manesses, is never content to accept the kind of work or station in life to which he is suited by birth and ability. The *Novelle,* a very slight one, tells how, preoccupied with grandiose and fruitless schemes, he loses one opportunity after another in life of making good in a humble way, and finally becomes mad and perishes miserably. He goes to live in Burg Manegg, the half-ruined ancestral castle of the Manesses and sets himself up as a *Minnesänger* with the aid of the Manesse *Liederhandschrift* which he has managed to steal. The theft is discovered, and Buz dies of fright when a crowd of young patricians and noblemen march on the castle and demand the surrender of the manuscript. He has paid the penalty for having pretended to be what he was not.

Der Landvogt von Greifensee concerns a genuine original, Salomon Landolt, who lived in and around Zürich in the late eighteenth century. Keller closely follows a biography by David Hess of the famous *Landvogt*. But Keller's hero is also in various respects a reflection of his creator. Landolt, magistrate of Greifensee, lives by the lake of that name in an ancient castle, waited upon by an old dragon of a housekeeper. An amateur painter and musician, a confirmed bachelor, a man of taste and good judgment, he is well able to administer justice even in matrimonial disputes. Once he invites to his castle all the five women whom he had loved, and spends a happy day surveying these gracious ladies, who had all for various reasons rejected him. The work is a most effective justification of the bachelor form of existence. What Salomon Landolt once regarded as a bitter cross to bear he now recognizes as a blessing. This work contains a wealth of unobtrusively introduced local colour, for Keller was well versed in the history of eighteeenth century Zürich and was learned in its literature. The ladies whom Landolt had loved are all depicted as having more or less recognizable characteristics of Keller's own loves; Hess says little about this aspect of Landolt's life, so that Keller was able to improvise freely and credibly from his own experience. *Der Landvogt* stands out as the most artistically satisfying of the *Züricher Novellen*.

In *Das Fähnlein der sieben Aufrechten* the Seven are elderly tradesmen of strong democratic convictions who have for years regularly met round a *Stammtisch*. They decide to march together to the Federal Marksmen's Competition with a banner they have had made and present a prize for the best marksman. A certain coolness has arisen between two of their number because the son of the poor tailor Hediger wishes to marry the daughter of the rich joiner, Frymann. On the day of the contest none of the Seven is prepared to speak in public for the group when they hand over their trophy to the chairman of the competition. Karl Hediger appears at the crucial moment, takes over this task and makes an effective little speech about his country's free institutions and the principles for which the old men have always stood. Karl's words reflect Keller's satisfaction with the constitutional improvements achieved in Switzerland in 1848. Then Karl goes off, and with Frymann's daughter aiding and abetting him wins high credit in the shooting competition. The Seven unanimously agree that the young couple should be allowed to marry. If we think of the *Eidgenössisches Schützenfest* as an event comparable in Switzerland to a Test Match in this country we may be able to summon up some sympathy for this frankly didactic little work.

Ursula, a story of the Reformation wars, tells how Hans Gyr, a peasant farmer, returns to his native Bachtelberg to find the populace there in the grip of sectarian delusions. His fiancée Ursula, is also affected by the false beliefs proclaimed by the *Winkelpropheten,* and he leaves the region again for the wars, intending to marry Ursula if and when she recovers her sanity. Hansli's wanderings and his eventual reunion with Ursula are interesting from the historical point of view, with accurate descriptions of the prevailing religious moods of that age and district, but the spectacular and sudden cure of Ursula's aberrations is hard to swallow.

VIII

Das Sinngedicht, first conceived in the 1850s, was not completed till 1883. The epigram in question was Friedrich von Logau's:

"Wie willst du weisse Lilien zu roten Rosen machen?
Küss eine weisse Galatee; sie wird errötend lachen."[4]

Reinhart, a young scientist, having strained his eyesight by overwork, goes out in search of a wife by way of relaxation. Following Logau's advice he seeks a girl who will both blush and laugh when he kisses her; after a few casual encounters he decides that his quest will not be easy. But then he comes across Lucia, the very person (the name is symbolical) who is calculated to bring sweetness and light into the life of a man who has become involved in scientific experiments to the exclusion of human interests.

Lucia is amiable and intelligent, rich, beautiful and extremely independent in outlook. Reinhart, having reached her country house late in the day, has to stay the night there, and the couple, along with Lucia's aged uncle, tell one another stories to pass the time. All the stories are concerned with love and marriage, relationships between the sexes and what factors can disturb or completely destroy a marriage.

Lucia begins with the story of Salome, a handsome inn-keeper's daughter whom Reinhart had just met on the way to her house. Salome had become engaged to a young townsman of good family, but, lacking a common background and having no shared interests at all to lend content to their relationship, they had become thoroughly bored with one another and quarrelled violently. That was the end of Salome's hopes of marriage.

Reinhart instances *Regine* in support of his contention that differing social backgrounds need not constitute an absolute bar to happiness in marriage. A rich young American of German descent goes to Germany in search of a wife. Having tried in vain to find one among young women of his own class, he finally marries Regine, a beautiful servant girl. By native intelligence, tact and adaptability Regine is well qualified to fulfil her new role with distinction, but foolish pride on Erwin's part prevents him from taking home his bride to Boston until she has lived longer in good society. Regine, left to her own devices while her husband returns to America, makes one or two comparatively harmless social mistakes, has some troubles with her own family, and, when Erwin after many months takes her to Boston, feels thoroughly insecure and miserable. Through a series of misunderstandings Erwin has lost confidence in Regine and she takes her own life. This tragedy is not due to her inability to make him a good wife, but to his failure to show confidence in her and provide her with sufficient moral support.

Die arme Baronin, also related by Reinhart, has a happier outcome. Hedwig von Hohenhausen has had a hard life and is forced to let rooms for a living after the collapse of her marriage and the loss of her child. Soured by her misfortunes, she has the reputation of a thoroughly unpleasant woman. Her lodger, Brandolf, brings affection and material prosperity back into her life and restores the foundation of wellbeing and happiness. Her character now improves out of all recognition. When she and Brandolf marry we are confident that theirs will be a sound and happy marriage. One element in this *Novelle* jars somewhat, namely Brandolf's revenge on Hedwig's rascally husband and brothers; in this incident Keller gives free rein to his love of grotesque fantasies, and we feel that it is in poor taste.

Lucia's uncle, who now joins in the conversation, contributes *Die Geisterseher,* an improbable story of a young woman, who, being unable to choose between two admirers, decided to test their courage by staging a mock haunting of their bedrooms. The man whose rational faculties remained unimpaired married her; he was Reinhart's father; the unsuccessful suitor was Lucia's uncle. The point made is this : A man worth his salt will not easily allow himself to be intimidated into forsaking the use of his reason.

Reinhart's long tale of *Don Correa* falls into two sections. The first tells of Admiral Don Correa's first marriage to a rich Portuguese noblewoman; he does not reveal his identity to her, and she takes him for a person of no consequence. As long as he complies with her wishes they get on very well, but as soon as he develops a

mind of his own she is angry with him. Don Correa finds himself
in the end presiding over the trial and execution of his own wife,
because Donna Feniza in her pride of birth and wealth has
assumed that a husband ought to be merely an accommodating
chattel. Don Correa's second marriage reminds us of the story of
Regine. In perfect humility and docility Zambo-Maria leans on her
rescuer, educator and protector; in return he saves her from servitude and savagery and makes of her a free human personality. The
closing scene of this *Novelle* is very impressive. Reinhart is clearly
anxious to establish the superiority of the male in matters of
marriage, but his Don Correa take a rather broad view of a husband's liberty by modern standards.

Lucia is stung into rebellion by the masculine view of the matrimonial estate expressed in *Don Correa* and relates *Die Berlocken,*
in which an unscrupulous young Frenchman is firmly put in his
place by a pretty Red Indian girl. M. de Vallormes had collected
a series of trinkets for his watch-chain from ladies young and old
whose affection he had managed to win, generally by thoroughly
unethical means. Arriving in North America with Lafayette's army
he fell sufficiently in love with the attractive Quoneschi to give her
his trinkets, imagining that by doing so he had won her heart.
Alas, she passed them to her Indian lover and quickly disappeared.
De Vallormes, who had behaved in exactly the same way towards
many women as Quoneschi towards him was more than a little
taken aback to discover what it must have felt like to be one of his
victims.

The last chapter of *Das Sinngedicht* is taken up with the story
of Lucia's and Reinhart's reconciliation and rapprochement in
idyllic country surroundings while the shoemaker sings Goethe's
Mit einem gemalten Bande with great feeling. At the climax of the
song the lovers kiss and Reinhart observes that Lucia is blushing
and laughing all at once. And so she has fulfilled the condition laid
down in Logau's epigram.

This summary gives little impression of the ripe wisdom and
practised art of *Das Sinngedicht*. A little artificial the work certainly is, with its elaborately stylized setting and the constantly
recurring symbolism of the epigram, but it has a charm and polish
all of its own. In this work Keller shows himself to be not merely
a profound writer, but also extremely accomplished. *Das Sinngedicht* is the greatest work of Keller's old age, as *Der grüne Heinrich*
is the greatest work of his youth.

IX

Martin Salander is a noble failure. Influenced by the later realists and not unaffected by the rising Naturalist school, Keller tried to write a book which would take into account the changing literary climate of the age. Alas, his genius was by now drying up, largely because his life had become arid and disappointing. His sister, Regula, was dying, his own health was failing, he disliked the flat to which they had just moved, and all these miseries of old age are reflected in the book. It concerns a typical Swiss citizen of the *Gründerzeit*. Martin Salander goes to Brazil to make money and returns home. There he loses all and has to go abroad again. He once more makes his fortune and comes home. His daughters make very unsatisfactory marriages with Julian and Isidor Weidelich, the twin sons of an ambitious washerwoman. It comes almost as a relief to Salander and his wife when both Julian and Isidor are convicted of embezzlement and sentenced to long periods in prison. It then becomes possible to dissolve the two girls' marriages. Martin Salander himself is not a very satisfactory figure for the hero of a novel. With his naive trust in human nature which causes him twice over to entrust his money to the rascally Wohlwend, his susceptible heart, which very nearly causes him to make a fool of himself with Wohlwend's beautiful but stupid sister-in-law, and his excessive faith in democratic politics, he is a strangely unimpressive successor to Keller's earlier heroes. His son Arnold, at one time intended as the principal character of a second volume, is too priggish and clear-sighted to be altogether agreeable. The novel represents an unsuccessful attempt by an ageing writer to come to terms with the new literary idiom introduced by the Naturalists.

X

Gottfried Keller's *oeuvre* is the most distinguished that has emerged fom German Switzerland. Although not a very prolific writer he had a lively artistic conscience, and even when, as often, he badly needed money, he always observed the highest standards of which he was aware. As a result all his work bears the unmistakable imprint of genius, though it is not, as we have seen, of altogether even quality. In spite of its weaknesses *Der grüne Heinrich* will always be regarded as a very great *Bildungsroman,* and in particular as one that shows a true appreciation of the difficulties of the child and adolescent. Each of his cycles of short stories has its own peculiar merits, and taken together they represent a valuable contribution to German and European literature. Keller was never content to relapse into a cosy and comfortable Swiss-ness; his work compares very favourably with anything that was being produced in Germany in his generation.

TRANSLATIONS

1. Here I feel a connection
   With the One and All.
2. The coarsest and most trivial art in the world to pull the shifts off over the heads of the female characters.
3. Seldwyla means according to the older language a delightful and sunny place, and indeed the little town of this name, which is situated somewhere in Switzerland, is just that. It is still confined within the same old town walls and towers as it was 300 years ago, and so it is still the same old hole; the original deep purpose of this siting is confirmed by the circumstance that the founders of the town stuck it a good half hour's journey from the nearest navigable river, as a manifest sign that nothing would ever become of it.
4. How will you make white lilies into red roses?
   Kiss a white Galatea; she will blushingly laugh.

BIBLIOGRAPHY

The standard edition of Keller's works is:
Sämtliche Werke, edited by Julius Fränkel and Carl Helbling, 24 vols. Berne, 1926–54.
The standard edition of the letters is:
Gesammelte Briefe in 4 Bänden, ed. Carl Helbling. Zürich, 1954.
The following collections of letters have been published separately:
Storm-Keller Briefwechsel, ed. A. Köster. Berlin, 1904.
Keller-Heyse Briefwechsel, ed. Max Kalbeck. Berlin, 1919.
At present available in English translation are:
Green Henry, translated by A. M. Holt, John Calder, London, 1960.
A Village Romeo and Juliet, translated by P. B. Thomas, 1955.

WORKS ABOUT KELLER

E. Ackerknecht, *Gottfried Kellers Leben, Berlin,* 1939 (a very full biography, not including the works).

E. Ermatinger, *Gottfried Kellers Leben*. Zürich, 1950 (The standard critical biography).

B. A. Rowley, *Keller: Kleider machen Leute* (an interpretation). E. Arnold, London, 1959.

Paul Schaffner, *Gottfried Keller als Maler*. Zürich, Atlantis, 1942.

See also the relevant sections of:

E. K. Bennett, *The German Novelle. Cambridge,* 1960.

R. Pascal, *The German Novel*. Manchester, 1956.

J. M. Lindsay, *Gottfried Keller: Life and Works*. London, 1968.

Lionel Thomas, ed. *Gottfried Keller. Two Stories* with introduction and notes. London, 1966.

Louis Wiesmann, *Gottfried Keller: Wirkung und Gestalt*. Frauenfeld, 1967.

Conrad Ferdinand Meyer

Conrad Ferdinand Meyer

by W. E. YUILL

IT would be difficult to imagine men more different in character, upbringing, taste and even appearance than the two celebrities who, as Meyer put it, occupied opposite ends of the literary see-saw in Zürich between 1870 and 1890. On one end perched Keller—a small, pugnacious figure, Bohemian in his habits, a Swiss patriot to the backbone; on the other end sat Meyer—large, lymphatic, neurotically reserved and punctilious, a convinced cosmopolitan. Little wonder that they disliked each other, that Keller complained of the other's "unnötiges Wesen und Sich-mausig-machen",[1] while Meyer accused Keller of rudeness and lack of "Bildung". The relations between them were tenuously sustained by Meyer out of a sense of propriety which even prompted him to visit Keller on his death-bed. One thing, it is true, they might seem to have in common with each other (and with the other great Swiss writer of the nineteenth century, Jeremias Gotthelf) : the long struggle to realize their poetic vocation. Even here, however, there was a significant difference. Keller struggled against the handicap of poverty—and an obstinate misapplication of his talents; Meyer spent nearly the first forty years of his life in overcoming a paralysis of the creative faculty. His were obstacles invisible to the onlooker : nothing could have seemed more propitious than the circumstances of his youth in a respected patrician family, nothing more natural than that he should continue a tradition of public service. Instead, his youth and early manhood were passed in a twilight dream :

> "Ich war von einem schweren Bann gebunden,
> Ich lebte nicht. Ich lag im Traum erstarrt."[2]

This was Meyer's later view of a youth spent in neurotic seclusion, so complete at one point that he was rumoured to have died. Amongst a people devoted to ideals of hard work, efficiency and success he lived a life tortured by a sense of inadequacy, tormented by vague ambitions. The early death of his father left him too much under the influence of his mother, a woman of somewhat morbid religiosity, given to referring to her son as "poor Conrad" and to praying for his salvation. While Keller took an active part in the hectic political events of the 1840s, Meyer was absorbing himself in lonely pursuits—fencing, rowing, walking in the mountains—and feeding his brooding melancholy on the Romantic works of Tieck, Lenau, Novalis and Victor Hugo. By the age of twenty-seven he had so lost contact with the outside world that he was sent to the mental hospital of Préfargier. To a similar refuge he was forced to return some forty years later. Between these withdrawals from the world Meyer built for himself a personality of precarious equilibrium and a series of brilliantly executed works of literature.

This emancipation was, however, relatively slow. His removal from the oppressive atmosphere of Zürich to French Switzerland and the consequent necessity of absorbing himself in another language was undoubtedly a first step. After a short stay in Préfargier Meyer went to Lausanne, where he was taken in hand by a friend of the family, Louis Vulliemin. Meyer remained grateful throughout his life for the benevolent influence of this man, to whose nobility of mind he has paid a tribute in the figure of Rohan in *Jürg Jenatsch*. Not only did Vulliemin discipline Meyer's literary ambitions by making him apply himself to translation from French, he also introduced him to the study of history, which was to become the indispensable element of this writer's art. By doing this he opened up for Meyer, who was incapable of effective action in the world around him, a world of the imagination in which he was given the possibility of creating a substitute for real experience. The other essential feature of Meyer's art, linguistic virtuosity, came to him in the long labour of translating Augustin Thierry's *Récits des Temps Mérovingiens*.

In 1856 Elisabeth Meyer committed suicide after her growing melancholy had led her to the same asylum which four years previously had received her son. In a sense her death represented a further stage in the liberation of the latter from the inhibitions of his youth. The freedom which the breaking of this bond entailed was further augmented by the inheritance of a modest fortune which enabled Conrad to travel to Paris and then, with his sister Betsy, to Italy. It was on these journeys that his eyes were opened to the contrast between the Latin and the Germanic cultures that forms such a frequent theme in his work. The contact with the Latin mode of life and the experience of Classical and Italian art seem to have turned his mind from a preoccupation with ethical matters and given the final impetus to his emergence as a poet : by 1860 he had compiled a collection of ballads, and although it was published until 1864, his new life had begun.

This emergence from the dark cell of the mind, the change from an ascetic to an aesthetic attitude, from contemplation to the release of energy is reflected and magnified in Meyer's work. He sees an image of his experience in the growth of bright new foliage over the old :

> "Eppich, mein alter Hausgesell,
> Du bist von jungen Blättern hell,
> Dein Wintergrün, so still and streng,
> Verträgt sich's mit dem Lenzgedräng?
> 'Warum denn nicht? Wie meines hat
> Dein Leben alt und junges Blatt,
> Eins streng und dunkel, eines licht
> Von Lenz und Luft! Warum denn nicht?' "[3]

In the notion of the flight from the cloister this experience occupies a very prominent place in his works. The identification of the cloister with moribund states of mind and the association of religion with the sufferings of his youth are no doubt the psychological basis of the anti-clericalism, and particularly the anti-Catholicism, that are for long a feature of his stories. The hero of one of Meyer's earliest works, the Reformer, Ulrich von Hutten, is inspired by Luther's escape from the cloister :

> "Ein sächsisch Mönchlein aus der Kutte schloff.
> Da, Ritter, habt Ihr einen guten Stoff !"[4]

The verse epic, *Engelberg,* revolves round this theme, as do the unfinished stories, *Clara* and *Die sanfte Klosteraufhebung*; Jürg Jenatsch exchanges the sword of the spirit for that of the soldier; Hans, the narrator in *Der Heilige,* is a runaway monk; *Die Hochzeit des Mönchs* contains, either in the "framework" or in the main story, no less than four such figures : Manuccio, Helene Manente, Astorre and Brother Serapion. The conflict of clerical and worldly values is perhaps clearest of all in *Plautus im Nonnenkloster.* Yet the opposition here is not between the cloister and the court, but between the cloister and the heart. Poggio Bracciolini, with his "feine Lüge" and his blasphemous identification of Pallas Athene and the Virgin Mary, is not the true hero of the story. He, no less than Brigitte, is a type of clerical degeneracy :

"Die Verweltlichung des hohen Klerus . . . der wahre Typus des Humanisten : Geist, Leichtsinn, Nachäffung und übertriebene Schätzung der Antike, Unwahrheit, Rachsucht . . ., Diebstahl und Bettelei."[5]

Meyer, who was often enough critizised by his pious countrymen as a mere "artist" and hence as immoral, is concerned that his views should be identified with those of Poggio :

". . . au fond et malgré la gaieté du récit je méprise cet humaniste, ce Poggio qui voit dans son fils devenu brigand ou peu s'en faut, sa facilité de vivre dégénérer en crime et ignominie. Ce n'est pas pour rien que j'ai mis cela au commencement de mon récit."

It is not the sophisticated paganism of the Renaissance humanist that Meyer sets against the superstition and fanaticism of the Church but the simple philosophy of Gertrude. She may stand for a pagan way of life, but it is an earthly paganism with its own roots : "Was mir taugt", she cries, "ist Sonne und Wolke, Sichel und Sense, Mann und Kind . . ."[6] This is the same affirmation of the idyllic life to which Meyer gives expression in such poems as *Veltliner Traube, Der Hengert* and *Bacchus in Bünden*—although, as in the last example, he often uses the figures of Classical mythology to express the thought.

In *Der Heilige* the change is from the worldly life to the life of asceticism. But in interpreting Becket's development from the man of the world to a saintly figure Meyer is simply substituting irony for direct attack. Becket's piety is the subtlest of attacks on the King, as Bertram de Born points out in the story :

"Du stiller, langsam grabender Mann, du duldest wie dein Meister, und lässest dich töten wie er. Du glaubst der Liebe zu dienen, aber der Haß ist der mächtigere, und dein Tod, wie der deines Gottes, ist die Verdammnis der Menschen."[7]

This is clear, too, from Meyer's comment on his hero :

"Dieser—eine geistig überlegene, fast modern humane, aber der Roheit des Mittelalters gegenüber wehrlose Natur—bedient sich ohne gläubig zu sein—die Legende und der Dichter geben ihm orientalisches Blut—der Kirche als einer Waffe."[8]

For all that he glorifies energy and vitality in so many of his works, Meyer is haunted by the spectre of death. He spoke to

Keller of "the insecurity of life", and was well aware of a fundamental difference in outlook between himself and the author of
such stories as *Kleider machen Leute* and *Spiegel, das Kätzchen:*

> "Keller hat der Menge gegenüber vor mir den Vorteil, daß
> er im Grunde Optimist ist. Daher ist er für die Menge. Denn so
> sind die Leute : sie drängen sich um den Brunnen des Lebens und
> sind froh, wenn sie mit ihrem Becherchen wenigstens ein
> Tröpflein auffangen. Die finden nun ihre Rechnung bei Keller,
> der alles gut enden läßt. Er kennt keine tragischen Ausgänge.
> Das ist ein Mangel, denn der Reiz des Daseins vollendet sich
> erst in beiden."[9]

Meyer's fault, if it is indeed one, lies in the opposite extreme—
he rarely achieves a happy ending. His taste was for the tragic and
he shows very few signs of a sense of humour : "Mir individuell
hinterläßt das Komische einen bittern Geschmack," he writes,
"während das Tragische mich erhebt und beseligt."[10] Keller,
himself by no means always free from a subtle form of sadism,
thought this quality pre-eminent in his compatriot's work :

> "Meyer hat eine Schwäche für solche einzelnen Brutalitäten
> und Totschläge. Wenn er so was hört oder liest, so sagt er :
> Vortrefflich! So hat jeder seinen Zopf."[11]

For Meyer death frequently represents the dramatic climax of
life, the crown of passion fulfilled : Jenatsch is struck down by
Lucrezia at the feast which celebrates his triumph: Astorre, plunged
into life like a glowing splinter into a stream of oxygen is con-
sumed in a blaze of passion, united with his lover in death;
"Komme, Tod, und raub mich, Tod, im Kusse!"[12] cries a girl
at her lover's breast (*Der Kamerad*); the harvesters toil beneath the
threatening storm and

> "Von Garbe zu Garbe
> Ist Raum für den Tod;"[13]

the victor in a duel, although his life is forfeit, revels in his
triumph :

> "Ich besitze den Kranz und verdiene den Tod."
> (*Der Ritt in den Tod.*)[14]

Leubelfing, Gustav Adolf's page, chooses the motto "Courte et
bonne" and longs for the hour of glorious life that culminates in
death :

"Ich wünsche mir alle Strahlen meines Lebens in ein Flam-
menbündel und in den Raum einer Stunde vereinigt, daß statt
einer blöden Dämmerung ein kurzes, aber blendendes helles
Licht von Glück entstünde, um dann zu löschen wie ein zuck-
ender Blitz."[15]

The flash of lightning invoked here frequently has symbolic value
in Meyer's work as the mark of a climax.

For Keller, Meyer was no doubt an inhabitant of that grisly
borough of Rüchenstein, with its garland of gallows and execution
blocks. In only one of his stories does he appear to breathe the
more congenial air of Seldwyla. Mythikon, an imaginary village on
the Lake of Zürich, is indeed "ein wonniger, sonniger Ort". The
whole story is suffused with a warm, Southern light :

"Eine warme Föhnluft hatte die Schneeberge und den Schwei-
zersee auf ihre Weise idealisiert, die Reihe der einen zu einem
einzigen stillen, großen Leuchten verbunden, den andern mit
dem tiefen und kräftigen Farbenglanz einer südlichen Meerbucht
übergossen, als gelüste sie eine bacchische Landschaft, ein Stück
Italien, über die Alpen zu versetzen."[16]

It is perhaps significant that this story was written not long after
the poet's marriage, at the age of fifty, to Luise Ziegler. At last he
seemed to have achieved full maturity. Although the story is set in
the seventeenth century, it is more closely linked, through its
location and through the relationship between Pfannenstiel and
Rahel, with the circumstances of Meyer's personal life than any
other of his prose works. The story illustrates the development in its
shy hero of a comfortable sensuality; its message is not that of
death in ecstasy or in triumph, but Keller's message of reconciliation with one's lot. Rahel reproves Pfannenstiel for his desperate
plan to become chaplain to a regiment stationed in the Balkan wilds :

"Ihr wolltet aus Eurer eigenen Natur heraus, und er hat
Euch heimgespottet . . . Warum auch? Wie Ihr seid, und gerade
wie Ihr seid, gefallt Ihr mir am besten."[17]

Meyer was aware of this rare affinity with Keller and feared
that he might be thought a mere imitator of the *Züricher
Novellen* :

". . . die Vortrefflichkeit von Keller's Züricher Novellen (wird)
mich sicher in Schatten stellen und vielleicht gar ungerechter-
weise als Nachahmer erscheinen lassen."[18]

In spite of the comic dénouement, however, in spite of the cheerfulness and the mild irony at the expense of the narrow-minded clergy and parishioners, there is a shadow on the sunlit landscape of the story—the shadow of Jürg Jenatsch, for, as Meyer pointed out, the story is, through the figure of Wertmüller, a continuation of the novel. Even here there is an element of the morbid : Wertmüller's dream of Jenatsch and himself as both dead. And Wertmüller himself is a problematic figure, a forerunner, in his scepticism and his traffic with the exotic, of Becket and of the figure who haunted Meyer's mind without ever emerging on the scale which the poet wished—the Hohenstaufen emperor, Frederick II. It is in such figures, rather than in Pfannenstiel, that Meyer expressed his inner nature. "Im *Jenatsch* und im Heiligen ... ist in den verschiedensten Verkleidungen weit mehr von mir, meinen wahren Leiden und Leidenschaften als in dieser Lyrik,"[19] he wrote to Louise von François. Into such men of destiny he projected a taste for power which he could never indulge in reality. There are many variations on the theme of the leader—Jenatsch, the ruthless; Rohan and Gustav Adolf, the saintly; Becket the subtle; Stemma, the sinful; Pescara, the loyal. Of these perhaps Becket is closest to Meyer's heart and exerts the most compulsive power over his imagination :

"Ich habe den Heiligen fast unbewußt, besessen, im Rausch geschrieben, weil ich ihn los werden mußte, er lag mir quälend auf der Brust wie ein Alp."[20]

Becket has the fastidiousness, the suavity, the subtle sense of superiority along with a certain lack of manliness that were characteristic of his creator. "Eines aber . . . mangelte dem Kanzler : das Ungestüm und die Schärfe eines männlichen Blutes."[12] There is something here of the poet described by Adolf Frey :

"Leidenschaftslosigkeit war ein Grundzug seines Wesens. Ich sah ihn niemals zornig und vermochte mir ihn auch nur schwer so zu denken."[22]

The analysis of motive in the enigmatic situation and figures of history and the infusion of his own modes of feeling into these figures constitute the most remarkable features of Meyer's use of historical material. He looks upon himself not as a rival to the historian but as his coadjutor; his aim, as he described it in an unpublished story, is to represent the psychological processes which gleam like fish through the wide meshes of the historian's net. By

and large, Meyer realizes this aim without giving too much offence
to the historian's conscience and justifies his claim : "Ich behandle
die Geschichte souverän aber nicht ungetreu."[23] If anything, his
stories are too richly embroidered with cultural reference, there are
traces of "Möbellust," an antiquarian relish, in his recreation of
the past. Occasionally, too, he is guilty of falsifying the spirit of an
age—in *Das Leiden eines Knaben,* for instance, there is evidence
both of an informality and a middle-class sentimentality that were
hardly characteristic of the court of Louis XIV.

The interest in historical themes was, as we have seen, first
dictated by objective considerations; it was in any case something
which lay in the air. Meyer lived in an age of great historians—
Mommsen, Ranke, Gregorovius, Burckhardt—an age when antiquarian interest was strong. The pervasion of this interest with his
own feeling was not something that was given him straight away.
His early ballads have the stiffness of historical vignettes. It is only
gradually that he came to realize both the relevance of the past to
contemporary political events that inspires *Huttens letzte Tage*
and the advantages of historical themes as a mask for his own views
and feelings. This function of the historical narrative he clearly
states in a letter to his friend Felix Bovet, written in January 1888 :

"Je me sers de la forme de la nouvelle historique purement et
simplement pour y loger mes expériences et sentiments person-
nels, la préférant au 'Zeitroman' parce qu'elle me masque mieux
et qu'elle distance davantage le lecteur. Ainsi sous une forme
très objective et éminemment artistique, je suis au dedans tout
individuel et subjectif."

It is this alienation, to use a current term, which prompts Louise
von François to describe Meyer as a "Telescopisten," as compared
with Keller, whom she calls "einen Microscopisten der Gegenwart." The use of a theatrical term is not inappropriate, because
Meyer, who long toyed with the notion of writing dramas, tends
to look upon history as a stage. Of many of his works it might be
said, as of the sermon heard by Gustav Adolf, that they "compare
life with a stage, with men as the actors, the angels for an audience
and death as the producer who rings down the curtain."

But even the historical remoteness of the theme is not sufficient
protection for the author : in many of his stories Meyer strives to
dissociate himself from his work through the technique of the
narrative. The use of the "framework" is characteristic :

"Die Neigung zum Rahmen dann ist bei mir ganz instinktiv. Ich halte mir den Gegenstand gerne vom Leibe oder richtiger gerne so weit als möglich vom Auge, und dann will mir scheinen, das Indirekte der Erzählung (und selbst die Unterbrechungen) mildern die Härte der Fabel."[24]

This device, clumsily used in *Das Amulett*, reaches a climax of refinement in *Die Hochzeit des Mönchs*. Altogether, this is a bravura piece, a self-conscious work of art. For once the story is presented, not as an account of authentic events experienced by the speaker, but as a piece of invention by the master, Dante. "Es schien mir," wrote Meyer to his sister, "Dante müsse erfinden, nicht erzählen."[25] The narrator weaves the characters and the relationships of his listeners into the story, selects and constructs with deliberate artistry: "Seine Fabel lag in ausgeschütteter Fülle vor ihm; aber sein strenger Geist wählte und vereinfachte."[26] The author indulges in a degree of elaboration here which subsequently seemed excessive even to him:

"Hier freilich wird der Verschlingung von Fabel und Zuhörer zu viel; die Sache wird entschieden mühsam. Ein non plus ultra! M'en voila guéri!"[27]

And cured he was, for this is the last of the stories in which the technique of the "Rahmen" is used.

Die Hochzeit des Mönchs demonstrates admirably not only Meyer's objectivity as a writer, but also the plasticity of his style. These were qualities first learned through the writings of F. Th. Vischer and confirmed by what Meyer saw in France and Italy, qualities which are summed up for him in the notion of "gesture":

"Kurz, was ich vom Romanischen bekommen habe, ist der Sinn für die Gebärde, Geste. Es ist mir nicht zu entbehrendes Bedürfnis gweorden, alles nach außen hin sauber, sichtbar zu gestalten, auch in der Sprache."[28]

In this Meyer consciously turned away from the traditional attributes of German poetry: its capacity for reflection, its musical quality and its power to evoke atmosphere. He once remarked to Hermann Friedrichs:

"Ja, wissen Sie, . . . ein paar stimmungsvolle Verse bringt schließlich jeder Backfisch zu Stande, der Heine, Geibel, Ritterhaus . . . verschlungen hat; aber in balladenartiger Form, ich möchte sagen, plastisch greifbare Gestalten hervorzuzaubern und sie handelnd auftreten zu lassen, das ist eine Kunst, die nur verschwindend Wenigen gegeben ist."[29]

On another occasion he criticized the lack of visual sharpness in most German writers :

"In der deutschen Literatur empfinde ich einen Mangel : das ist nicht scharf genug gesehen, nicht sinnlich herausgestellt, es ist unbildlich verschwimmend. Die Gleichnisse und Bilder im Deutschen sind schwach, sie erhellen und beleuchten nicht. Dagegen die Ariosts sind immer, wenn auch übertrieben grotesk, so doch scharf gesehen, erleuchtend . . ."[30]

This sharpness of definition is evident in almost every aspect of Meyer's work—in the rapid, unreflective narrative of his early stories (which owe a good deal to Mérimée, in the concise similes : "So redete Victoria aufwallend und überquellend wie ein römischer Brunnen"; "Das Spiel seiner Natur war ehrlich wie ein Stoß im Hifthorn und überquoll wie der Schaum am Gebiß eines jungen Renners."[31] Contrasts of faith, outlook, national idiosyncrasy or destiny are embodied in figures placed in dramatic opposition : Schadau and Boccard, the grave Calvinist with his belief in Predestination and gay, superstitious Catholic; Jenatsch and Rohan, the unscrupulous Gewaltmensch and the gentle Gewissensmensch; Becket and Henry II, the fastidious intellectual and the gross sensualist; Lucrezia and Angela Borgia, as Meyer said, "zu wenig and zu viel Gewissen." And across the span of the poet's work as a whole something of the same contrasts : Jenatsch pursuing unrepentant a career of crime and apostasy, Stemma succumbing to the perennial pressure of conscience and judging herself as she had judged so many others; Becket avenging himself ironically through his death for the injury done him by his sovereign, Pescara refusing in the presence of death, to avenge a like injury. The increasing prominence of conscientious scruples in such contrasts represents a significant development in Meyer's attitude.

This striving for the concrete, for the visual effect permeates the texture of the works. Thought and feeling are expressed in gesture : Otto von Gemmingen sketches Hutten's fate in a graphic sign (*Die Gebärde*); the Emperor Otto pardons his brother with a gesture (*Der gleitende Purpur*); Jenatsch utters not a word of grief at the murder of his wife, he is *seen* as "dieses Nachtbild sprachlosen Grimms und unversöhnlicher Trauer."[32] Events and relationships are epitomized in objects or gesture : "Drei Hindernisse erschwerten eine Brautfahrt : die hohen und oft finstern Brauen Dianas, die geschlossene Hand ihres Vaters und die blinde Anhänglichkeit ihres Bruders Germanos an den Tyrannen"[33]; ". . . die weggeschleuderte Kutte des Mönchs . . . die vereinigten Hände Dianas und Astorres."[34] Posture can be the clue to the soul : "Ich sehe, wie er sitzt und sinnt," says Michelangelo of Julianus Medici, "und kenne seine Seele"[35] (*Il Pensieroso*).

The affinity of Meyer's descriptions with painting and sculpture is clear : his masters are Titian and Michelangelo. Everywhere he reveals a love of the sumptuous and the statuesque—and nowhere more than in those scenes where the actors are frozen by death or grief : Lucrezia posed with the body of Jenatsch beneath the figure of Justice, Becket prostrate by the body of his daughter :

"Ich schaute in das Halbdunkel der Burgkapelle. Aber da war kein Kruzifix und kein ewiges Licht und statt eines heiligen Leichnams unter dem Altare lag in einem Schrein vor demselben, ebenso reich geschmückt, die tote Gnade. Ein Lichtstrom, der durch das einzige, hochgelegene Fenster sich ergoß, beleuchtete ihre überirdische Schönheit. Ihr Haupt ruhte auf einem Purpurkissen und trug ein Krönchen von blitzendem Edelgestein. Der zarte Körper verschwand in den von Goldstickerei und Perlen starrenden Falten ihres über die Wände des Schreins ausgebreiteten Gewandes. Die kleinen durchsichtigen Hände lagen auf der Brust gekreuzt und hielten keusch den schwarzen Schleier ihres Haares zusammen, der vom Scheitel fliessend die zarten Wangen einrahmte, und die zwei Wunden des Halses bedeckend, sich unter den blassen Marmorkreuz ihrer Arme wieder vereinigte.

Neben dem lieblichen Todesantlitz aber lag ein anderes hingesunken, von demselben Sonnenstrahle gebadet, lebloser und gestorbener als das der Leiche, ein Antlitz, über das die Sterbenot der Verzweiflung gegangen und von dem sie, nach getanem Werk, wieder gewichen. Es war der Kanzler, der mit zerrauftem Haar und aufgerissenem Gewande neben dem Sarge lag, die Arme aud den Rand desselben stützend.

Lautlose Stille herrschte. Nur ein Laubgeflüster regte sich im offenen Fenster und leichte Blätterschatten tanzten über das Purpurkissen und die beiden Angesichter."[36]

This description does not depend for its effect on the musical quality of the language, on richness of metaphor, on overtones or the evocation of associations, but on the creation of an individual, objective, visual impression in the mind of the reader. It is essentially plastic rather than musical : its statuesque quality emerges even in expressions like "starrend" and "Marmorkreuz".

This predilection for the visual can seem artificial and mannered, particularly when it leads Meyer to attempt a reproduction in words of the painter's or sculptor's work, as in the poem, *Das Joch am Leman,* or when it prompts him to see a landscape or a human situation through the prism of art (*Auf Goldgrund; Venedig*). This occasional artificiality is perhaps most noticeable in the lyric where a certain spontaneity and musicality are normal. The rigid, tense, often staccato rhythms and the lapidary expression of Meyer's lyric suggested to poets of a more fluid idiom that he lacked spontaneity of feeling, and hence the authentic lyric voice. Storm wrote to Keller :

"Ein Lyriker ist er nicht; dazu fehlt ihm der unmittelbare, mit sich fortreißende Ausdruck der Empfindung, oder auch wohl die unmittelbare Empfindung selbst."[37]

Meyer himself was of a very different opinion and deplored "a sentimental streak which I recognized in myself and despise but which appears as a matter of course in my lyric." In support of Storm it must be admitted that there is often enough in Meyer's lyric a strange discord between mood and form. A striking instance is the poem, *Stapfen,* where the nostalgic and sentimental theme— the sight of the beloved's footprints in the snow—is oddly at variance with the terse style. In the absence of a direct expression of emotion, however, this disparity vanishes, and Meyer is capable of achieving—often by a process of refining and filing that extended over years—a perfection of form, a coincidence of rhythm, sound and image that has rarely been surpassed in German. The qualities of Meyer's lyric at its best are shown in what is perhaps his most famous poem, *Der römische Brunnen,* a refinement over the years of a diffuse first version twice as long :

"Aufsteigt der Strahl und fallend gießt
Er voll der Marmorschale Rund,
Die, sich verschleiernd, überfließt
In einer zweiten Schale Grund;
Die zweite gibt, sie wird zu reich,
Der dritten wallend ihre Flut,
Und jede nimmt und gibt zugleich
Und strömt und ruht."[38]

From the energetic opening to the dark, restful vowels of the last line, the poem traces the motion of the fountain; its pauses mark the contrast of rest and flow; the combination of dark and light vowels seems to suggest the solidity of the stone and the fluidity of the water; the whole epitomizes in the images of giving and receiving, of rest and motion a cosmic process. It is a poem of perfect "objectivity".

Something of the same objectivity appears in poems describing the Lake of Zürich (e.g. *Schwarzschattende Kastanie* and *Im Spätboot*). Elsewhere, the picture has a symbolic value—the Bacchic reapers saving their sheaves from the threatening storm in *Erntegewitter,* or the gondolas in *Auf dem Canal grande,* whose rapid passage through a band of evening sunlight symbolizes the brief span of human life :

> "Eine kleine, kurze Strecke
> Treibt das Leben leidenschaftlich
> Und erlischt im Schatten drüben
> Als ein unverständlich Murmeln."[39]

But amongst these poems, uniformly controlled and epigrammatic, there are some which hold fast a moment of intense feeling or a mood of profound melancholy. It was not the case, as the poet claimed in the verses which open a section of his collected lyric, that "It was all a game." *Eingelegte Ruder,* although it is again the product of many revisions, describes a despondency none the less genuinely felt. In *Schwüle* there is a suggestion of panic as the poet scans the sky for the first stars, the symbol of hope which will deliver him from the dark fascination of the depths beneath, the depths in which his mother had found her end :

> "Fern der Himmel und die Tiefe nah—
> Sterne, warum seid ihr noch nicht da?"[40]

Against such despair, against the havoc wrought by passion and the torment of moral misgivings, Meyer's talisman was the concept and the practice of art. Art represents a timeless, passionless world. The Medici envies the statues of Michelangelo : "Leidlose Steine, wie beneid ich euch," [41] and the master himself apostrophises his creations :

> "Ihr stellt des Leids Gebärde dar,
> Ihr meine Kinder, ohne Leid !"[42]

Art is the escape from mortality; its element is eternity :

"Den Augenblick verewigt ihr,
Und sterbt ihr, sterbt ihr ohne Tod.
Im Schilfe wartet Charon mein,
Der pfeifend sich die Zeit vertreibt."[43]

At the peak of his career, between 1875 and 1885, Meyer seems to be sustained by this faith in art, moral issues are subordinate to aesthetic considerations. Not only does the author dissociate himself from his creations, the tone of the stories is fatalistic. Even the pious Gustav Adolf succumbs momentarily in Wallenstein's presence to a sense of fatality, while Ezzelino in *Die Hochzeit des Mönchs* is the very personification of fate. The characters, particularly in this Novelle, are driven on by circumstance and overpowering passion. Once Astorre has taken the decisive step of leaving the monastery he is blind to all sense of obligation, to everything but the love which possesses him entirely. The problem of guilt hardly enters into the work. With *Die Richterin,* however, a new phase seems to begin in Meyer's development. A moral problem, the problem of guilt and atonement occupies the foreground. Meyer pointed to the parallel with *Crime and Punishment,* which he described as "a pathological masterpiece" :

"Meine *Richterin* hat ein verwandtes Motiv, doch als mittelalterliche Burgfrau stärkere Nerven als das russische Studentchen."[44]

Instead of being driven simply by instinct, the characters here are torn by an inner struggle; a conflict such as is elsewhere embodied in two opposing figures is compressed into the person of Stemma. There is indeed a pathological element in the story, and certain emotional problems in the mind of the author do not yield as formerly to the discipline of art. The suspected incestuous relationship between Wulfrin and Palma seems to hint at some psychological disturbance in the poet and might be taken as a belated echo of the long and intimate association with his sister Betsy that preceded his marriage. The turmoil of emotion in the characters is matched by the wild and fantastic scenery of the Alps. These landscapes are not objectively described, they represent symbolically the feelings of the characters, they are externalizations of mental states; the idyllic setting of the pool into which Wulfrin and Palma gaze, the savage gorge through which Wulfrin passes, believing that he lusts after his own sister—these are powerful images of psychological conditions. *Die Richterin* stands out among Meyer's

Novellen as being entirely his own invention, and it may well be that it springs more immediately from psychological sources than his other stories. He hints at something of the kind when he writes to Louise von François : "(ich) schloß klüglich die Augen und ließ das Saumroß . . . meiner Einbildungskraft den Fuß setzen, wie es für gut fand."[45]

His next work, *Die Versuchung des Pescara* (1887), shows Meyer back on more familiar ground with a historical theme from the Italian Renaissance. Here, again, there is a moral problem, Pescara's choice of loyalties between the Imperial cause and the cause of Italian unity. It never becomes a real problem, however, for the hero is doomed by a mortal wound. Death in *Pescara* is for once not a sudden and brilliant climax, but something which paralyses action and makes choice vain, an insidious enemy who can only be met with resignation. In spite of all its glowing scenes the story is pervaded by melancholy and an abhorrence of death that springs more from fear than fascination. Meyer felt an alien element creeping into his work, "a mystical or phantom element à la Kleist," and in the midst of creating he was visited with intimations of mortality :

> "Wenn ich sehe, welche Arbeitskraft mir noch zu Diensten steht, wenigstens an schönen trockenen Tagen und bei offenen Fenstern, könnte ich versucht sein, große Pläne zu entwerfen, doch ich fühle zugleich die Ungewißheit menschlichen Glücks. Zwei Jüngere als ich, nahe Bekannte, sind mir in den letzten Wochen weggestorben."[46]

The sombre note grows deeper in the last of the Novellen, *Angela Borgia,* a story heavy with foreboding and full of nightmare and hypnotic states. Its gloom is not entirely relieved, as Meyer claimed, by an ending which is "conciliatory, almost idyllic". The blinding of Don Giulio epitomizes the turning of the poet's gaze inwards, a narrowing of his world, an incipient withdrawal to the cloister of the mind. Humility and renunciation are the virtues of which Angela Borgia bears the symbolic cross on her brow, imprinted there by the bars of Don Giulio's prison, spiritual poverty is the lesson preached by Father Manette to the sightless Don Giulio in a favourite image of the poet's :

> "Werdet arm und ärmer, damit Ihr empfangen und geben könnt, wie ein Brunnen, der Schale um Schale überfließend füllt."[47]

The gaiety, the energy and brutality of the Renaissance is overlaid with the spirituality of Tolstoy; irony gives way to faith.

It may be the more intensely personal nature of this work which leads to a relaxation of the strict form which Meyer customarily imposed on himself : the two figures of Angela and Lukrezia, although they form a pattern, tend to divide the work into phases, and hence to disrupt its unity, the narrative is episodic, even the language is less plastic, more haunting and lyrical. There is a slackening of control; in fact, the author found it difficult to achieve the necessary concentration, and managed to complete the work only by an effort of the will : *"Angela Borgia* is finished, if not a work of art, at least a powerful act of the will."

It was his last creative achievement. Ill-health heralded a return to the neurotic condition of his youth, he slipped back into the twilight world. In the summer of 1892 he once more entered a mental hospital—this time in Königsfelden—his condition diagnosed as "senile melancholia". A little over a year later he was able to return to Kilchberg, but he never fully recovered and his poetic voice was silenced for ever. In November 1898 there came to an end a career which he himself described as "incredibly remarkable". Remarkable it was as an example of a double life, not only in its successive phases, but also in the contrast between the man and his art, between the tranquil, withdrawn, uneventful life of the Swiss villa and the restless, brilliant, savage life of the stories and ballads. C. F. Meyer's art is essentially a mask and a substitute for real experience. What saves it from appearing mere fantasy is its visual quality, its full-bloodedness, its linguistic discipline and its psychological truth. Although he works with settings remote in time and space and describes events and emotions of which he can have had only an imaginative experience, nevertheless Meyer can claim to be a realist : "I go to bed every evening more realistic than I rose," he wrote to Spitteler. His aim is not "to make the poetic real," but "to make the real poetic". Where Keller realizes poetic themes of universal validity in familiar Swiss settings, Meyer seeks to evoke, by imaginative interpretation, the inner, poetic truth of recorded history. These are very different approaches, but both writers might be described as "poetic realists". There is little point in assessing the merits of one against the other; as far as popularity with his fellow-countrymen goes, the see-saw will probably always come down in favour of Keller. There is never likely to be a *Jürg Jenatsch* restaurant in Zürich to rival *Der grüne Heinrich*. It may be, however, that Meyer's appeal is more universal. Nor is he without successors : his irony, his morbidity and his use of symbols are carried into the twentieth century by Thomas Mann, another offspring of a patrician race who found salvation in his art.

TRANSLATIONS

1. All his carry-on and hoity-toity ways.
2. I lay in bondage to a heavy spell,
   I did not live. I lay as in a trance.
3. Ivy, my old house-mate
   You gleam with young leaves.
   Your wintry green, so grave, austere,
   Does it well consort with the riot of spring?
   "Why not? Like mine,
   Your life has leaves both old and new,
   One grim and dark, one bright
   With spring and air. Why not?"
4. A petty Saxon monk did doff his habit.
   There, Sir Knight, you have a splendid theme.
5. The secularization of the higher clergy . . . the authentic type of the humanist: wit, frivolity, emulation and exaggerated respect for antiquity, insincerity, vindictiveness . . . theft and mendicancy.
6. What I need is sun and cloud, sickle and scythe, husband and child . . .
7. You silent man, working slow subversion, you are long-suffering like your master and you encompass your own death as he did. You believe that you are serving charity, but hatred is the stronger and your death, like the death of your God, is the damnation of men.
8. This man—an intellectually superior nature, humane almost in the modern way, but defenceless in the face of medieval barbarity—this man uses the Church as a weapon without being himself a believer—legend and the poet both endow him with Oriental blood.
9. As far as the majority of the people are concerned, Keller has the advantage over me that he is at heart an optimist. That is why he is a man for the masses. People are like that: they crowd round the spring of life and are pleased if they catch at least a drop in their little cups. In Keller they find what they are looking for, because he always contrives a happy ending. Tragic dénouements are a thing unknown to him. That is a fault unknown to him. That is a fault, for to have its full charm existence must include both.
10. As far as I personally am concerned, the comic leaves a bitter taste in my mouth, whereas the tragic elevates and inspires me.
11. Meyer has a weakness for particular brutalities and slaughters of

this kind. Whenever he hears or reads about this sort of thing he says: Excellent! Everyone has his eccentricities.

12. Come, death, and bear me off, death, in the fervour of a kiss.

13. From one sheaf to another.
There is space for death.

14. I have gained the palm and merited death.

15. I want all the rays of my life to be joined in one blaze of fire and in the space of a single hour, so that instead of a senseless gloom there might be generated a brief but blinding light of rapture which would vanish like a fleeting flash of lightning.

16. A warm southerly breeze had idealized the snow-capped mountains and the Swiss lake in its own manner, blending the chain of the former into one vast, serene luminosity, submerging the latter with the deep and vividly glowing colours of a Southern bay, as though eager to transport a Bacchic landscape, a portion of Italy, across the Alps.

17. You were trying to divest yourself of your own nature and he sent you about your business by making fun of you . . . And why? I like you best of all as you are, and just as you are.

18. . . . the excellence of Keller's *Züricher Novellen* will certainly put me in the shade and even make me look, quite unjustly, like an imitator.

19. In *Jenatsch* and in *The Saint* there is far more of me in various disguises, my true sufferings and passions, than in these lyric poems.

20. I wrote *The Saint* almost without knowing it, obsessed and intoxicated, because I had to get rid of it, it lay on my chest like a tormenting nightmare.

21. But one thing, however, the Chancellor lacked: the energy and asperity of a manly temperament.

22. Impassivity was a fundamental feature of his character. I never saw him angry and could not even easily imagine him so.

23. I treat history in a sovereign manner, but not inaccurately.

24. The propensity for the framework is quite instinctive in me. I like to keep my subject at a distance, or rather as far as possible from my eye, and, again, it seems to me that the indirect nature of the tale (and even the interruptions) mitigates the harshness of the plot.

25. It seemed to me that Dante must invent and not narrate.

26. The plot lay in scattered profusion before him; but his astringent mind chose and simplified.

27. Here, admittedly, there is too much intertwining of plot and listener: the whole thing becomes decidedly tiresome. A non plus ultra! I am cured of it!

28. In short, what I have gained from the Romance world is a sense of gesture. For me it has become essential and imperative to shape everything so that it is outwardly observable, visible, even in language.

29. Yes, you know . . . when you come to think of it, any flapper who has read Heine, Geibel, Rittershaus . . . can put together a few lines full of atmosphere; but to conjure up in ballad-like form what I might call

plastic and substantial figures, and to make them appear in action, that is an art that is given to an infinitely small number of people.

30. I feel a lack in German literature; it is not keenly enough observed, not made obvious to the senses, it is abstract and blurred. The similes and metaphors in German are feeble, they do not shed light and illuminate. Ariosto's, on the other hand, even although they are exaggeratedly grotesque, are nevertheless sharply observed and illuminating.

31. So Victoria spoke in surging and overflowing words like a fountain of Rome.

The motion of his nature was as honest as a blast on a hunting-horn and overflowed like the foam on the bit of a young charger.

32. This nocturnal phantom of speechless wrath and inconsolable grief.

33. Three obstacles hindered a match: the high and often sombre brow of Diana, the close fist of her father and the blind attachment of her brother Germano to the tyrant.

34. . . . the cast-off habit of the monk, the linked hands of Diana and Astorre.

35. I see how he sits and ponders and I know his soul.

36. I looked into the semi-darkness of the castle chapel. But there was no crucifix there and no eternal lamp, instead of a holy corpse beneath the altar, in front of it and just as richly decked there lay in a coffin the body of Grace. A flood of light that poured through the one window high in the wall, lit up her ethereal beauty. Her head rested on a purple pillow and wore a coronet of glittering gems. Her slight body was hidden in the folds of her dress, which, stiff with pearls and gold embroidery, spread over the sides of the coffin. Her small, transparent hands lay crossed on her breast and modestly held together the black veil on her hair which, flowing down from both sides, made a frame for her delicate cheeks, and covering the two wounds in her neck, was joined again beneath the marble cross of her arms.

By the side of the lovely dead face, however, reclined another bathed in the same shaft of sunlight, more lifeless and more dead than that of the corpse, a countenance across which the mortal pang of despair had passed, leaving it again after its work was done. It was the Chancellor who lay with disordered hair and doublet torn open by the side of the coffin, resting his arms on its edge.

Complete silence reigned. Only a whisper of foliage stirred by the open window and the light shadow of leaves danced across the purple pillow and the two faces.

37. A lyric poet he is not; he lacks the immediate and compulsive expression of emotion, or probably even the emotion itself.

38. Up springs the spray and falling fills
    The marble basin's curving rim
    That, veiled in water, ceaseless spills
    To reach a second basin's brim;
    The second sheds its lapping swell

To flood the third one as it goes,
And each one takes and gives as well
  And rests and flows.

39. One brief little space
Life drifts on in passion,
And dies away in the shadows yonder
As an indistinct murmur.

40. Far the heavens and the depths are near—
Stars, why are you not yet here?

41. Passionless, how I envy you.

42. You shape the gesture of grief,
You my children, who know not grief.

43. The moment is by you eternalized
And when you die you know not death.
While in the sedge old Charon waits for me
And whistling whiles the time away.

44. My *Richterin* has a related motif, but as a medieval Chatelaine she has stronger nerves than the little Russian student.

45. I closed my eyes prudently and let the pack-horse of my imagination pick its way as seemed best to it.

46. When I see what energy is still at my disposal, at least on fine dry days and with open windows. I might be tempted to make great plans, but I feel at the same time the uncertainty of human happiness. Two younger men than I, close acquaintances have been taken from me by death in the last few weeks.

47. Become even poorer, that you may receive and give, like a fountain, which fills one basin after another as it overflows.

BIBLIOGRAPHY

Works

Sämtliche Werke, hrsg. von R. Faesi. Th. Knaur Nachf., Berlin, 1926. 4 vols., with an essay condensed from Faesi: *C. F. Meyer,* Frauenfeld, 2nd ed., 1948.

Sämtliche Werke, Droemersche Verlagsanstalt, Th. Knaur Nachf., München, Zürich, 1959.

One volume, with an account of Meyer's life and works by Hans Schmeer.

Sämtliche Werke, Dieterich Verlag, Leipzig, 1956.

Two volumes, with a long introduction and (rather elementary) notes by Chr. Coler.

Sämtliche Werke. Historisch-kritische Ausgabe. Besorgt von Hans Zeller und Alfred Zäch, Benteli-Verlag, Berne, 1959 ff.

Letters

Briefe C. F. Meyers. Nebst seinen Rezensionen und Aufsätzen. Hrsg. von A. Frey. Leipzig, 1908. 2 vols.

C. F. Meyers Briefwechsel mit Luise von François, hrsg. von A. Bettelheim. Berlin, 1905 (2nd ed., 1920).

C. F. Meyer, La crise de 1852–6. Lettres de C. F. Meyer et de son entourage, ed. by R. d'Harcourt. Paris, 1913.

Biography and Commentaries

F. J. Beharriel, "Conrad Ferdinand Meyer and the origins of psychoanalysis" (*Monatshefte für den deutschen Unterricht,* xlvii, 3, 1955).

H. Henel, *The Poetry of Conrad Ferdinand Meyer.* Univ. of Wisconsin Press, 1954.

L. Hohenstein, *Conrad Ferdinand Meyer.* Bonn, 1957.

B. Meyer, *C. F. Meyer in der Erinnerung seiner Schwester.* Berlin, 1903.

W. Oberle, "C. F. Meyer: ein Forschungsbericht." (*Germanisch-Romanische Monatsschrift,* xxxvii, 3, 1956).

L. Wiesmann, *Conrad Ferdinand Meyer, der Dichter des Todes und der Maske.* Berne, 1958.

W. D. Williams, *The Stories of C. F. Meyer.* Oxford, 1962.

Carl Spitteler

Carl Spitteler

by WERNER GÜNTHER

Carl Spitteler was born in Liestal, near Basle, on April 24, 1845. His father, who had played an active role in the *Sonderbundskrieg,* was a high official in both cantonal and federal circles. The boy began his education in schools at Liestal and Berne, before moving to the "literary-humanist" *Obergymnasium* in Basle, where he studied under both W. Wackernagel and Jacob Burckhardt. He later read law and theology at the Universities of Basle, Zurich and Heidelberg, and after overcoming considerable difficulties, was ordained without, however, taking up office as a priest. From 1871 to 1879 he worked as a private tutor in Russia. Then, on his return to Switzerland, he took up a position in a girls' school in Berne, as a teacher of history. He completed *Prometheus and Epimetheus* in 1880, but when this achieved no recognition, he was compelled to go on teaching, this time at the *Progymnasium* in Neuveville, where he remained for four years. Here he married a Dutch girl, Maria Op den Hooff.

He spent several years after this in journalism, with the *Grenzpost* in Basle, as well as with the *Thurgauer Zeitung and the Basler Nachrichten,* and from 1890–92 acted as editor of the *Neue Zürcher Zeitung.* This period also saw the birth of *Literarische Gleichnisse.*

The death of his wife's parents brought financial independence, and Spitteler moved with her and their two daughters to Lucerne, in order to devote himself completely to literature. It was by the Lake of Lucerne that *Olympischer Frühling* and *Prometheus der Dulder* were created. In December 1914, the author delivered in Zurich a lecture entitled "Our Swiss Standpoint", which brought him a great deal of criticism and hostility from Germany. In 1919, mainly through the special intercession of Romain Rolland, Spitteler was awarded the Nobel Prize. He died in Lucerne on December 29, 1924, a few months before his eightieth birthday.

ONE can distinguish four stages in the development of Carl Spitteler's reputation as an artist. The first runs from *Prometheus and Epimetheus* to *Olympischer Frühlung*, i.e. approximately between 1880 and 1905. During this period he received little or no response from critics. The second (roughly 1905–20) is one of growing fame. It began with the clarion call of the musician and conductor Felix Weingartner, in *Carl Spitteler, Ein künstlerisches Erlebnis* (1904), and was crowned with the award of the Nobel Prize, in 1919, together with a number of introductory and analytical studies of his work. The third period embraces two decades, beginning shortly before the death of the poet, and is characterized chiefly by some extremely sharp criticism. The final period, which brings us up to the present day, is one of a certain degree of alienation from Spitteler—a respectful but, one feels, almost ceremonial silence surrounds his name, tending here and there towards embarrassment, and even the celebration of his centenary (1945) failed to mitigate the situation. Is this the temporary obscurity into which the names of so many great authors fall immediately after their deaths, and from which they eventually arise in a stronger light? It is difficult to be a prophet here, but it does seem doubtful that critics will ever come to full agreement about the greatness of Spitteler.

For what is questioned is not, as it once was with Gotthelf, the outer form, but rather the innermost nature of the work, the genuineness of his creative personality. The critical attacks which hit deepest are those directed not only against this or that idiosyncrasy which may give offence, but against the very essence of his art. Has Spitteler's poetry a foundation of artistic maturity and integrity? That is the question; and the difference between the critics who affirm this and others who concur only with strongest reservations seem to indicate that any overall agreement is far away. Spitteler himself knew that he would never be widely read. His main creations are mythical or mythically adorned epics, and the epic is no longer fashionable—at least not in the garish compounds of myth and realism, phantasy and pessimism which Spitteler evolved. Thus the problem remains one for a small number of initiates and for those with a critical interest.

Fundamentally, the question of the origin of his poetry revolves around the essentially lyrical nature of his creativeness: lyrical, that is, in the modern aesthetic sense, applied to the unconscious, emotional sources of art. Writers of epics and dramatists must also be lyrical in this sense if they wish to be truly poetic, as Spitteler himself recognized :

"In every poet there hides, by definition, a lyricist, as there is in the dramatist and in the author of epics."[1]

Even his most unwavering supporters and apostles admit that Spitteler was not a born lyricist. He called himself a "geborener Epiker", an epic writer of cosmic, mythological and symbolic poetry. By "forfeiting lyricism", he claimed, possibly hoping thereby to blunt any future criticism, one can achieve "epic greatness". He described his own ballads, thus censuring them too strongly, as "Formgymnastik", or "early drafts for a projected future epic"; even his *Schmetterlinge* he defined as "optimistic lyricism" rather than *Gefühlslyrik*; and elsewhere he insists, "My verse does not set out to be musical" for the reason that his soul itself is steeped in music—"My soul was and is my lyricism".[2] He even speaks of a "contempt for language" :

"Language has no naturalness, it is an artificial and quite lothsome means of conveying poetic images."[3]

These and other of his pronouncements are not always, of course, to be taken literally. Yet one thing remains certain : we will find not lyrical outpourings in Spitteler's work. The question is, does he possess instead lyricism in its broader sense : that lyricism of the epic, sublime, brimming over with the fullness of man? He attributes to himself two qualities : first, the fundamentally epic predisposition—joy in the outward splendour of life, taste for adventure, a strong belief in the richness and variety of events, the vast possibilities of the world; and secondly, in contrast, the need for something more ethereal, the reluctance to be limited to and to draw his poetry from normal routine existence. Unlike Mörike, whom, significantly, he here quotes, he longs to build "a higher, broader arch, up and away from the real".[4] His wish it not to indulge in "analysis of the soul", in the manner of the novelist ("The novelist is no epic poet, he is the opposite"), but to escape "nach oben", "far above the surface of the earth into unrestricted heights", where one can treat Gods with "Übermut"—bravado— and even with a touch of irony.[5] It is on the basis of these two elements that critics have propounded Spitteler's greatness : he has been called a realistic poet and a visionary. But the big question remains—whether these two factors alone can produce a great poet, without that "little invisible and indefinable something" which "gives a work of art eternal salvation".[6] This "something" is precisely that hidden nucleus of lyricism of which we spoke, which nourishes all art and without which true art cannot subsist.

Could the absence of this in Spitteler perhaps be connected with the undeniable role of the will in his work, to which he himself admits, and even deliberately stresses? In a sort of "fever of the will" he took, as a young man, the "Entschluss zur Poesie", the conscious decision to be a poet, after renouncing what appear to have been his natural talents, music and painting. True, he speaks of "visitations" in the form of poetic images, which does assume an unconscious, intuitive process of creation, and it would be an error to discount this. Yet at the same time, one senses clearly the part played by the will, which frequently gives to his poetry an air of unnaturalness and strain, extending even to a sort of violence against both subject-matter and language. The fact is, poetry only rarely allows itself to be dictated to : that being when the intuitive faculty is firmly at the artist's command. For intellectuality, artistry and personal elements tend to appear at times when intuition falters. In Spitteler's case, this is undoubtedly the case of the overemphasis on autobiography in certain passages, and of their excessively hard realism, just as it is the source of the allegories, the exaggerated personification and the violence of the language.

Spitteler's *Weltanschaung* presents us with huge difficulties. It was against Spitteler the philosopher and not the artist that Edith Landmann, a protagonist of Stefan George, directed her attack, still during the poet's lifetime. "It is absurd for a poet to give himself over to Ananke"[7] was the centre of her criticism. And in truth, despite his joy in the richness of life, despite his epic "Übermut", Spitteler's work conceals an abyss of pessimism. In his view, the tragedian may look up from his individual calamity into a moral world-order, but the epic poet looks down, through the sunshine of the outer world, into hollow darkness.[8] Such pessimism, of course, was rife at the time. Like Nietzsche, like Jacob Burckhardt, Spitteler had been weaned on the thoughts of Schopenhauer, and had reached the position of the convinced non-Christian, denying the world and scorning mankind. For all Christian beliefs about the next world, as well as for all "philosophical sleight-of-hand", he had nothing but angry contempt. His symbol for the cruel meaninglessness of the world is the unfeeling automaton, behind whom and in whom, in *Olympischer Frühling*, Ananke, "der gezwungene Zwang",[9] lies concealed.

As an antidote to this basic meaninglessness, Spitteler emphasises the sublime resignation of great men (Prometheus, Hercules), while showing pity for suffering and, above all, maintaining his faith in beauty, art and imagination. This belief in beauty amidst the decay of moral order puts him somewhat in line with the "Absolute" poets of his time, who, lacking a faith, and yet thirsting for one, clung to their own creative forces, and, like the young Nietzsche, found justification for the world only as an aesthetic phenomenon. Yet none of them had gone as far as Spitteler, who removed the soul from the Universe, reducing it to a gigantic laboratory of physics and chemistry, the "Weltenmühle".[10]

Of course, a pessimistic *Weltanschaung* does not necessarily have to be anti-aesthetic. It becomes so only when it puts a curse, as it were, upon the creative impulse, and distorts the artist's perception of true human values. This is what happened to Spitteler. Admittedly, Edith Landmann did not see it in this way, for she praised him as an artist while referring to his work as "a monument to the hopelessness of mankind". However, strictly speaking, the hopelessness of man is also the hopelessness of the artist, and Spitteler was severely handicapped by his view of the world : not only did it prevent him from considering and portraying sympathetically such important character-types as the mother-figure or the saint, but, moreover, it not infrequently distorted his concept of the complete human being, thereby depriving his work of any true "heroes". We may cite Gottfried Keller's judgment of Spitteler :

> "If only the poor man would use his talent and his strong imagination to create some really human poetry, he would be one of the best."

Again, in a letter to C. F. Meyer, Keller sums up his opinion in the brief but telling phrase : "he is embarrassed by the simple and the human".

Spitteler did not regard man and his soul with much seriousness, but, in fact, only what Goethe called "heiliger Ernst" can raise life on to the eternal plane. Certainly, Spitteler had a powerful imagination at his command, but it was from this, his most valuable asset, that he removed the driving force—the belief in the dignity of man. If he possessed basic insights of great worth, but failed to fill this framework with living poetry, it was due to deficiencies in his intuitive faculty, and hence in the source from which this is fed—that is, the quality of humanity. In Spitteler, both these qualities lacked a firm root, and were therefore too weak to combine effectively in order to resist non-artistic forces. Both as man and as poet he was a creature of contradiction. His greatness lies in the amount he managed to squeeze out of this rather barren nature.

The most perfectly tuned strings of his lyre were, obviously those where the least room was given to any anti-artistic strains. Generally speaking, we can distinguish three factors which helped in this. First, his work is capable of achieving an enchanting purity whenever the cosmic vibrations in his soul produce images which stem from a genuinely serious conception of human life, and whenever human forces are facing one another with defiance or serenity, notwithstanding the tragic surroundings in which they may exist.

In a second way, purity is often attained through Spitteler's child-like nature. "Il y a un mot qui vous expliquera tout en moi, ni grand homme ni homme célèbre, ni poète, ni citoyen, ni rien—seulement . . . un enfant." Indeed, perhaps no word can get nearer to the true Spitteler, and if this is remembered, much of his work becomes clearer. Even in his poetry, he often plays like a child, and yet the cosmic visionary and the child form complementary opposites, acting and reacting together, witnesses to the breadth of his nature.

The third realm in which Spitteler is at home is that of the sophisticate, the man-of-the-world. Although he strikes a discordant note in his rather limited, puppet-like portrayal of the lower classes (e.g. in *Conrad der Leutnant*), on the other hand he finds precisely the right tone when describing the atmosphere of a court, as for instance the ultra-refinement of Versailles in *Der Neffe des Herren Bezenval*. It was no accidental that he found such brilliant words to write of the French classical era. The aristocratic manners which he acquired in Russia suited his temperament perfectly, endowed as he was with wit, elegance and natural self-assurance.

It is an idle question to ask whether Spitteler wrote better poetry in his introvert or his extrovert vein. The true poet, as he creates, must also be introspective, for at that time he is inhabiting an imagined world, belonging only to himself; according to the degree in which he can adapt this world to normal reality, he may become more outward-looking. Even as a "realist", Spitteler remained an introvert.

A far more important question than this for the critic is that of the choice of theme. Spitteler gained much by restricting the number of subjects he treated to a minimum, and one cannot reproach him at all for this. Richness of artistic imagination, so Jacob Burckhardt had taught him, shows itself not in the number of themes one can invent, but in the mastery of one important motif, treated in various different ways. His Promethean epics, *Imago, Gustav, Der Neffe des Herrn Bezenval, Conrad der Leutnant,* all pertain to the theme of greatness, or the recognition of greatness. It is also touched upon in *Mädchenfeinde,* as well as in several scenes of *Olympischer Frühling.* Greatness, in his view and not only artistic greatness entails the renunciation of happiness, especially of happiness through love, and is bought at a terrible price. This theme, which had occupied the Romantics, had been clearly formulated by Schopenhauer, and subsequently appeared in many forms. It is certainly the stuff of tragedy, and has enormous artistic potential, but it is still nevertheless doubtful whether Spitteler did the right thing in devoting so much of himself to it. For quite clearly, in his case, the theme stems far less from the joy and suffering of a warm human heart than from the defiance and self-assurance of his own ego. With so much preoccupation with the self, the danger was that he could easily slip into a consciously intellectual or over-personal art-form. This is the case with, for instance, the novel *Imago,* where Spitteler definitely succumbs to the temptations of writing biography. His treatment of human experience is most effective and memorable in those works where he clothes it in mythology (e.g. *Prometheus*) or else sets it in an idyllic, if rather bitter atmosphere (as in *Gustav* or *Mädchenfeinde*).

Spitteler's genuine pathos reveals itself most clearly in *Prometheus und Epimethus* (1880). It is easy to list the faults of this early poem : its imbalance, the decline of artistic standards in the second half, the lack of inner motivation in certain episodes, imprecision in the drawing of Prometheus' character, the rational element : above all, the allegories, the excessive length of the work and the monotonous iambic metre, maintained with iron discipline, to the point where it obstructs the search for fresh imagery. It is much more difficult to say why, despite all its faults, the book remains a work of art (if not an "eternal" work as Romain Rolland claims).

"Und sprach ein Lied mit dunkler, weichumhüllter Stimme",[11] says the poet and minstrel in the castle of King Epimetheus. Like the audience there, we are gripped by Spitteler's "Lied" and we, too, see "auf dem dunklen Grunde heller leuchten all die lebensvollen Bilder".[12] If we are to understand logically why we are so moved, we must first of all appreciate the powerful harmony between the mythical atmosphere and the poetic expression : in other words, the artistic unity of the work. This is particularly true of the first half, where there issues, from a huge reservoir, a flood of vision which cannot be denied expression. There are lapses and errors, because the intuitive source lacks balance and consistency, but usually the right tone is found, in tune at the deepest level with both theme and mood.

A second reason for our involvement is the profound belief in the soul which pervades the work. It is not simply the fact that he altered the character of Prometheus which is important—that is the prerogative of any poet—but that he gave him such primitive majesty, such austerity and solid faith in himself. It is the contrast between the basically sombre, almost dull, mood of the poem, and the shining strength of this conviction which gives the book its strange attraction. When we remember this, the criticism that the personality of Prometheus is too vague becomes less important. He lives by his faith in his own soul, upright and blameless, hard with himself, but mild with his brother; the tension of his love for the Goddess of his soul pulsates through the work, bringing it alive even during the long scene in the wilderness, where Prometheus undergoes tough physical labour and guards his master's flocks.

These two factors, the basic atmosphere and the faithfulness to an idea, form the cross-threads of the poetic fabric; and at certain points, the whole lights up, as if it were prose suddenly becoming poetry—for example, in the famous scene where Prometheus meets his Goddess at the top of the mountain, and offers himself to her. Another scene which is rightly well known is the description of Pandora's descent to earth : she imagines herself as a mortal woman, "enduring in her dreams human desire and human suffering", sees herself in the role of a wife at the side of a loving man, happily undergoing need, worry, fatigue and illness, and comes to regard the misery and death of mankind as less bitter than her "desolate existence, removed from the world and all its pains".

Or again, consider King Epimetheus' conversation with his friend before the marble statue representing a man leaning on his club and staring enraptured at the little box he is holding aloft in his right hand. The irony is that King Epimetheus himself will not recognize Pandora's box when the peasants bring it to him a little later. Or, finally, there is the moving scene when, after Epimetheus and the Behemoth, to cheers from the crowd, have exchanged their coats as a sign of friendship, the poet suddenly lifts the veil from the enormous graveyard, ruled by "Proserpina with the soulful eyes". Here, merciful sisters comfort the souls of the dead, still trembling from "the dreadful illness of being", and now descending to the realm of Proserpina while, in Adam's dark cave, the father of all men and his son Atlas sit, spurning sleep and peace, formulating plans to improve the lot of mankind. They will not listen to the Goddess, who tells them to rest, for there is no cure for the world, the taste of the earth's crust is bitter . . . Then from the land of men they hear a great shout of jubilation. What, has a saviour been born? Has God taken pity upon his world? The father sends his son to discover the truth, but when Atlas reappears, he spits contemptuously upon the floor. What was the cause of the jubilation? "One man has swopped his smock with another!" Thereupon Adam tears his plans and his books page from page, saying to his son : " 'True enough, why should we sow? All we shall reap here is shame, if we spend ourselves any more upon these creatures.' Thus he spake and they departed in peace to their eternal home."

To sum up Spitteler's first work, one is tempted to employ the words spoken by Pandora when she meets a shepherd boy, who is painting on a canvas the fields, mountains and woods, the clouds and the birds :

> "And all drawn with few strokes, somewhat childish and groping, with no certainty; here and there an object changed its form, bushes and hedges becoming lambs; but always there reigned an inward strength, and soul led the gentle lines from the dark foreground with its rough shadows towards the distant, fragrant, hazy land. . . ."

Written in his old age (in 1924), *Prometheus der Dulder,* by his own admission a "second book on the same theme", has only the dark and bitter shadows of the foreground, but lacks the "distant, fragrant, hazy land" behind. The earlier work is more appropriate to its theme, and therefore more solid. One may perhaps describe the change as the move from "poet" to "artist", but in doing so, the usual connotations of value judgment must be removed from these terms. For in this case, in calling him an "artist" we mean that the original creative or "poetic" impulse (which is more or less unconscious, and automatically finds the right verbal expression for its message) has yielded to a *conscious* application of artistic methods : in other words, as the intuitive power decreases, the so-called outer form assumes more importance. In a perfect work of art, the distinction is removed and "artist" and "poet" become one, although one can still—e.g. with Gotthelf—sometimes accuse the poet of "artistic" errors. Naturally, there are almost as many transgressions as there are works of art, for the perfectly blended work is an extreme rarity. In Spitteler's *Dulder,* the effect of the more intellectual approach is felt in three fields : the versification, the "realistic" style, and the overall structure.

In the first *Prometheus,* the hero, escaping from the noisy feast, seems almost lost in the "secret" which drifts up out of the valleys; hour after hour he strides up and down, till the snow buries the land under a soft white carpet and the forest looms black and white under the stars. He is trembling with expectation, listening, peering, staring at the entrance to the forest. When the austere woman suddenly appears, the scene continues in silence. Yet underneath, life is bubbling through its veins.

In the second *Prometheus,* the defiance and restlessness of the hero—who takes a much more active, central role—are depicted in a more plausible fashion. However, it often happens that, to achieve this, too many words are required, and what he says does not make the scene any more impressive; the Goddess, too, loses much of the bewitching power of her beauty, by talking too hastily and too long, and the lines which describe her entry are too round-about and vague, hindered by the demands of rhyme. The magic has gone.

However, in *Dulder,* too, there are many moments of individual beauty. The quest for a wider symbolism certainly bears much fruit, especially in the various secondary motifs which have been well chosen and delightfully executed; we can point, for instance, to the seductive fan which the Angel of God played with, as if casually, as he asks Prometheus a second time to renounce his soul; or the "bird of doom", who glides like a ghost from the forest as the Goddess Soul hurls her curse upon the Angel, on his kingdom, Epimetheus and the whole cowardly race of man; or, finally, there is the Goddess's vision of the future : "I hear the river of life, gushing through the caverns . . .", etc., to which Prometheus, slurring his words like a drunkard, gives not only the reply to which the Goddess counsels him : "Ich !", but the committed "Ich Alle !"

What we have said so far offers enough pointers as to how *Olympischer Frühling* should be judged. Here Spitteler, following all kinds of "experimental works" and practice "on the silent piano", attempted to bridge the gulf between mythology and symbolism on the one hand and realistic poetry on the other. He was trying to fill a cosmic vision with human colour and life. The undertaking required great caution, to say the least, and the result was bound to contain weaknesses. The reasons for this are easily enumerated : first, because Spitteler was tempted to confuse the epic element with mere adventure stories; secondly, because the deeper human insights were too readily lost sight of, obscured by the bitterness of the poet's general outlook; and thirdly, because, in any case, the work could never really hold together, the "realistic" element being conceived far too much in terms of the external, thus robbing the world of the Gods of a large part of its mythical flavour. Even apart from all this, there is still another problem inherent in the basic idea : how could he produce a satisfactory ending, after all the high-spirited wedding celebrations of the new set of Gods? We know how uncomfortable the poet felt about this problem. In the final version of 1910, he split the ending into two sections, "Ende und Wende", originally the last quarter of the first version, becoming "Der hohen Zeit Ende" and "Zeus"; but the division is purely superficial.

Yet how should he finish off the work? With the fall of the Gods at the end of the modern era? That would require a much longer epic—and where would he find the material for it? Spitteler had long before cut himself off from the greatest source of fresh (and real!) experience : the world of man is forbidden to the Gods. Although there was nowhere else to find the material he required for effective poetic conflicts, it would have gone against his basic premises to come too close to the human sphere. "Des Lebens Zweck ist Schmutz" patters the rain, in his Dionysus-song, "im Stein ist Wahrheit";[13] and on the Morgenberg it brings to the Gods the terrible message : "Kein Raum von Ewigkeit, den nicht der Jammer füllte".[14] Zeus himself learns to his cost what it is to become involved with the "human breed", and henceforth his wish is to suffocate the entire human "horde" in a gigantic cloak and to set a hound upon the lord of the earth! We are left wondering, then, what good Hercules, the "complete human being", can do as he strides towards earth.

Spitteler, sensibly enough, restricted himself to showing us only the Olympic "spring". What might happen in the "summer" and the "autumn" we cannot tell—nor, perhaps could the author. After the exciting high nuptials, is what follows simply a sort of Olympic banality, no longer worth recording? The theme, which has begun splendidly enough, tails off into nothing. The "basic impulse" of *Olympischer Frühling*, the "need for unlimited elbow-room for the creative imagination" carried in it the seeds of its own destruction. When, towards the middle of the work, the "hohe Zeit", the huge "spring feast of the earth", begins, the ground suddenly falls away

from under the poet's feet. What for Spitteler was the central core
—the string of colourful adventures—appears to the sensitive
reader as no more than richly imaginative ornamentation, while
the part which for us has the most artistic weight—i.e. the opening
poems *Auffahrt* and *Hera die Braut*—was almost, so the poet tells
us, absent-mindedly omitted, at a time when he was without the
advice of his friend Jonas Fränkel.

What raises *Die Auffahrt* to such poetic heights can be summed
up in three main principles. For one thing, the theme of the ascent
of the Gods, from Erebos, up the "Morgenberg", to Mount
Olympus, with their detour through Heaven, springs from a blissful
vision : there is a flavour of pure art about this journey. Then
again, the scenery here is still clearly described and easily imagined :
mostly an Alpine landscape seen through fresh eyes. And finally,
most important : while the Gods are generally unnamed, we can
conceive of them as one unit, and their opponents likewise. Because
of this, Spitteler's poetic vision is able to emerge at full strength,
not yet diverted or disturbed by other conflicting forces. Is it not
remarkable that out of almost a thousand crudities of language in
Olympischer Frühling, an exceedingly small number fall in the
first half? For here the poet, much more than the artist, was at
work.

Structurally the most powerful scene in the whole book, and one
to which the three principles mentioned also apply, is, unquestionably, the confrontation between the old and the new Gods.
The latter have already seen Hades, which they passed by on their
climb. And with horror they recognize the "scheussliche Lawinen-
bett"[15] which is made even more ghostly by the white bones, the
overhanging medlar-trees, and the deep silence broken only by the
trickling of water. As they rest by the fountain, they find, carved
in wood, the names of the earlier Gods who had also passed by
long ago. They too, engrave their names. . . . Climbing further,
during which time an argument over who is to be their king reveals
jealousies and hate, they come upon flagstones which have been
worn smooth by the steps of Gods, walking this way since time
immemorial. "Wie ist die Welt vom Alten", sighs a voice, "Für
welchen Jammer hat sie Raum bereits enthalten".[16] Like an echo,
booming from the chasm, come the words "Kein Raum von
Ewigkeit, den nicht der Jammer füllte",[17] and suddenly the old
Gods come rushing towards them. The two groups speak together.
The older Gods are envious; once more they climb up and down
the "golden ladder of memories"; alternately silent and weeping

bitterly, they hand each other the "giant miracle flowers" of memory, while in their tears is reflected the shining Olympus. The new Gods make their reply : we lay groaning in the prison of night while you enjoyed sunshine, pleasures and light; "uns aber schwingt Anankes Schaufel heut nach oben".[18]

Then, like a ghost, Orpheus the seer appears, and all stand back to give him space. His eyes are fixed and glazed, he gazes into the very core of the world, into the heart of eternity. How the world was created, whence evil came, he does not know . . . "I was there, and no more". Shattered, the new Gods stare after the exhausted prophet as he leaves, "ein Unheil ahnend, das die Schwingen weiter spannt".[19] Thereupon, Prometheus appears, pride in his face. Lamentation is not worthy of immortal Gods, he says. Man's body rots away from his soul, his mind and body are destroyed by death, but Fate attacks the Gods only outwardly. "Value, pride, self-assurance, these dwell inside me." He does not drink from the treacherous fountain, thus avoiding the trap of anger. He moves on "as if his path were concern of Fate, not his own".

Kronos, the king, arrives, seated on a charger, his sword hanging from the pommel of his saddle. He shakes his defiant lion's head, and seeing the group of new Gods, flies into a rage. So, any young upstart can aspire to his heritage ! . . . "I know I have not been conquered. Only treachery has brought me low." (This is the treachery of his daughter Hera.) He turns about, whipping on his army in an attempt to retake Olympus by storm. But the earth trembles, an avalanche sweeps down the valley, and the whole army is carried off in a whirlwind of rocks. The king stands firm for a few moments, and hurls his curse upon whoever shall marry his daughter : may he never find honour upon the throne, nor love in any bed. Then, like a mighty oak falling, he disappears with his charger into the abyss—watched in helpless confusion by the new Gods. Bitterly they reflect upon what one day will be their fate, too—"Why? For what reason? To what purpose?" Despondently, they flop to the ground, awaiting Ananke's command. When nothing happens, they humbly continue their journey.

In such scenes, Spitteler produces the genuine epic atmosphere, steeped in deepest emotion and humanity. These are the visions of a great poet, and the language used is correspondingly effective. For their sake, we must acknowledge *Olympischer Frühling* as a work of art. The second part, *Hera die Braut,* has its living moments, too, scenes which in their own way possess great depth. (For example, there is the union of guilt and lust on Zeus' wedding-night.) However, this section is generally overshadowed by the hardness and cruelty of Hera's character, and by her ultimate treachery.

Genuine pathos, where the particular and the universal become fused, is also to be found in the occasional poem where Spitteler, having achieved a certain level of poetry, manages to sustain it; not, however, in the "visual" lyric of *Schmetterlinge,* nor yet in the more acoustic one of the *Glocken—und Gras-lieder,* where one sees and hears little more than the occasional sally into higher poetry. In the *Balladen* and the *Literarische Gleichnisse,* more undulating strains are to be perceived, though the latter will certainly not be appreciated first and foremost for their lyricism. Even here, however, one still finds no wholly perfected pieces. Only rarely does Spitteler manage to achieve the tonal contrasts of the true literary ballad, so well demonstrated by Goethe.

It is chiefly in the two stories, *Gustav* and *Die Mädchenfeinde,* that the childlike playfulness of Spitteler's "idyllic" temperament reveals itself. In *Gustav* (1892), the theme of greatness is developed out of a not unalluring idyll, which one would scarcely connect with the early satirical *Kleinstadtroman* (never published by Spitteler) on which it is based. A girl imparts to a young artist, who has failed as a medical student, the most precious gift a woman can give to a man—the belief in his vocation. The work certainly has many charming touches, but its basic structure lacks maturity, thus hampering any real refinement of language.

Artistically much more important is the Novelle, *Die Mädchen-feinde* (1907). Only at intervals is this story of a boys' world threatened by the intrusion of the poet's adult personality. As a whole, its evenness of tone, its sureness of touch in the depiction of the child mind, and the power and spontaneity of its epic pictures compel admiration. In his "Früheste Erlebnisse", Spitteler conjures up the prime of his early years with love and moderation, tinged with a sort of bashfulness. In *Die Mädchenfeinde,* boyhood is transmitted on to a higher, more idealised, yet still semi-realistic plane. Thus the idyll, a delightful vision of youthful souls awakening, is embedded in an apparent commonplace of events and in a landscape intimately familiar to the poet. The Novelle is a summer's ramble, a summer's rapture. Yet, over the nimble alertness, the innocence and artlessness of child experience, there hovers the reflection of another ramble, of another, somehow deeper sensual rapture : the gently gliding entry into maturer human experiences. The story strides with consummate skill up the narrow ridge where the innocent child world is overtaken by disillusioned adolescence. Adults play a part in the story only in so far as the plot requires them, and yet they provide a meaningful framework, since the experiences of the youngsters overflow into their domain. The obvious antithesis to the world of child joy is the crazy student. Through this human oddity Spitteler has expounded with extraordinary acuteness his pet theme of the suffering artistic genius.

The mundane temperament of the poet at last reveals itself in engaging fashion in the long story *Der Neffe des Herrn Bezenval* (1889). This is a historical novel set at the time of the French Revolution. Just as in Conrad Ferdinand Meyer's *Amulett*, a young Swiss arrives in Paris and gets himself entangled in love and politics. The theme is the development of a somewhat gauche but morally upright young idealist into a fully aware adult, who finally sacrifices himself for the sake of his convictions.

In *Conrad der Leutnant* Spitteler is dealing with a world far outside his natural sphere. The story was an "art gageure", a challenge to the despised guild of naturalists. It was an attempt to attack his opponents with their own weapons, having first refined them—or so he believed. Refined, that is, not in terms of psychological analysis, which Spitteler considered inartistic and anyway superficial, but through the acceptance of the formal laws of classical tragedy—in particular the French.

With this technique, it is only immediately before the dénouement that he unites the main dramatic themes, imposing upon himself the unity of character and perspective, as well as a regular time-sequence, in order to achieve the most intense involvement possible in the plot. There are two main reasons why the attempt was doomed to failure. As a poet, Spitteler had little feeling for ordinary human love. The popular heart remained amazingly alien to his own. The individual was after all for him not sufficiently noble to warrant any creative interest, *sui generis*. This being so, how could the material he chose ever have provided him with a poetic stimulus? Moreover, Spitteler's self-imposed principles only increased the disparity. For the figures do not live in their own right, but only in order to do justice to a preconceived idea of plot and character. From the outset they are treated like puppets. For the problems of authority and the generation-gap to be presented clearly, and so that the plot will develop in a terse and compact fashion, Conrad's father, who is immersed in ineluctable gloom, must appear to his son and daughter as a loathsome monster. And Conrad himself in his rank of lieutenant must appear as almost childishly obsessed in his hunger for power. Any subtle nuance in the story's fabric is thus precluded, and one is immediately struck by the glaring artificiality, even affectedness, of the work. Between the two main characters, father and son, no single spark of intimacy is ever kindled. There is therefore no basis on which tragic suspense can breed.

Imago, by Spitteler's own admission, was "not just a work of art, but . . . 'life-blood' ". Yet he was "nauseated by this Sisyphus-like toil in prosaic filth". How, one may ask, can life-blood become nauseating? How can "life-blood" transform itself into prosody? If Spitteler preferred to present his innermost spiritual life in a "veiled and disguised" way, why then so sudden and naked a confession? Some personal thorn, some extra-artistic motive must surely have been at work. Was it some insuppressible grudge, a wound that refused to heal—an almost pathological need for revenge? This suspicion is now confirmed by what we know of the work's origins : there could anyway be no other answer to the question. *Imago* was an unfortunate book not only for the author but also for the sensitive reader—in fact, one of the most unedifying among the better-known works of contemporary literature.[20] "The love story of Felix Tandem" (Spitteler published his first two works under this pseudonym) "in the year when he wrote Prometheus." This is Spitteler's own definition. Certainly a love story of a very strange kind ! One lover between two women, one earthly, one unearthly, both with the same face, and after a fight in which he makes a fool of himself, he devotes himself completely to the unearthly. Prometheus with fainting fits—so one might just as well dub it ! Not a Prometheus in an imaginary, mythical world, but a Prometheus "among the democrats", in a bourgeois environment. However, what once—in Prometheus' human weakness and stupidity, is developed in *Imago* into a biting satire of bourgeois society : "Idealia" as the mirror image of a complacent bourgeoisie flowing with "ideals" but in fact selfish and narrow.

This satire is not charmingly presented, but quivering with scorn and resentment. Resentment is the word, perhaps, which most accurately characterises the work. Resentment on the one side, delusions of grandeur—one cannot avoid the expression—on the other. And this implies the presence of an element which makes the work profoundly unartistic : the personal, the all too personal. The satire is born out of resentment, as is the hero's anguish when he is prevented from loving the woman. The hero is simply not a human being, but the marionette-like creation of the poet's resentful, almost monomanic, mind—a mind which here turns the vacuum of a growing sense of inferiority and aversion into a euphoria of artificial characters, without ever finding a way to translate its own "life-blood" into any redeeming artistic form.

In his essay on Spitteler, C. A. Bernouilli pronounced that *Imago* was at best an instinctive and violent "Aufschrei", and at worst a completely artificial creation.[21] One is bound to go along with this verdict, adding, too, that there are strains in this "outcry" which cast a shadow on the poet's human decency.

This essay is a considerably shortened version of Professor Werner Günther's (Neuchâtel) important essay on Carl Spitteler, which appeared in *Dichter der neueren Schweiz* (Francke Verlag, Berne, 1963).

(Translated by E. M. W. Maguire.)

ANNOTATIONS AND TRANSLATIONS

1. *Aesthetic Writings,* p. 171.
2. *Autobiographical Writings,* p. 300.
3. *Aesthetic Writings,* p. 71.
4. *Autobiographical Writings,* p. 281–82.
5. *Aesthetic Writings,* p. 185.
6. *Aesthetic Writings,* p. 466.
7. Viz. *Carl Spittelers poetische Sendung,* Schweizer Monatshefte fur Politik und Kultur, 3 vol. (1923).
8. *Aesthetic Writings,* p. 193.
9. Literally, "the compelled compulsion".
10. The world-mill.
11. And spake his song in dark velvet tones.
12. Against the sombre background shining a world of teeming images.
13. Life's purpose is dirt. The truth is in the stone.
14. Not an inch in eternity which is not filled with anguish.
15. The terrible bed of the avalanche's debris.
16. What has become of the world of the Ancients! For what anguish it has already left a space!
17. See 14.
18. But now Ananke's shovel swings us upwards.
19. Foreseeing the doom which will spread its wings ever wider.
20. It testifies to the original fame of the novel that Sigmund Freud published a "Periodical for the application of Psychoanalysis to the Humanities" under the title of *Imago* from 1912. One of the editors, Dr.

Hanns Sachs, praised Spitteler's novel, as early as 1913, as a manual for the phenomenon of the Oedipus-complex.

21. C. A. Bernouilli cit. by R. Matzog-Schmauss, *Prometheus-Fate. Essays about Carl Spittler,* 1930, p. 87.

BIBLIOGRAPHY

Gesammelte Werke in neun Bänden, vermehrt um zwei Geleitbände, Zürich, 1945–58. Herausgeber: G. Bohnenblust, W. Altwegg, R. Faesi.

Briefe von Ad. Frey und C. Spitteler, Hsg. von Lina Frey, Frauenfeld, 1933.

G. Spitteler, *Laughing Truths,* 1927.

C. Spitteler, *Selected Poems,* 1928.

O. Kluth, *Carl Spitteler,* 1918 in French.

E. Boyd, *Studies of Ten Literatures,* 1923.

R. Gottschalk, *Carl Spitteler,* 1928.

F. Weingartner, *Carl Spitteler. Ein künstlerisches Erlebnis,* 1904.

Th. Roffler, *Carl Spitteler. Eine Literarische Feststellung,* 1926.

R. Faesi, *Spittelers Weg und Werk,* 1933.

J. Fränkel, *Carl Spitteler. Hundigungen und Begegnungen,* 1945.

W. Frels, *Eine Bibliographie Spittelers in "Die Schöne Literatur",* 1925.

Robert Walser

Robert Walser

by H. M. WAIDSON

Robert Walser was born on 15 April 1878 at Biel, where his
father was proprietor of a stationery and toy shop. He had seven
brothers and sisters, of whom one, Karl Walser (1877–1943),
became a well-known painter. On leaving school in 1892, Robert
Walser was employed at a local bank, but soon gave up this work
and took a succession of posts, frequently as a clerical worker,
interrupted by periods when he undertook long walks and gave
himself to writing. He published individual poems and wrote some
short verse dramas before *Fritz Kochers Aufsätze* was published
by the Insel Verlag in 1904. For much of the time from 1905 to
1913 Robert Walser lived with his brother Karl in Berlin, where
apart from prose sketches he wrote the novels *Geschwister Tanner*
(1907), *Der Gehülfe* (1908) and *Jakob von Gunten* (1909), which
were published by the Verlag Bruno Cassirer. His stay in Berlin
was terminated by a personal crisis. He returned to Switzerland,
but found the struggle to devote himself to writing continuingly
difficult. The manuscript of a novel *Theodor* seems to have disappeared. In 1929 Walser agreed to undergo treatment at a mental
hospital in Berne, and in 1933 he transferred to the hospital at
Herisau. He died on 25 December 1956 during the course of an
afternoon walk. Walser's life and personality are described by
Robert Maechler in his biographical study of the author.

ROBERT WALSER'S first extended prose publication, *Fritz
Kochers Aufsätze* (1904), anticipates his later work in its
themes and presentation. It is true that here there is a
tenuous framework, which the later collections of prose sketches do
not have; Fritz Kocher, a boy who died shortly after leaving
school, has left behind him a collection of school-essays which the
editor wishes to publish. The essays are on subjects such as "Man",
"Autumn" or "Friendship", themes set by the teacher and
developed by the pupil into delicate arabesques that characterize
them unmistakably as the work of Walser. A theme is presented
with simplicity, then diverted by a small touch into satire, or less

frequently into a direct expression of the writer's sensibility of heart. There is the vision of the writer and artist as representing man in his noblest state, the admission of a secret enthusiasm for art, praise of the posssession of a sensitive temperament, a determination to live intensely only for the passing moment, an appreciation of the joys of friendship, descriptions of autumn and winter, contrasts between poverty and wealth, indecision about a future career, descriptions of Christmas or a fairground, and an invocation of the spirit of music. Then the fiction is tacitly dropped, and there follows a series of descriptions of the problems of a clerical worker; the essays concern someone who has now left school and who between the age of eighteen and twenty-four is making wry discoveries about the world of business. A new framework is now devised; the author brings to the reader's notice "leaves from the notebook of a painter". Here is an early indication of the relationship between Robert Walser and his elder brother Karl. The painter has been living in poverty, finds the patronage and affection of a wealthy lady, later tires of this protected life and sets off once more on his travels. "Why is it that artists can find no rest?" he asks himself. The volume concludes with an essay on "Der Wald", which is more rhapsodic in tone than the ealier ones. The author remains dissatisfied with his attempt :

Über etwas Schönes exakt und bestimmt schreiben, ist schwer Gedanken fliegen um das Schöne wie trunkene Schmetterlinge, ohne zum Ziel und festen Punkt zu kommen.[1]

In this image one senses the seriousness with which Walser approached his writing, for all the self-deprecating gestures he often made, and one senses too the tension that he may well have felt between his volatile-impressionistic imagination and the desire to control his themes within a firm formal structure. Here was a problem which he rarely resolved successfully, and preoccupation with which seems to have caused him to express himself, apart from the novels, in a series of essays and short stories which elaborate, sometimes repetitively, themes many of which are foreshadowed in *Fritz Kochers Aufsätze*. The problem is indicated again in *Die Geliebte*, from *Die Rose* (1925), the last new collection of his prose writing in bookform which Walser himself brought out : "Dich binden, Macht des Geistes, wem gelänge das?"[2]

The precision of detail and lightness of touch with which Walser writes may be illustrated most simply by reproducing one of Fritz Kocher's essays. Here, then, is *Unsere Stadt* :

Unsere Stadt ist eigentlich mehr ein großer schöner Garten als eine Stadt. Die Straßen sind Gartenwege. Sie sehen so sauber und wie mit feinem Sand bestreut aus. Über den Dächern der Stadt erhebt sich der Berg mit seinen dunklen Tannen und mit seinem grünen Laub. Wir haben die prächtigsten Anlagen, unter anderem eine Allee, die von Napoleon herstammen soll. Ich glaube zwar nicht, daß er mit eigener Hand die Bäume gesetzt hat, dazu war er doch wohl zu stolz, zu großmächtig. Im Sommer geben die breiten alten Kastanien einen herrlichen erquickenden Schatten. An Sommerabenden sieht man die Bewohner der Stadt, welche spazieren mögen, in dieser Allee auf und ab wandeln. Die Damen nehmen sich in ihren hellfarbigen Kleidern besonders schön aus. Auf dem abenddunklen See wird dann mit Lust gegondelt. Der See gehört zu unserer Stadt wie die Kirche, oder wie das Lustschloß eines Fürsten zu einer Residenz in Monarchien. Ohne den See wäre unsere Stadt nicht unsere Stadt, ja, man würde sie nicht wiedererkennen. Unsere Kirche, die protestantische, liegt auf einer hochgelegenen Plattform, die mit zwei wunderbar schönen, großen Kastanienbäumen geziert ist. Die Fenster der Kirche sind mit den feurigsten Farben bemalt, was ihr ein märchenhaftes Aussehen gibt. Oft ertönt der lieblichste vielstimmige Gesang aus ihr. Ich stehe gern draußen, wenn drinnen gesungen wird. Die Frauen singen am schönsten. Unser Rathaus ist würdig, und sein großer Saal dient zu Bällen und sonstigen Anlässen. Wir haben sogar ein Theater. Alle Winter besuchen uns auf zwei Monate fremde Schauspieler, welche sehr feine Manieren haben, ein sehr feines Deutsch sprechen und Zylinder auf den Köpfen tragen. Ich freue mich immer, wenn sie kommen, und helfe unsern Bürgern nicht mit, wenn sie verächtlich von dem "Pack" reden. Es kann sein, daß sie ihre Schulden nicht bezahlen, daß sie frech sind, daß sie sich betrinken, daß sie aus schlechten Familien herstammen, aber wofür sind sie Künstler? Einem Künstler sieht man großmütig dergleichen durch die Finger. Sie spielen auch ganz herrlich. Ich habe die "Räuber" gesehen. Es ist ein wundervolles Theaterstück, voll Feuer und Schönheiten. Kann man sich auf eine feinere und edlere Weise amüsieren, als, indem man das Theater besucht? Große Städte gehen uns ja in dieser Hinsicht mit dem besten Beispiel voran.—Unsere Stadt hat viel Industrie, das kommt, weil sie Fabriken hat. Fabriken und ihre Umgebung sehen unschön aus. Da ist die Luft schwarz und dick, und ich begreife nicht, warum man sich mit so unsauberen Dingen abgeben kann. Ich bekümmere mich nicht, was in den Fabriken gemacht wird. Ich weiß nur, daß alle armen Leute in der Fabrik arbeiten, vielleicht zur Strafe, daß sie so arm sind. Wir haben hübsche Straßen, und überall blicken grüne Bäume zwischen den Häusern hervor. Wenn es regnet, sind die Straßen recht schmutzig. Bei uns wird wenig für die Straßen getan. Vater sagt das. Schade, daß unser Haus keinen Garten hat. Wir wohnen im ersten Stock. Unsere Wohnung ist schön, aber es sollte ein Garten dazu gehören. Mama klagt oft deshalb. Der alte Stadtteil ist mir am liebsten. Ich schlendere gern in den alten Gässchen, Gewölben und Gängen. Auch unterirdische Gänge haben wir. Im ganzen : wir haben eine sehr hübsche Stadt.[3]

The sketch flows in one paragraph, its sentences being short and often simple. It can be imagined as an exercise, where the thought pours out in a succession of impressions which are linked together by association, not by argument. The panorama moves from one section of the view to another, description of the physical surroundings being interrupted by factors such as the singing in church, the visits of the actors and the comments from father and mother. The frequent use of "schön", "hübsch" and "fein" can indicate an ironical sense of distance from the objects described; elsewhere Walser sometimes uses diminutives for similar effect. One senses the conflict of two worlds. Citizens like Fritz' parents are proud of the orderly world of tree-clad streets, and of the town's other amenities—church, chestnut-trees, lake and so on. Napoleon is the remote, patriarchal provider of an avenue of trees, associated with the burghers and their "dignified" town hall. Opposed to the securely established citizens are the actors and industrial workers. The actors, being artists, are not to be measured by ordinary, civic standards. They are the wanderers who do not share the stability of the settled burgher. The industrial poor are for the most part unseen and out of mind, and Fritz Kocher reflects and parodies the general attitude of the middle-class section of the inhabitants. There is no narrative tension in this sketch; the effect depends upon the unity of mood and style which is achieved. There are hints here of the inconsequentiality that at times becomes tiresome in some of the later sketches. No doubt *Unsere Stadt* is less memorable than some others of the short works, but it is recognizably Walser's work.

The short sketch, occasionally expanded into a short story, is the literary form which accompanied Walser throughout the course

of his life as a writer. But although it is through this briefer form
that Walser's work is likely to be introduced to readers, the present
essay wishes to concern itself mainly with the author's longer works.
Der Spaziergang (1917), of Novelle length, has much in common
with the shorter works. Walking is a frequent theme in Walser's
writing, and is expressed here with a vigour and enthusiasm that
have made this work one of his best known writings. The narrator's
principal business in the town which he visits is to have lunch with
a patroness, to try on a suit at a tailor's, and to convince an
income-tax official that, as a poorly paid writer, he is entitled to
the lowest possible assessment. These encounters are expressed as
a series of speeches which are themselves sketches in miniature—
Frau Aebi's comic encouragement to the protagonist to do justice
to her food; his indignation about his suit and the tailor's equally
indignant reply; his justification to the tax official of his way of
life as a poor but independent writer. In anticipation of these
central points of the outward action the protagonist describes with
playful zest the figures whom he meets on the first part of the walk,
the professor, the bookseller, the bank-official, the woman who, he
imagines, was once an actress, a girl whose singing is heard from
an open window, and a number of others. They are not important
as participants in any plot, but we are asked to cherish them as
impressions in their own right which have become memorable because of the vivid eagerness with which the author has seized them :

Die morgendliche Welt, die sich vor meinen Augen ausbreitete,
erschien mir so schön, als sähe ich sie zum erstenmal.[4]

The quality of freshness which Walser conveys in *Der Spaziergang*
endows everyday scenes with the uniqueness of a personal vision.
In his statement to the tax official the narrator equates the man
who writes with the man who walks, and describes his concern as
being extended over the small as well as the great :

Die höchsten und niedrigsten, die ernstesten und lustigsten Dinge
sind ihm gleicherweise lieb und schön und wert . . . Er muß
jederzeit des Mitleides, des Mitempfindens und der Begeisterung
fähig sein, und er ist es hoffentlich. Er muß in den hohen
Enthusiasmus hinaufdringen und sich in die tiefste und kleinste
Alltäglichkeit herunterzusenken und zu neigen vermögen, und er
kann es vermutlich. Treues, hingebungsvolles Aufgehen und Sich-
verlieren in die Gegenstände und eifrige Liebe zu allen Erschei-
nungen und Dingen machen ihn aber dafür glücklich . . .[5]

The narrator combines idyllic description with fantasy. A pine forest which is "quiet as in the heart of a happy human being" reminds him of the interior of a temple or an enchanted castle. The vision of the tired giant Tomzack looms unexpectedly into the protagonist's solitude, to disappear as inexplicably as he came. The poet-walker must make considerable effort to prevent the ordered world of consciousness from disintegrating :

> . . . er muß sich fragen : "Wo bin ich?" Erde und Himmel fließen und stürzen mit einmal in ein blitzendes, schimmerndes, übereinanderwogendes, undeutliches Nebelgebilde zusammen; das Chaos beginnt, und die Ordnungen verschwinden. Mühsam versucht der Erschütterte seine gesunde Besinnung aufrecht zu erhalten . . .[6]

What is seen is described with sharpness and precision, and an additional dimension is provided by the imaginative reactions of the protagonist to the scene before him. The common-sense world is continually liable to lose its shape, perhaps by being overlain with a fantasy, or by being transmuted by ecstasy or by being overcome by chaos. An important climax lies in the narrator's vision at the level-crossing shortly after the conclusion of his friendly interview with the tax authorities. After the opening of the barrier at the crossing he senses that he has come to the highlight of his walk :

> Hier beim Bahnübergang schien mir der Höhepunkt oder etwas wie das Zentrum zu sein, von wo aus es leise wieder sinken würde.[7]

The commonplace scene on the road is transfigured and is interpreted in these terms :

> Gott der Allmächtige, unser gnädiger Herr, trat auf die Straße, um sie zu verherrlichen und himmlisch schön zu machen. Einbildungen aller Art und Illusionen machten mich glauben, daß Jesus Christus heraufgestiegen sei und jetzt mitten unter den Leuten und mitten durch die liebenswürdige Gegend wandere und umher wandle. Häuser, Gärten und Menschen verwandelten sich in Klänge, alles Gegenständliche schien sich in eine Zärtlichkeit verwandelt zu haben. Süßer Silberschleier und Seelennebel schwamm in alles und legte sich um alles. Die Weltseele hatte sich geöffnet, und alles Leid, alle menschlichen Enttäuschungen, alles Böse, alles Schmerzhafte schienen zu entschwinden, und von nun an nie mehr wieder zu erscheinen.

Frühere Spaziergänge traten mir vor die Augen; aber das wundervolle Bild der bescheidenen Gegenwart wurde zur überragenden Empfindung. Die Zukunft verblaßte, und die Vergangenheit zerrann. Ich glühte und blühte selber im glühenden, blühenden Augenblick . . . Im süßen Liebeslichte erkannte ich oder glaubte ich erkennen zu sollen, daß vielleicht der innerliche Mensch der einzige sei, der wahrhaft existiert.[8]

The impression of the moment has acquired visionary significance, emphasizing man's inward spirit and its closeness to the earth's beauty. After this experience, the walk takes its return journey as evening approaches with an elegiac tone and with a less emphatic manner than earlier. The author does not offer novelties to the reader, and asserts rather his conception of nature and human life as a "flight of repetitions", a phenomenon that he regards both "as beauty and as blessing". Evening brings with it thoughts of loneliness, tiredness and the transience of all life and its impressions.

Der Spaziergang is rich in its varied associations of ideas and the luminous intensity of its prose. It blends the playful, the satirical and the sensitively imaginative aspects of Walser's writing in a form which is simple, but without the tenuousness of a number of the short sketches. This is one of the few occasions when Walser used the middle-length prose form, though he gave much of his creative energies to wrestling with the novel form, with varying success. The years in Berlin in particular saw his preoccupation with novel writing. In his *Wanderungen mit Robert Walser,* Carl Seelig reports Walser as having said that he might well have burnt three novels in Berlin; a later novel *Theodor* was written in Switzerland between 1917 and 1922, but this too has been lost. There remain the three published novels : *Die Geschwister Tanner, Der Gehülfe* and *Jakob von Gunten.* In later life Walser looked back to the period in Berlin as his time of greatest opportunity. He said to Seelig in January 1937 :

"Könnte ich mich nochmals ins 30. Lebensjahr zurückschrauben, so würde ich nicht mehr wie ein romantischer Luftibus ins Blaue hineinschreiben, sonderlingshaft und unbekümmert. Man darf die Gesellschaft nicht negieren. Man muß in ihr leben und für oder gegen sie kämpfen. Das ist der Fehler meiner Romane. Sie sind zu schrullig und reflexiv, in der Komposition oft zu salopp. Um die künstlerische Gesetzmäßigkeit mich foutierend, habe ich einfach drauflosmusiziert."[9]

Six years later he expressed regrets combined with ironic defiance that he did not meet the reading public half-way during his productive period :

"Ich hätte ein wenig Liebe und Trauer, ein wenig Ernst und Beifall in meine Bücher mischen sollen—auch ein wenig Edel-romantik . . ."[10]

In the conversations with Seelig Walser criticizes the subjective element in *Die Geschwister Tanner* as having irritated its first readers; he feels that he has spoken too intimately of his own brothers and sisters, and that he would prefer to cut the work by seventy or eighty pages in preparing it for a new edition. The sketch *Geschwister Tanner*, from the *Kleine Dichtungen* of 1914, throws a more positive and poetic light upon the genesis of this work in the Berlin flat which he shared with his brother Karl. The act of creating something that he knows to be beautiful is a blissful experience, and is described in rapturous terms :

Der Dichter muß schweifen, muß sich mutig verlieren, muß immer alles, alles wieder wagen, muß hoffen, darf, darf nur hoffen . . . Ich hoffte nie, daß ich je etwas Ernstes, Schönes und Gutes fertigstellen könnte.—Der bessere Gedanke und damit der Schaffensmut tauchte nur langsam, dafür aber eben nur um so geheimnisreicher aus den Abgründen der Selbstnicht-achtung und des leichtsinnigen Unglaubens hervor.—Es glich der aufsteigenden Morgensonne. Abend und Morgen, Vergangen-heit und Zukunft und die reizende Gegenwart lagen wie zu meinen Füßen, das Land wurde dicht vor mir lebendig, und mich dünkte, ich könne das menschliche Treiben, das ganze Menschenleben mit Händen greifen, so lebhaft sah ich es.—Ein Bild löste das andere ab, und die Einfälle spielten miteinander wie glückliche, anmutige, artige Kinder. Voller Entzücken hing ich am fröhlichen Grundgedanken, und indem ich nur fleißig immer weiter schrieb, fand sich der Zusammenhang.[11]

Die Geschwister Tanner is an episodic work, liable to dissolve into series of descriptions, letters and monologues. Its unity lies in the first place in the personalities of the Tanner family, reflected through their encounters with Simon. His elder brother Klaus reproaches Simon in a letter for not having a settled career and for his restlessness in moving from one post to another. Simon is a wanderer who wants to live in the present moment; he says on first meeting Frau Klara :

Ich habe nie etwas besessen, bin nie etwas gewesen, und werde trotz den Hoffnungen meiner Eltern nie etwas sein.[12]

Rather more than a year later Simon wanders into a state convalescent home, glad of the temporary shelter of warmth in midwinter. A friendly woman-supervisor persuades him to talk about himself and his family, and the novel closes with this conversation, which consists largely of Simon's summing up of himself and of his near relatives, reminding us of the ties of affection that exist between this group of individualists. It is here, in Simon's last speech, that he gives some hints as to the reason for the particular character of the bonds between these brothers and sisters which gives the novel its distinctive quality. The memory of their mother's dignity, the accounts of her sufferings as a child, and later the witnessing of the collapse of her personality in her last years form a common emotional experience of depth which her children carry with them, hardly consciously, in their adult lives. Simon says of his mother :

Ihre Eltern waren nicht gut zu ihr, so lernte sie früh die Schwermut kennen und stand, als sie Mädchen war, eines Tages an ein Brückengeländer angelehnt und dachte darüber nach, ob es nicht besser wäre, in den Fluß hinab zu springen. Man muß sie vernachlässigt, hin und her geschoben und auf diese. Art mißhandelt haben. Als ich als Knabe einmal von ihrer Jugend hörte, schoß mir der Zorn ins Gesicht, ich bebte vor Empörung und haßte von nun an die unbekannten Gestalten meiner Großeltern. Für uns Kinder hatte die Mutter, als sie noch gesund war, etwas beinahe Majestätisches, vor dem wir uns fürchteten und zurückscheuten; als sie krank im Geist wurde, bemitleideten wir sie. Es war ein toller Sprung, so von der ängstlichen, geheimnisvollen Ehrfurcht ins Mitleid überspringen zu müssen.[13]

Both parents grew up in isolated mountain districts, and came into the town to share the newly developing prosperity introduced there by industrialization. Simon has not yet found the solutions to the problems involved in his parents' lives :

Ich stehe noch immer vor der Türe des Lebens, klopfe und klopfe, allerdings mit wenig Ungestüm, und horche nur gespannt, ob jemand komme, der mir den Riegel zurückschieben möchte.[14]

In the course of the novel Simon's closest ties are with his brother Kaspar and his sister Hedwig. With his firm vocation as painter

Kaspar has an immediate purpose in life which Simon lacks; at the same time his carefree self-confidence enables him to take life more easily than Simon :

"Was geht alles in der Welt vorüber. Man muß schaffen, schaffen und nochmals schaffen, dazu ist man da, nicht zum Bemitleiden."[15]

Simon finds the furnished room and thus begins the connection with Frau Klara, but it is Kaspar with whom she falls in love. For Kaspar is more defined as a personality by his artistic mission and by the easiness of his approaches to the other sex. Simon rejects the possibility of a more intimate relationship with her, and asserts his independence by going for a lonely walk. As an artist and a Bohemian, Kaspar is following an expected pattern of development, and his move to Paris is in keeping with his sense of purpose. As Frau Klara says, Simon is different and "can scarcely be grasped". Simon likes to confide in his friend Rosa, but she is secretly in love with Kaspar. Simon's affection for his brother allows of no feelings of jealousy; he is glad for Kaspar when Frau Klara becomes closely bound to the latter.

When winter finds him out of work and homeless, Simon goes to his sister Hedwig, a village schoolmistress, and stays with her for three months. Hedwig's attitude to him is protective, but she is much less settled than at first appears; she is anxious to escape, perhaps as a governess in Italy, or more probably by marrying a local farmer. "Ich werde das Leben verspielt haben,"[16] she says, as she thinks of the type of marriage she is likely to make. But she feels, as Simon puts it later, a mixture of affection and contempt for him :

"Nein, nein, Simon, wegen dir wird niemand weinen. Wenn du fort bist, bist du fort. Das ist alles. Glaubst du, um dich könnte man weinen? Keine Rede."[17]

Simon is more closely bound to Kaspar and Hedwig, who are nearer to him in temperament, than to his other brothers. For Klaus is separated from them by his more positive acceptance of the standards of normal society, while Emil, in a mental hospital, lives in total estrangement from the world around him.

Der Spaziergang focuses our attention on the events of the walk and on the immediate impressions they make on the narrator; the personality of the narrator is kept deliberately in the background. To discover a further dimension to such a personality we can turn to *Die Geschwister Tanner*, where Simon, a self-effacing wanderer, is the main personage. Of the various walks that Simon undertakes in the course of the novel, the most memorable is perhaps the three days' trek to Hedwig in the winter, in the course of which he comes across the frozen corpse of the poet Sebastian and resolves to see that his poems are collected and published. *Die Geschwister Tanner* has an emotional directness that is less clearly observed in Walser's other writings; it is a work which invites above all affectionate reading.

Der Gehülfe is in the first place a comic novel depicting the relationship of Joseph Marti with the Tobler family during the months when he is in their house as clerical assistant and secretary to the engineer Tobler. Joseph Marti seems to be less vulnerable than Simon Tanner, but at heart he too is a wanderer; the events of the novel take place during an interval between one phase of restlessness and another. He would like to keep the whole of his experience of people on a light, ironical, non-committal, distant level. His reflections as he first awaits admission to the house indicate a characteristic mood :

> Eines Morgens um acht Uhr stand ein junger Mann vor der Türe eines alleinstehenden, anscheinend schmucken Hauses. Es regnete. "Es wundert mich beinahe," dachte der Dastehende, "daß ich einen Schirm bei mir habe." Er besaß nämlich in seinen früheren Jahren nie einen Regenschirm.[18]

An attention to details of everyday life suffuses this realistic novel, and a variety of precisely observed impressions can be united in Joseph's mind to an experience of beauty. After a few weeks with the Tobler family, Joseph is permitted to take a trip to the nearby city (the novel is based on a similar period in Walser's life spent near Zürich), and he feels the impact of the sunny Sunday with a gaiety and heightened awareness :

> Es war alles so mild, so bedeckt, so leicht und hübsch, es war ebenso groß wie klein geworden, ebenso nah wie fern, ebenso weit wie fein und ebenso zart wie bedeutend. Es schien bald alles, was Joseph sah, ein natürlicher, stiller, gütiger Traum geworden zu sein, nicht ein gar so schöner, nein, ein bescheidener, und doch ein so schöner.[19]

Here it is as if Joseph is capable of double vision, of harmonizing a close examination of detail with a broad conspectus of the whole scene; the series of contrasting adjectives indicates the combination of the miniature and the panoramic which is successfully achieved in this vision of the city. He speculates about the personalities of the strangers sitting on the public seats, imagining the complexity of living that could be developed from the material of his passing glances:

> Das Leben ließ sich nicht so leicht in Kasten und Ordnungen abteilen . . . Ah, das Leben machte bitter, aber es konnte auch froh und innig demütig machen, und dankbar fürs Wenige, für das bißchen süße, freie Luft zum Einatmen.[20]

From the point of view of its stylized description this impression of Zürich is one of the outstanding sequences in the work. It is perhaps inevitable, and part of the comedy, that it should later be reduced by Tobler to a commonplace level :

> "Ja so? In der Stadt sind Sie gewesen? Und wie hat es Ihnen denn dort nach der längern Abwesenheit wieder gefallen? Nicht schlecht, was? Jawohl, die Städte vermögen manches zu bieten, aber man kommt schließlich doch auch gern wieder zurück. Habe ich recht oder nicht?"[21]

The tension between Joseph and his employer is the main motor force of the novel. Tobler's first words to Joseph are an irritated enquiry as to why he has arrived two days earlier than expected, a misunderstanding for which Joseph is not responsible. The final quarrel on New Year's Day which causes Joseph abruptly to leave is not primarily about Joseph, but about his predecessor Wirsich to whom Joseph has been giving protection and shelter, though without Tobler's personal permission. It appears as if Joseph is diametrically opposed to Tobler, his own quietness, for instance, contrasting with the latter's loud and decided manner. Tobler is essentially a comic figure. Having inherited some money, he has taken over an elegant house and devoted himself to inventions such as the "Reklameuhr", advertising novelties by means of which he hopes to make his fortune. He makes much of the August 1st holiday, organizing illuminations and fireworks for the household :

> Wie glücklich sah Tobler aus! Das war etwas für ihn. Für Feste und deren schöne Inszenierung schien er wie kaum ein zweiter geschaffen zu sein.[22]

This thought comes again to Joseph Marti as he silently participates in Tobler's celebration of the completion of his fairy-grotto,

> . . . ein höhlenartiges, mit Zement ausgeschlagenes und tapeziertes Ding, länglich wie ein größeres Ofenloch, etwas zu niedrig, so daß die Besucher mehr als einmal die Köpfe anstießen.[23]

Characteristic too are Tobler's frequent, busy-seeming train journeys, which are mainly motivated by his wish not to "waste" a
season-ticket he has taken out.

Already at an early phase of the novel, we acquire little confidence in the nature of Tobler's enterprises, and as with the
passing of the months his affairs approach inevitably nearer to
bankruptcy, Tobler and his assistant seem to be bound more closely
together. Tobler is rebuffed by his mother, while Joseph is at odds
with his father; neither of them is at home in the middle-class world
of Swiss enterprise which surrounds them; they irritate and stimu-
late each other, and both are romantic at heart. Joseph is a freer
man than Tobler, and Frau Tobler, tied to her husband and her
four children, tells him to count his blessings :

> "Sie, Marti, haben es eigentlich recht gut, viel besser als mein
> Mann und als ich, aber von mir will ich gar nicht reden. Sie
> können von hier weggehen. Sie packen einfach Ihre paar Sachen,
> setzen sich in die Eisenbahn und fahren nach wohin Sie wollen
> . . . An nichts Dauerndes sind Sie gebunden, an nichts Hem-
> mendes gefangen und an nichts Allzuliebevolles gefesselt und
> angekettet."[24]

Joseph Marti's encounters with Wirsich offer a sequence of
action that forms a counterpart to his relations with Tobler. If
Joseph seems elusive and irresponsible to the Toblers or to Klara,
the friend he visits in the city, he can with justification assume a
protective rôle to the unfortunate Wirsich. When the latter and
his mother have left after their first meeting with Joseph at Toblers', Joseph reflects upon the fatality with which suffering may fall
upon an old woman or a poor child. Although he expects to put
the man and the old woman aside as memories that will soon turn
pale, as most memories do in his vagrant life, chance is to bring
him on two other occasions into contact with the forlorn Wirsich.
Joseph's conviction of the rightness of his caritative assistance to
Wirsich seems to be confirmed by the landscape around him :

> Und dazwischen war es ihm beinahe heilig zumut. Die ganze
> Landschaft schien ihm zu beten, so freundlich, mit all den leisen,
> gedämpften Erdfarben.[25]

Both Silvi, Frau Tobler's neglected child, and Wirsich appeal to
Joseph because they are in distress and unloved; similarly Frau
Weiss, Frau Tobler and Klara feel a need to offer help, sympathy
or advice to Joseph; and Tobler himself, though apparently secure

enough, is ultimately a figure to be loved and pitied. *Der Gehülfe* is a friendly novel, and the support which Joseph gives to Wirsich comes to take a prior place to his assistance of Tobler. The mood of the lake forms a colourful background as the narrative moves from summer to winter, while the decline of the Tobler fortunes is mirrored in the changing weather outside the house.

Although considerably shorter than the two earlier novels and written in diary form, *Jakob von Gunten* is equally distinctive. It has an elusive quality of self-conscious distance from everyday reality that marks it out as contemporary in spirit as well as in time with Rilke's *Malte Laurids Brigge* and the work of Kafka. Seelig has reported Kafka's admiration for this particular work, and Jakob's attitude to the Institut Benjamenta, together with other features of the novel, seems to foreshadow the relationship of Kafka's protagonists to their environment, particularly in *Der Prozeß* and *Das Schloß*. The Institute gives little to its pupils, whose instruction is largely limited to learning by heart regulations and studying a book on the aims of the school. There is only this one lesson, which is repeated indefinitely; it is taken by Fräulein Benjamenta, sister of the principal. Outward decorum is emphasized, and laughter is out of place. One of Jakob's first reactions is indignation at the sleeping quarters offered to him. But he soon comes to accept the lack of furniture in the classroom, to take part willingly in the scrubbing and sweeping operations, to conform with the requirement that all food should be eaten up, to be resigned to unjust punishments and to the elaborate ceremonies during interviews with Benjamenta. The pupils, Jakob comments, are cheerful but without hope. There is a derelict garden to which the pupils are forbidden access, and the "inner rooms" of the principal and his sister are also normally out of bounds. The school is placed in an apartment in a shabby city block. Inside the school complicated regulations are supposed to be followed, but from three o'clock in the afternoon onwards the pupils are left to themselves and are free to explore any part of city life that attracts them. The institution is in fact a training-school for personal servants. Walser spent a short time at such a school in Berlin and for a time tried this form of work; Simon, in *Die Geschwister Tanner,* has an episode as a domestic servant.

Kraus is the pupil whose personality stimulates Jakob most. For much of the time he is patronizing to this youth with the "monkey-like" appearance. Kraus has the temperament that will make for an ideal servant, and sees it as part of his duty to persuade Jakob to accept his point of view on such subjects as willingness to work, the need for contentment and humbleness. Kraus is never bored, and is indignant that Jakob should have such feelings. When Kraus leaves, Jakob feels that a sun has set: "Adieu, Jakob, bessere dich, ändere dich," Kraus advises him, and: "Arbeite mehr, wünsche weniger." Unlike Jakob, Kraus is indifferent to the glitter and bustle of the city. School routine and life outside the school, including the interludes when he is the guest of his artist-brother, offer Jakob neither comfort nor hope, but Kraus' personality gives Jakob a faith that he finds nowhere else:

> . . . dieser ungraziöse Kraus ist schöner als die graziösesten und schönsten Menschen. Er glänzt nicht mit Gaben, aber mit dem Schimmer eines guten und unverdorbenen Herzens, und seine schlechten, schlichten Manieren sind vielleicht trotz alles Hölzernen, das ihnen anhaftet, das Schönste, was es an Bewegung und Manier in der menschlichen Gesellschaft geben kann . . . Ja, man wird Kraus nie achten, und gerade das, daß er, ohne Achtung zu genießen, dahinleben wird, das ist ja das Wundervolle und Planvolle, das An-den-Schöpfer-Mahnende . . . Ich glaube, ich, ich bin einer der ganz wenigen, vielleicht der einzige, oder vielleicht sind es zwei oder drei Menschen, die wissen werden, was sie an Kraus besitzen oder besessen haben.[26]

Jakob's presence at the school is more unexpected than that of Kraus. It is to a considerable extent an act of rebellion against his childhood environment; he has run away from his father and a wealthy home, and does not write to his mother, though he knows that she will be distressed on his account. The presence of his successful elder brother in the city gives him an opportunity of experiencing different circumstances from those of the school, but the link with Johann is less important to him than the relationships within the school. Jakob is here because he has decided to cut himself off from all dependence on his family, to build up his own life without their help; and if he fails, this will be in his eyes more creditable than remaining within the confines and protection of the Guntens. He and his fellow-pupils have as prospects only servitude. If Kraus accepts this contentedly, Jakob is pessimistic about these implications:

> Vielleicht aber besitze ich aristokratische Adern. Ich weiß es nicht. Aber das Eine weiß ich bestimmt: Ich werde eine reizende kugelrunde Null im späteren Leben sein. Ich werde als

alter Mann junge, selbstbewußte, schlecht erzogene Grobiane
bedienen müssen, oder ich werde betteln, oder ich werde
zugrunde gehen.[27]

These are among Jakob's first thoughts in his diary, and he comes
back to them as he approaches its end, when he envisages the possibility of his life collapsing and decides that such a collapse is of
little importance, as his individual personality is a cipher.

Yet the school dominates Jakob. At first he is indignant and
rebellious (hence his first friendship with Schacht), but his hatred of
the Institute gradually changes to fondness and sympathy as he
realizes its precariousness and the need which Benjamenta and his
sister have for his affection and support. Jakob soon comes to
identify himself, in hate and then in love, with the environment he
has chosen. His admiration for Fräulein Benjamenta begins as if
towards a distant being, and when she approaches him alone in the
darkening schoolroom, he realizes that she is in need of his sympathy. Her death is foreshadowed, though when it takes place,
Jakob is surprised at the coldness of his own emotions at this point.
Jakob's relations with Benjamenta undergo a comparable transformation from dislike to friendship. Fairly soon Jakob feels something akin to commiseration for Benjamenta's solitary life. An
important moment in their relationship is the interview in which
Benjamenta, to Jakob's astonishment, confesses his special feelings
for his pupil. Love and hatred alternate for a time; the invitations
become more pressing, until after the death of Fräulein Benjamenta and the departure of Kraus, Jakob agrees to throw in his lot
with Benjamenta, who has hated the world until he found Jakob.
The school has disintegrated into non-existence, and Benjamenta
and Jakob prepare for a new life—that of the wanderer. For a time,
a peculiar setting has satisfied the restless protagonist, as in *Der
Gehülfe,* but here the union between the two antagonists has in
the end been realized, and a strange harmony prevails at the close.
The individual at first seems powerless against the rules which press
upon him, but the forms of society fall away, leaving the personal
relationship with Benjamenta, paradoxical as it is, as the centre
and essence of Jakob's life.

The element of fantasy repeatedly breaks into the narrative of *Jakob
von Gunten.* Soon after his arrival at the Institute Jakob notes:

Weiß Gott, manchmal will mir mein ganzer hiesiger Aufenthalt
wie ein unverständlicher Traum vorkommen.[28]

He dreams once about his mother, and another time creates in his imagination a whole series of teachers who might have held office in the school. He develops fantasies connected with wealth and power, and sees himself as a medieval leader or as a soldier of Napoleon. One of his most elaborate visions is of Fräulein Benjamenta escorting him over unknown regions of the house explaining to him allegories of happiness, poverty, deprivation, care, freedom, quiet and doubt. When he and Kraus are admitted to the "inner rooms", he is disappointed to find no element of wonder or secrecy there. Satirical humour asserts itself again :

> Es sind allerdings Goldfische da, und Kraus und ich müssen das Bassin, in welchem diese Tiere schwimmen und leben, regelmäßig entleeren, säubern und mit frischem Wasser auffüllen. Ist das aber etwas nur entfernt Zauberhaftes? Goldfische können in jeder preußischen mittleren Beamtenfamilie vorkommen, und an Beamtenfamilien klebt nichts Unverständliches und Absonderliches.[29]

His imagination can extend the apartment into a huge building with winding-staircases and a maze of corridors. And Jakob's final decision to go with Benjamenta is foreshadowed by his dream, in the course of which Jakob follows Benjamenta into the desert :

> Es war lächerlich und herrlich zugleich. "Der Kultur entrücken, Jakob. Weißt du, das ist famos," sagte von Zeit zu Zeit der Vorsteher, der wie ein Araber aussah.[30]

The closeness of reality to fantasy, of ridiculousness to magnificence, and the contrast of civilization and solitude, of stability and restlessness, are recurring themes in Walser's work. *Der Gehülfe* is the most normally realistic novel, and *Jakob von Gunten* the most elusive and problematic. The short essays and stories are often prose-poems, and are the literary form to which Walser turned most regularly and spontaneously in the main course of his career as a writer. His work as a poet, finally, may be briefly noted, for here too the proximity in themes and approach to the prose sketches is evident. The collection of *Gedichte,* published in 1909 with illustrations by Karl Walser, contains short lyrics, mostly of consciously unassuming and simple shape and content. Nature, wandering, poverty, fear, solitude and inner quiet are among the themes. "Zu philosophisch" is the title of this poem :

> Wie geisterhaft im Sinken
> und Steigen ist mein Leben.
> Stets seh ich mich mir winken,
> dem Winkenden entschweben.

Ich seh' mich als Gelächter,
als tiefe Trauer wieder,
als wilden Redeflechter;
doch alles dies sinkt nieder.

Und ist zu allen Zeiten
wohl niemals recht gewesen.
Ich bin vergeßne Weiten
zu wandern auserlesen.[31]

Walser's later verse is more rugged and reflective, often with a colloquial directness and a dry quality of language and thought. Carl Seelig records in his postscript to the *Unbekannte Gedichte* how Walser took up lyrical poetry anew in his later years, at the time when he was becoming increasingly aware that his gift of prose-writing was becoming exhausted. "Beten ist ja wie dichten. Jedes Gedicht ist eine Art von Gebet,"[32] he wrote in an essay of 1919 which Seelig quotes. Perhaps the undated poem "Beschaulichkeit" belongs to a late phase of his writing; evidently it looks back rather than forward :

Die Bücher waren alle schon geschrieben,
Die Taten alle scheinbar schon getan.
Alles, was seine schönen Augen sah'n,
Stammte aus früherer Bemühung her.
Die Häuser, Brücken und die Eisenbahn
Hatten etwas durchaus Bemerkenswertes.
Er dachte an den stürmischen Laertes,
An Lohengrin und seinen sanften Schwan,
Und üb'rall war das Hohe schon getan,
Stammte aus längstvergang'nen Zeiten.
Man sah ihn einsam über Felder reiten.
Das Leben lag am Ufer wie ein Kahn,
Das nicht mehr fähig ist zum Schaukeln, Gleiten.[33]

[I should like to express my indebtedness to Herr P. Müller and Dr. M. Schäppi for their help during the writing of this essay.]

TRANSLATIONS

1. To write exactly and definitely about something beautiful is difficult. Thoughts fly around what is beautiful like drunken butterflies, without coming to a destination and a firm point.
2. "O power of the spirit, who could bind you?"

3. Our town is actually more a large, beautiful garden than a town. The streets are garden-paths. They look so clean, and as if strewn with fine sand. Above the roofs of the town rises the mountain with its dark fir-trees and its green foliage. We have the most magnificent parks, including an avenue which is said to date from Napoleon. It is true, I do not believe that he planted the trees with his own hands, for after all he was surely too proud, too powerful for that. In summer the wide, old chestnut-trees provide splendid, refreshing shade. On summer evenings one sees those inhabitants of the town who like to take a walk strolling up and down this avenue. The ladies look particularly beautiful in their bright-coloured dresses. It is a pleasure to go boating on the evening-dark lake. The lake belongs to our town like the church, or as in a monarchy the summer palace of a duke belongs to his town-residence. Without the lake our town would not be our town, indeed, one would not recognize it. Our church, the Protestant one, is situated on an elevated platform that is adorned by two wonderfully beautiful, large chestnut-trees. The windows of the church are painted with the most fiery colours, and this gives it a fairy-like appearance. Often the most delightful part-singing is heard from it. I like to stand outside, when there is singing inside. The women sing most beautifully. Our town hall is dignified, and its large hall serves for balls and other occasions. We even have a theatre. Every winter we are visited for two months by strange actors who have very elegant manners, speak very elegant German and wear top-hats. I am always glad when they come, and do not collaborate with our citizens when they speak contemptuously of the "mob". It may be that they do not pay their debts, that they are insolent, that they get drunk, that they come from bad families, but what are they artists for? One makes generous allowances to an artist for that sort of thing. They act quite splendidly too. I have seen "The Robbers". It is a wonderful play, full of fire and beautiful passages. Is it possible to amuse oneself in a more elegant and a nobler manner than by going to the theatre? Big cities set us the best example in this respect. Our town has much industry, the reason being that it has factories. Factories and their surroundings look ugly. The air there is black and thick, and I do not understand why people can occupy themselves with such unclean things. I don't care about what is made in the factories. I only know that all the poor people work in the factory, perhaps as a punishment for being so poor. We have pretty roads, and everywhere green trees look out between the houses. When it rains the streets are really dirty. In our town little is done for the streets. Father says so. A pity that our house hasn't a garden. We live on the first floor. Our flat is nice, but there ought to be a garden to it. Mama often complains about this. I like the old part of the town best. I like strolling in the old streets, arcades and passages. We have underground passages too. All in all: we have a very pretty town.

4. The morning world spread out before my eyes appeared as beautiful to me as if I saw it for the first time.

5. The highest and the lowest, the most serious and the most hilarious things are to him equally beloved, beautiful and valuable . . . He must at all times be capable of compassion, of sympathy, and of enthusiasm, and it is hoped that he is. He must be able to bow down and sink into the deepest and smallest everyday thing, and it is probable that he can. Faithful, devoted self-effacement and self-surrender among objects, and zealous love for all phenomena and things make him happy in this however . . .

6. . . . he must ask himself: "Where am I?" Earth and heaven suddenly stream together and collide, rocking interlocked one upon the other into a flashing, shimmering, obscure nebular imagery; chaos begins, and the orders vanish. Convulsed, he laboriously tries to retain his normal state of mind . . .

7. Here at the railway-crossing seemed to be the peak, or something like the centre, from which again the gentle declivity would begin.

8. God the Almighty, our merciful Lord, walked down the road, to glorify it and make it divinely beautiful. Imaginings of all sorts, and illusions, made me believe that Jesus Christ was risen again and wandering now in the midst of the people and in the midst of this friendly place. Houses, gardens, and people were transfigured into musical sounds, all that was solid seemed to be transfigured into soul and into gentleness. Sweet veils of silver and soul-haze swam through all things and lay over all things. The soul of the world had opened, and all grief, all human disappointment, all evil, all pain seemed to vanish, from now on never to appear again. Earlier walks came before my eyes; but the wonderful image of the humble present became a feeling which overpowered all others. The future paled, and the past dissolved. I glowed and flowered myself in the glowing, flowering present . . . In the sweet light of love I realized, or believed I realized, that perhaps the inward self is the only self which really exists. (The English passages from *Der Spaziergang* are taken from Christopher Middleton's translation, *The Walk and Other Stories,* by kind permission of John Calder (Publishers) Ltd.

9. "If I could screw myself back to the age of thirty, I would not again write into the blue like a romantic will-o'-the-wisp, eccentric and not caring. It is wrong to deny society. We must live in it, and fight either for or against it. That is the fault of my novels. They are too odd and reflective, often too slack in structure. Not caring about artistic propriety, I simply fired away."

10. "I should have mixed into my books a little love and grief, a little earnestness and applause—a little of the nobly romantic too."

11. The poet must roam, must boldly lose himself, must always venture everything again and again, must hope, may, may only hope . . . I never hoped that I should ever be able to complete anything serious, beautiful and good. The better thought and at the same time the courage to create appeared only slowly, but precisely because of this with all the more

secret splendour from the abysses of lack of self-respect and of frivolous unbelief.—It was like the rising sun. Evening and morning, past and future and the attractive present lay as if at my feet, the land close before me came to life, and I felt as if I could grasp hold of human activities, the whole of human life, with my hands, it looked so alive to me.—One image came after the other, and the ideas played with each other like happy, charming, good children. Full of rapture I clung to the cheerful central thought, and as I just went on writing busily, the connections were established.

12. I have never possessed anything, have never been anything, and in spite of the hopes of my parents shall never be anything.

13. Her parents were not good to her, and so she knew melancholy at an early age, and one day when she was a girl she stood leaning against the railing of a bridge and considered whether it would not be better to jump down into the river. She must have been neglected, pushed about and in this way maltreated. When as a boy I once heard about her youth, my face flushed with anger, I trembled with indignation and from now onwards hated the unknown figures of my grandparents. When she was still in good health mother had for us children something that was almost majestic about her which we feared and of which we fought shy; when she became mentally ill, we pitied her. It was a crazy leap, to have to jump in this way from fearful, secret reverence to pity.

14. I still stand in front of life's door, I knock and knock, it is true with little impetuosity, and I only listen tensely in case someone should come and push back the bolt for me.

15. "What is there in the world that does not pass by. We must create, create, and again create, that is what we are there for, not to pity."

16. "I shall have gambled away my life."

17. "No, no, Simon, nobody will cry on your account. When you are away, you are away. That is all. Do you believe that anyone could cry about you? There is no question of this."

18. At eight o'clock one morning a young man stood at the door of a detached, apparently elegant house. It was raining. "I am almost surprised," the man standing there thought, "that I have an umbrella with me." For in his earlier years he never possessed an umbrella.

19. It was all so gentle, so protected, so light and pretty, it had become so large as small, so near as distant, so far as fine and so delicate as significant. Soon everything that Joseph saw seemed to have become a natural, quiet, friendly dream, not a particularly beautiful one, no, a modest one, and yet one that was so beautiful.

20. Life did not let itself be divided so easily into boxes and orders . . . Ah, life made one bitter, but it could also make one gay and inwardly humble, and thankful for the little that was given, for the little sweet, fresh air to breathe.

21. "Oh yes? You've been in the town? And how did you like it there again after a fairly long absence? Not bad, eh? Indeed, the towns can

offer a great deal, but in the end it is always a pleasure too to come back. Am I right, or not?"

22. How happy Tobler looked! That was just right for him. He seemed to be suited almost uniquely to celebrations and to producing them in fine style.

23. . . . a cave-like thing, lined and decorated with cement, longish in shape like a fairly large oven-hole, rather too low, so that the visitors bumped their heads more than once.

24. "You, Marti, are really in quite a good position, much better than my husband and myself, but I don't want to talk about myself. You can go away from here. You simply pack your few things, sit in the train and travel wherever you like . . . You are not tied to anything permanent, not caught by anything that restrains and not bound and chained to anything that is all too endearing."

25. And in between his mood was almost holy. The whole landscape seemed to him to be praying, in such a friendly fashion, with all the gentle, muted colours of the earth.

26. . . . this ungraceful Kraus is more attractive than the most graceful and attractive of human beings. He does not shine with talents, but with the light of a good, unspoilt heart, and his bad, simple manners are perhaps, in spite of everything that is wooden about them, the most beautiful thing in the way of movement and manner that there can be in human society . . . It is true, Kraus will never be respected, and precisely the fact that he will live out his life without enjoying respect is indeed what is beautiful and purposeful, what reminds us of the Creator . . . I believe that I, I am one of the few, perhaps the only one, or perhaps there are two or three people, who will know what they have, or have had, in Kraus.

27. But perhaps I possess aristocratic blood in my veins. I don't know. But one thing I know definitely: in later life I shall be a charming, spherical cipher. As an old man I shall have to serve young, self-confident, badly brought up louts, or else I shall be a beggar or come to ruin.

28. God knows, sometimes my whole stay here seems to me like an incomprehensible dream.

29. Certainly there are goldfish there, and Kraus and I regularly have to empty the bowl in which these creatures swim and live, and fill it with fresh water. But is that something even distantly magical? One can find goldfish in every Prussian family of the middle official class, and there is nothing incomprehensible and strange about officials' families.

30. It was ridiculous and magnificent at the same time. "To get away from civilization, Jacob. You know, that's grand," said the principal, who looked like an Arab, from time to time.

31. How ghostly is my life as it falls and rises. Always I see myself beckoning to myself and disappearing from the one who beckons.

I see myself as laughter, or again as deep mourning, or as a wild orator; but all this sinks down.

And it has probably never really existed at any time. I have been chosen to wander through forgotten distances.

32. "After all praying is like writing poetry. Every poem is a kind of prayer."

33. The books had all been written, the deeds apparently had all been accomplished. Everything that his fine eyes saw derived from earlier effort. The houses, bridges and railways had something wholly remarkable about them. He thought about stormy Laertes, about Lohengrin and his gentle swan, and everywhere what was great had already been accomplished, and derived from long since forgotten times. He could be seen riding lonely across fields. Life lay on the bank like a boat that is no longer capable of swaying and floating.

SELECT BIBLIOGRAPHY

Fritz Kochers Aufsätze, Leipzig, 1904.

Geschwister Tanner, Berlin, 1907. (Second ed. Zürich, 1933.)

Der Gehülfe, Berlin, 1908.

Jakob von Gunten, Berlin, 1909. (Second ed. Zürich, 1950.)

Gedichte, Berlin, 1909. (Third ed. with preface by Carl Seelig. Basle, 1944.)

Der Spaziergang, Frauenfeld, 1917. (Second ed. Herrliberg-Zürich, 1944.)

Poetenleben, Frauenfeld, 1918.

Die Rose, Berlin, 1925.

Unbekannte Gedichte, ed. with a postscript by Carl Seelig. St. Gallen, 1958.

Dichtungen in Prosa, ed. by Carl Seelig. Geneva. Vol. 1, 1953: *Aufsätze, Kleine Dichtungen.* Vol. 2, 1954: *Unveröffentliche Prosadichtungen.* Vol. 3, 1955: *Der Gehülfe.* Vol. 4, 1959: *Fritz Kochers Aufsätze, Die Rose, Kleine Dichtungen.* Vol. 5, 1961: *Komödie, Geschichten, Der Spaziergang.*

Robert Walser: Kleine Auslese, ed. by Paul Müller, on behalf of the Stiftung Pro Helvetia for the opening of the Walser Memorial, Herisau, Herisau, 1962.

Prosa, ed. by Walter Höllerer, Frankfurt am Main, 1960.

The Walk and Other Stories, translated by Christopher Middleton, London, 1957.

Hans Bänziger, *Heimat und Fremde. Ein Kapitel "Tragische Literaturgeschichte" in der Schweiz: Jakob Schaffner, Robert Walser, Albin Zollinger,* Berne, 1958.

Karl Joachim Wilhelm Greven, *Existenz, Welt und reines Sein im Werk Robert Walsers,* Diss. Cologne, 1960.

Robert Maechler, *Das Leben Robert Walsers. Eine dokumentarische Biographie*, Geneva/Hamburg, 1966.

Christopher Middleton, "The Picture of Nobody. Some Remarks on Robert Walser with a Note on Walser and Kafka", *Revue des langues vivantes*, Vol. 24, Brussels, 1958, pp. 404–28.

Paul Müller, "Aufbruch, Einfahrt, Zerfall. Bemerkungen zu Robert Walsers Prosa", *Neue Zürcher Zeitung*, June 17, 1962.

Carl Seelig, *Wanderungen mit Robert Walser*, St. Gallen, 1957.

Albert Soergel and Curt Hohoff, *Dichtung und Dichter der Zeit*, Vol. 1, Düsseldorf, 1961, pp. 815–28.

Otto Zinniker, *Robert Walser der Poet*, Zürich, 1947.

"A Miniaturist in Prose", *Times Literary Supplement*, July 21, 1961.

The above essay was first published in 1963. After the death of Carl Seelig, editor of the *Dichtungen in Prosa*, Jochen Greven undertook the preparation of a new edition of Robert Walser's work. The plan of this edition is:

Das Gesamtwerk. Vollständige Ausgabe in zwölf Einzelbänden. Geneva and Hamburg. Vol. 1: *Fritz Kochers Aufsätze, Geschichten, Aufsätze.* Vol. 2: *Kleine Dichtungen, Prosastücke, Kleine Prosa.* Vol. 3: *Poetenleben, Seeland, Die Rose.* Vol. 4: *Geschwister Tanner, Jakob von Gunten.* Vol. 5: *Der Gehülfe.* Vol. 6: *Phantasieren—Prosa aus der Berliner und Bieler Zeit.* Vol. 7: *Festzug—Prosa aus der Bieler und Berner Zeit.* Vol. 8: *Olympia—Prosa aus der Berner Zeit* (1). Vol. 9: *Maskerade—Prosa aus der Berner Zeit* (II). Vol. 10: *Der Europäer—Prosa aus der Berner Zeit* (III). Vol. 11: *Versdichtungen und Dramoletts.* Vol. 12: *Briefe und verschiedene Schriften.*

The editor explains in his "Nachwort" to vol. 6 (1966) the way in which he has collected and edited, for vols. 6–10, those prose pieces which were not published in book form in Walser's life-time. These include work published in periodicals or newspapers as well as hitherto unpublished items. The extent of this material, that is only becoming generally accessible with the publication of these later volumes of the *Gesamtwerk*, is very considerable.

A full-length study of Walser is now available in English: George C. Avery, *Inquiry and Testament. A Study of the Novels and Short Prose of Robert Walser*, Philadelphia, 1968.

Max Frisch

Max Frisch

by MARTIN ESSLIN

Max Frisch was born in Zürich on May 15, 1911. His grand-father on the paternal side had come to Switzerland from Austria; he was a saddler. On the mother's side his great-grandfather had come to Zürich from Württemberg; his name was Wildermuth and he was director of the city's Arts and Crafts School. After two years of reading German and Philosophy at the University of Zürich, the death of his father, who was an architect, compelled him to start earning a living. So, at twenty-two he became a journalist. As a freelance reporter he travelled widely in Eastern Europe. Having written a first novel, he was, at the age of twenty-five, enabled by the generosity of a friend, who undertook to support him for four years, to resume his studies. He decided to become an architect and gained his diploma at the Eidgenoessische Technische Hochschule (ETH) at Zürich. While still studying he was called up at the outbreak of the Second World War and spent some time guarding the frontiers of his native country to protect its neutrality. After the fall of France he was able to get back to work, completed his studies and married. In 1943 a novel, *J'adore ce me brûle oder die Schwierigen*, appeared and had a favourable reception from some of the critics. Among the reactions was a letter from Kurt Hirschfeld, then the *Dramaturg* of the Zürich Schauspielhaus, suggesting that he might try his hand at writing a play. At about the same time Frisch won an architectural competition for a public building—the Municipal Swimming Baths at Letzigraben in Zürich—and was enabled to open his own office as an architect. This in turn gave him the freedom to arrange his own time and to devote more time to writing. In 1947–8 Frisch befriended Bertolt Brecht who had temporarily settled near Zürich after his return from the United States and before he decided to go to East Berlin. Frisch has travelled widely : in 1951–2 he spent a considerable time in the United States and Mexico. After attaining fame as a writer he gave up his architect's practice.

WHEN German civilization collapsed in 1933—and it is a matter for argument whether the rise of Hitler was the cause of this collapse or merely its chief symptom—only one German-speaking area of Europe remained untouched by this calamity : German Switzerland. It is therefore no coincidence that some of the best writers now active in the German language are Swiss—members of that very generation which has remained totally sterile in Germany itself, the generation born between 1910 and 1920 whose formative years fell into the Nazi period. Among these Swiss writers, two, Friedrich Dürrenmatt and Max Frisch, have attained world fame.

Dürrenmatt is the scion of an old Bernese patrician family, Frisch the grandson of an Austrian immigrant. Yet it has rightly been pointed out that this makes Frisch the more typically Swiss; a higher percentage of present-day German Swiss citizens have an ancestry like Frisch. While Dürrenmatt comes from a family of statesmen, professors and parsons, Frisch has a background of artisans and "artists". He himself has described the artistic pretentions of his maternal great-grandfather, who "called himself a painter, wore a considerable cravat which was much bolder than his drawings and paintings . . . My mother, to see the great wide world, once worked as a governess in Czarist Russia; she has often told us about it. My father was an architect. Being the son of a saddler he had not been able to afford a professional education and so it was his ambition to see his sons as university graduates."[1] So Frisch has the more artistic background, yet he has striven much harder than Dürrenmatt to find a place in his society : as an architect he is a technologist and a very typical embodiment of our contemporary world, a world where construction and production play so decisive a part. In discussing his position with one foot in the camp of literature, the other in the camp of scientific technology, Frisch clearly reveals that he sympathises with some of the men he worked with who considered his writing as a somewhat crazy aberration : "Having a dual profession as a writer and as an architect is, of course, not always easy, however many fruitful effects it may have. It is not so much a question of time as of strength. I find it a blessing to work every day with men who have nothing to do with literature; some of them may know that I write, but they don't hold it against me so long as my other work is all right."[2]

And yet for Frisch writing has always been a necessity, an almost compulsory activity, an effort at self-exploration. In a brief note, headed *About Writing,* in his published diary he gives a fascinating and ruthlessly sincere insight into the motives of his work as a writer: "Years ago, in my capacity as an architect, I once visited one of those factories where our glorious watches are being made; my impression was more shattering than any I have ever received in a factory; and yet I have never succeeded in conversation to reproduce this experience, one of the strongest of my life, in such a way that it was relived by my interlocutor. Once it has been talked about, this experience always remains trivial or unreal, real only for the one who went through it, incommunicable like any personal experience—or rather: every experience remains basically incommunicable so long as we hope to express it through the real example that actually happened to us. Real expression can be found for me only through an example that is as far removed from my own self as from that of the person listening: that is, the fictional example. Communication is essentially possible only through the fictitious, transformed, reshaped instance; and that is also why artistic failure is always accompanied by a feeling of suffocating loneliness."[3]

Frisch has enabled us to follow the process of transformation of his experience into fiction through a series of autobiographical writings, mainly journals and diaries, which are among the most remarkable writers' notebooks of our time. *Blätter aus dem Brotsack* (1940) is his diary of military service at the outbreak of the war; *Tagebuch mit Marion* (1947) was later reprinted in the wider *Tagebuch 1946–49.*

His first novel *Jürg Reinhart* which deals with a young man's attainment of maturity during a trip to Dalmatia, has clearly autobiographical character. (Frisch travelled in south-eastern Europe before the war as a freelance journalist.) The delightful novella *Bin oder die Reise nach Peking* which describes the lyrical musings of a young man who holds long conversations with Bin, his alter ego or second romantic self, on an imaginary journey to Peking, the ever unattainable goal of the German romantic tradition, also barely rises above the level of autobiographical statement. In Frisch's later plays and novels the transmutation of the material into truly fictional terms is far more complete, but the basic connection with the author's quest for his own self nevertheless always remains clear.

Frisch's origin and background account for some of the main themes of his writings: to be Swiss means to be a citizen of a relatively small, self-governing community with its inevitably petty

local politics that tend to loom very large in the foreground even
in times of world upheaval; the sensitive, artistic temperament tends
to react against this by a violent yearning for the great, wide
world : Frisch spent his *Wanderjahre* as a journalist in south-
eastern Europe before the war, he has since travelled widely in the
United States and Europe : the yearning for exotic climes,
romantic distant islands is a recurring theme in his plays and
novels; and so is scorn against the narrowness and pettiness, the
complacency and arrogance of a small, self-contained community
which feels itself free from the taints and crimes of other, less
fortunate countries. For to be Swiss also means to be the citizen of
a country that has escaped two world wars. *Andorra,* Frisch's
most widely performed play, is among other things, an attack on
this Swiss complacency. Andorra in the play is a small, mountain
country, proud of its freedom, proud of being better and morally
superior; convinced that this moral superiority makes it immune to
any foreign attack : "As Perin, our great poet once said : Our
weapon is our innocence. Or the other way round : our innocence
is our weapon. Where else in the world is there a republic that can
say this? I ask you : where? A nation like ourselves who as no
other can appeal to the conscience of the world, a people without
guilt . . . Andorrans I tell you : no nation on earth has ever been
attacked without someone having been able to reproach them with
a crime. What can they reproach us with? The only thing that
could happen to Andorra, would be an injustice, a gross and open
injustice. And that they will not dare. Tomorrow even less than
yesterday. Because the whole world would defend us. At one fell
swoop. Because the conscience of the world is on our side."[4]
And yet Andorra is attacked, and the Andorrans sacrifice young
Andri, whom they believe to be a Jew, to the anti-Semitic in-
vaders. They have prided themselves on being free from the sins
of those powerful neighbours, but they have carried the seeds of the
same moral corruption within themselves all the time. They have
been free from the crimes that great powers become guilty of, only
because being a small power they have never exercised any responsibility, they have never taken an active part in history; their
innocence springs from their insignificance, from their pettiness,
from their provincialism, from their bourgeois respectability. One
of the impulses behind Frisch's writing is the passionate resolve *not*
to feel himself free from the guilt and responsibilities of his age, to
detect within himself the seeds of the crimes that sully the record
of the great powers : in the plays *Nun singen sie wieder* (1945) and

Als der Krieg zu Ende war (1949) as well as in *Andorra* (1961) he comes to grips with the problem of the extermination of the Jews; in *Die chinesische Mauer* (1946) the problem of the atom bomb is boldly confronted : "The flood can now be manufactured by man !" And the young poet, the "contemporary man" (and thus undoubtedly an image of the author himself) who has come to inform the Emperor of China and all the great figures of history of this fact reveals himself as not only unable to act to defend the suffering people; having delivered an impassioned plea against the bomb, having uttered a terrible warning to the Emperor, he is awarded a prize for fiction and ignored. Because he is helpless to change the course of history the poet, the intellectual, who knows the horrors to come and cannot act effectively, shares in the final guilt.

To be Swiss also means having been brought up to an ideal of bourgeois rectitude, to have lived in a small community where neighbours know each other only too well and where one has to do one's utmost to maintain a façade of strict, puritanical respectability. This respectability is merely another aspect of the features of Swiss life against which a sensitive, artistic personality like Frisch is bound to react strongly : the narrowness of local politics, the righteous complacency of guiltless and petty neutrality it will appear to such an individual as a refusal to face the world and human life as they really are, an escape from responsibility, from guilt, from temptation—and therefore from life itself. For such respectability is bought at a terrible price : by running away from any valid experience, by hiding behind barriers of timidity and moral cowardice.

This is one of the main themes of *Biedermann und die Brandstifter* (1957–8) (known in England as *The Fireraisers* and in the United States as *The Firebugs*). Biedermann (in German the name is also a generic term for a complacent, respectable citizen, a *faux bonhomme*) is a ruthless businessman, he has just driven an exploited employee to suicide; yet he prides himself on the fact that his daily life is amiable, well-ordered, superficially that of a "good man". And that is why he cannot believe that the two sinister characters who have infiltrated themselves into his house can really be plotting to use the drums of petrol and the bales of inflammable stuff they are hoarding in the attic to burn down Mr. Biedermann's respectable house, and the whole respectable city he inhabits. For, after all, Biedermann manages to be on friendly conversational terms with them, he has invited them to dinner even, that shows that he is human, friendly, benevolent, free from guilt and therefore he cannot, he will not be attacked (exactly as the citizens of Andorra are convinced that nobody can attack them because they are innocent of ever having furnished good reason to be attacked). And so he even offers the incendiaries the match with which they will blow up his world. His false values, the in-authentic life and the lack of awareness, of consciousness they entail, lead Biedermann directly to destruction.

The Fireraisers also has a direct political implication, quite different incidentally from that imposed upon it by a number of performances in Britain, notably Lindsay Anderson's production at the *Royal Court*. Far from being a play about the atomic bomb which we are having in our attic and which will blow up our world, *The Fireraisers* deals—or dealt originally—with the Western world's inability to see through Communist tactics of infiltration. In Frisch's published diary for 1946–9 the idea of Biedermann is noted immediately after the entry about his consternation at the Communist take-over in Czechoslovakia. "Worries about our friends. And to all this the glee of my acquaintances towards whom I have always presented Czechoslovakia as an example of a Socialist democracy; and all this topped by the general conceit: such a thing could not happen here!" These words are clearly the germ of the idea . . . Only if the fireraisers can be seen as revolutionaries threatening the bourgeois world will the play make sense. And it is significant that the other interpretation which will fit the play and at which Frisch hints in the Epilogue in Hell that he added after the success of the original radio version refers to the inability of the German bourgeoisie to see the rise of Hitler in its true significance. Frisch despises the bourgeois precisely because having forced himself into the image of *bonhomie* (which is a lie for it is merely a mask for the cruelties of a system based on exploitation, merely a refusal to see the obvious hardships and sufferings of our world), having suppressed the spontaneous human reactions by a dry, heartless and calculating respectability, he has become incapable even of defending the values on which his well-being is founded.

How is one to react against bourgeois respectability and its dangers? The conventional reaction is to fall into Bohemianism, to flaunt one's defiance of respectable values. Swiss cities like Zürich have their own brand of Bohemian, artistic communities. And Frisch certainly frequented this world in his youth. But if anything these small enclaves of Bohemianism are even narrower than the

narrow bourgeois world they defy. Hence the Swiss nostalgia for
the romantic, the exotic and the far off. In Frisch's earliest published play *Santa Cruz* (1944) everything revolves round the conflict between the respectable and narrow circle of everyday lives,
and the mysterious pull of distant and exotic lands. The Cavalry
Captain and his wife Elvira have lived together in a humdrum
marriage for seventeen years. And all that time Elvira has been
dreaming of the vagabond whom she once loved and who may be
the father of her daughter; and all that time the Captain has been
dreaming of the friend with whom he once planned to roam the
world and to visit the Southern Seas. Pelegrin the vagabond comes
to visit them, as he is about to die, and the ageing couple recognize
that they have been dreaming of the same man, the same romantic
ideal. But they also recognize that the real flaw of their lives was
that each concealed his secret longing from the other. It is not the
escape to remote romantic islands that is the solution, but the
courage to be oneself and the courage to love. This question, the
problem of identity, the problem of how man can find his true self,
an authentic existence, is the central pivot around which most of
Frisch's work revolves. It is also the main problem of existential
philosophy and although there is no evidence that Frisch has ever
been preoccupied with the work of writers like Camus and Sartre,
his approach to it coincides with many of their ideas. For Frisch
is above all appalled by the influence that the opinions of other
people have on our own identity : "Some fixed opinion of our
friends, our parents, our teachers . . . may weigh upon us like an
ancient oracle. Half a lifetime may be blighted by the secret
question : will it come true or will it not come true . . . A teacher
once said to my mother she would never learn how to knit. My
mother often told us about this assertion; she never forgot, never
forgave it; she became a passionate, extraordinarily skilful knitter;
and all the stockings and knitted caps, all the gloves and pullovers
I ever received, in the end I owe them to that objectionable
oracle . . . ! To a certain extent we really are what others see in
us, friends as well as enemies. And the other way round : we too
are the *authors* of the others; in a mysterious and inescapable way
we are responsible for the face they show us . . ."[5] We create the
others in the image we make ourselves of them. And this for
Frisch is the ultimate sin, the extinction of their authentic existence,
the origin of all the troubles of our time. For the image that we
thus make is a fixed, a dead thing, an imposition that can kill. If
thus "being-for-others" by fixing an image reduces human freedom,

love that accepts a human personality as "being-for-itself" creates
freedom : "Love frees from all images. That is the exciting, the
adventurous, the truly suspenseful thing about love, that with
those human beings we love we never reach an end : because we
love them; as long as we love them. Listen to the poets when they
are in love : they search for similes, as though they were drunk,
they grasp for all the things in the universe, flowers, animals,
clouds, stars, and oceans. Why? Just as the universe, God's inexhaustible spaciousness, is boundless, so boundless, pregnant with
all possibilities, all mysteries, unfathomable is the human being we
love . . . If we think we know the other, that is the end of love,
everytime; but perhaps cause and effect are reversed . . . not
because we know the other person is our love coming to an end,
but the other way round : because our love is at an end, because
its strength is exhausted, we have finished with the other person . . .
We deny him the claim of all living things, which must remain
unfathomable, and at the same time we are astonished and disappointed that our relationship is no longer alive. 'You are not', says
the disappointed man or woman, 'what I took you to be.' And what
did one take the other for? A mystery, that man, after all, is, an
exciting riddle we have become tired of. Now we make ourself an
image. That is the loss of love, the betrayal."[6] This beautiful
passage in Frisch's published diaries for the years 1946–9, the most
fruitful, formulative period of his creative life, certainly is the key
to a great deal of his subsequent work. It defines the subject of his
great novel *Stiller* (English title : *I'm not Stiller*) (1954) and of a
number of his most interesting plays.

Anatol Ludwig Stiller, a successful sculptor at Zürich had disappeared without a trace for more than six years when a man
resembling him in all particulars was picked up at the Swiss frontier because his passport, made out in the name of White, was
obviously not in order. Is the stranger Stiller? He refuses to
acknowledge his identity, any identity, and the bulk of the novel is
taken up by this unidentified man's diaries in prison. He denies
that he is Stiller and yet in the end he has to accept that he is
Stiller. He wanted to escape from the image that was constricting
him, but the world with all its powers of official and sentimental
pressure through his wife, family and friends effectively puts a stop
to any such attempts. Seen from one angle the hero of the novel is
a clinical case of split personality, seen from another he is a human
being trying to assert his uniqueness, his freedom to choose himself
(in Sartre's sense); and, moreover, he is also a legendary hero, a

Rip Van Winkle, who returns to his former surroundings as a changed man. (Frisch has written a radio play on the theme of *Stiller* which has the title *Rip van Winkle*.)

As a novel *Stiller* is a remarkable *tour de force*. We are made to witness the gradual rediscovery of his self by a man who has rejected not only the world's former image of his personality, but his own image of himself. And at the end we feel with him that, although he must bow to the overwhelming evidence of his physical identity with Stiller, mentally and spiritually he remains as unconvinced as ever. He returns to his image as we slip back into an old suit we had discarded; the self the world imposes on Stiller is an alien, dead thing. He tried to discard his former self because he felt himself a failure as an artist and as a husband. Now he is pushed back into these roles and again he therefore must end up as a failure.

And yet, perhaps, Stiller's failure is an even deeper one: he refused to accept the image of himself that society imposed on him, but he also could not make up his mind to be himself. As Stiller's wife lies dying, the public prosecutor, who conducted the case and later became Stiller's friend, tries to sum up the lesson of his life: "As far as I know your life, you have again and again thrown everything away because you have been uncertain of yourself. You are not the truth. You are a human being and you have often been ready to abandon an untruth to be uncertain. What else does this mean, Stiller, but that you do believe in a truth? A truth, that is, which we cannot alter and which we cannot even kill—which is life itself . . . Again and again you have tried to accept yourself without accepting something like God. And that has turned out to be impossible. He is the power that can help you to accept yourself truly. All this you have experienced! And in spite of it you say that you cannot pray . . . you cling to your own powerlessness which you take for your personality; and yet you know your own powerlessness so well—and all this as though from stubbornness, only because you yourself are not the power . . ."[7] Stiller himself makes no comment on these observations and the question remains open. We merely learn that Stiller's return to his wife, the renewal of his failed marriage, in the end killed the woman he loved and that after that he lived on as a broken man. And yet Stiller, who refuses the world's image of himself, who is unable to accept his own image of himself, is, and this is the subtlest turn in the labyrinthine complexity of this brilliantly conceived novel, himself a maker of images, a sculptor: "Whether there is not something inhuman in the mere attempt to make a picture of a living human being, that is a big question. It essentially concerns Stiller", says the public prosecutor in his commentary that forms the final part of the book. Thus Stiller stands for the artist in general—and for his own creator, who, as a playwright and novelist, has also embarked on the dangerous and perhaps deadly pursuit of making images of human beings.

Stiller is a deeply serious, searching and philosophical work. In a lighter and more ironical vein Frisch has dealt with the same subject in the play *Don Juan oder die Liebe zur Geometrie* (1953) which was written almost at the same time. Don Juan is here shown as a man whose ruthless determination to be true to himself creates a wholly false image. Far from being a seducer or voluptuary, he really is only interested in geometry. Betrothed to Donna Anna, and truly in love with her, he refuses to pronounce the marriage vows merely because he feels himself morally unable to pledge his future conduct so far ahead, for after all we can only know what our present self intends, never what may be the sincere feelings of our future selves. Having killed Donna Anna's father and having acquired the reputation of a wicked voluptuary as a result, he is so much sought after by the ladies that he finally decides to end it all by staging his own death in the most gruesome circumstances : the arrival of the dead Governor's statue and the swallowing up of Don Juan by the mouth of hell are elaborately stage-managed at his own expense in the presence of a multitude of his mistresses. It seems as though Don Juan, now believed to be in hell, could safely start a new life (just like Stiller after he had shed his old self) and devote himself to his true love, geometrical research. But one of the ladies who loves Don Juan knows his secret and so she can blackmail him into a life at her side—marriage and domesticity. This is boring and irritating, but at least Don Juan *has* shed his former image. But no—as the play ends a visitor arrives with a book, the newly published comedy about Don Juan, the seducer of Seville. The image has become immortal and will outlive the real Don Juan.

But the problem of man's identity has other facets as well : it is not merely a question of the image that the outside world imposes on us. It is also one of which of the multitudinous potentialities in ourselves is our real self. Are we what we appear to be in our self-controlled, conscious waking hours; or are we the wild wishes and violent desires of our dreams. In *Graf Oederland* (first version 1951, third and final version 1961) Frisch approaches this problem

in a play which is probably his most intriguing virtuoso performance. An official of the utmost respectability, a public prosecutor,
one day finds that he is identifying himself with the murderer
whose trial he has been conducting in court—a humdrum little
man who killed without motive, merely because he could not en-
dure the deadly routine of a pointless existence. The public prosecutor helps the murderer to escape, takes to the woods, becomes
the leader of a revolutionary force of outlaws which overthrows the
legal government and thus the dictator of his country. Having
entered the capital at the head of his victorious forces he returns to
his own house and finds himself there in exactly the same position
and situation as at the moment when the whole fantastic sequence
of events began. In a flash, and greatly relieved, he realises that it
has all been a nightmare, the wild fantasy of a man dreaming by
the fireside at the end of a hard day in court. The public prosecutor, and the audience with him, can now see the whole violent
sequence of events in all its extravagant improbability. Of course,
it *was* all a dream! But then the maid asks: "Do you want me to
take off your muddy boots?" And the public prosecutor looks at his
boots: the nightmare was reality after all. It was *not* a dream. Or
is it merely part of the nightmare that we ask ourselves whether
we are dreaming and still are so deeply immersed in the dream
that we must answer that it is reality after all . . .? Frisch has here
brilliantly succeeded in putting a most elusive human situation on
the stage: the situation when we are going through some terrible
event and hope it is a dream, or when we are dreaming and are
hoping it is a dream and yet cannot but accept the dream as real.
But beyond the mere virtuosity of recreating such a highly ambi-
valent psychological state, Frisch here says something very important: namely, that dream or not, each human being really *is* what
his hidden desires represent, as much as he really *is* the well-
behaved and respectable shell that he presents to the outside world.
The public prosecutor followed *his* real desires when he became an
outlaw and it is therefore relatively irrelevant whether at the end
of the play it all turns out to have been a fantasy or whether it all
really happened; the violence was potentially present from the very
beginning.

The public prosecutor's nightmare adventure merges into myth,
the myth of Count Oederland, a fairy-tale figure that has been
haunting the public prosecutor. And indeed our subconscious wishes
and fantasies are closely akin to myth, in which the archetypal
fears and desires of human beings have found lasting form. In the

novel *Homo Faber* (1957) Frisch has attempted another *tour de force*—to create an ancient myth in the terms of our technological age. Walter Faber, the hero of this tale, which Frisch has sub-titled "A Report", is a technologist, an engineer. But he is also a modern Oedipus, a man fated to become the bridegroom of his own daughter. The role of the blind fate which drove Oedipus into guilt in the Greek myth is here played by the pitiless, impersonal directing force of our own lives : the workings of our mechanical civilization. Faber's fate is shaped by engine failures of aircraft, by a slight defect in his electric razor : if a bit of nylon thread had not stopped the razor he would not have been at home when the ship-ping line phoned to confirm his booking and would not have been able to take the boat on which he met the girl with whom he fell in love and who later turned out to be his own daughter. The engineer who prides himself on controlling machines is constantly controlled by the whims of minute pieces of machinery. And what is more : the further we are removed from the true sources of human feeling, the more isolated we seem from the raw, primeval workings of humanity, the more certainly we are thrown back into the primeval human situation—subjected to the blind workings of an impersonal fate, involved in monstrous guilts. The image of Auschwitz in which technological man could be seen as merely a more monstrous, because more powerful, repetition of the Stone-Age savage, stands behind the subtle and delicate imagery of *Homo Faber*.

In *Andorra* Frisch returned to the problem of human identity, but he put it against the background of this terrible guilt of our age. The play is about anti-Semitism, but it also deals with the existential situation of man as the product of the opinions of his neighbours. Andri, the hero of the play, is the illegitimate son of an Andorran schoolmaster and a woman from beyond the borders of Andorra, 'the country of the Blacks'. Ashamed to confess his transgression to his wife the schoolmaster has taken the boy into his home by pretending that he is a Jewish orphan, a victim of the anti-Semitic excesses of the Blacks. The schoolmaster is an idealist who wants to teach his countrymen a lesson about racialism. When the boy is grown up and generally accepted as a Jew he will reveal that he is his own son and no Jew and this will prove the fallacy of all racial prejudices and theories.

But Andri is not only regarded as a Jew; being looked at as a Jew imposes on him the patterns of Jewish character. The car-penter to whom he is apprenticed, for example, simply will not

believe that he likes making furniture; he forces him to become a
salesman because that suits his Jewish talent. Andri has fallen in
love with Barblin, the schoolmaster's daughter. When he asks his
"fosterfather" for her hand, he meets a horrified refusal—and he
is convinced that this is due to his Jewishness. When the schoolmaster tells him the real reason he simply cannot accept it. Having
been seen as a Jew by the others, he has now *become* a Jew and
cannot but *be* a Jew. And so he goes to his death as a Jew when
the Blacks invade Andorra and demand a scapegoat for the
murder of a Black woman (who is none other than Andri's own
mother) at the hands of the xenophobic Andorrans. The image we
have made for ourselves has killed the real human being, and now
we kill the image *and* the man who bears it.

Andorra tells the story of Andri in retrospect. Each scene is pre-
faced by the self-justification of one of "the others" from a witness
box—or is it a dock?—at the side of the stage. None of us want to
have been responsible afterwards, when the consequences of our
thoughtless actions have resulted in tragedy. *Andorra* not only became a major success in the theatre in the German-speaking world
and elsewhere (it was the first contemporary foreign play to reach
the stage of Britain's new National Theatre in 1964), it also headed
the best-seller lists of books in Germany for a considerable period.

Frisch's next work, the novel *Mein Name sei Gantenbein* (1964)
also became an almost immediate best-seller.

Here Frisch pushes his preoccupation with identity a step
further: the novel consists of the unnamed narrator *imagining*
himself in a number of different identities—Enderlin, a scholar
who has an affair with a woman he casually meets in a foreign
city; Svoboda, that woman's betrayed husband; Gantenbein, a
man who undergoes an eye operation and, when the bandage is
taken off pretends that he has become blind although his sight
has returned, and later marries a successful actress whose infidelities
he delights in observing as she neglects to conceal the evidence
from her "blind" husband. We never learn who the narrator
actually is, but gradually the impression builds up that he must
himself be a betrayed husband obsessed by variations on the theme
of his predicament. The scenes of love-making, adultery and its
concealment are so vividly imagined in such meticulously convincing detail, that the reader tends to forget that he is merely
following the daydreams of the narrator and is repeatedly brought
to confront this fact with a jolt. Images of incurable sickness
and suicide, the melancholy dissolution of a household, the empty

apartment, the loneliness of an abandoned spouse are interwoven like the musical strands of a symphonic poem. It all adds up to a kind of "alienation effect"—a subtly intriguing puzzle which each reader is free to try to solve in the manner most congenial to his own personality, his own mood. Yet, again, what it all adds up to is the impossibility of escaping the identity which the world, the environment, the blind chance of life, the "others" impose upon the individual. The Gantenbein-character of the narrator's imagination seems to come nearest to an escape—but only at the cost of maintaining the fiction of his own blindness, that is, by insisting that he does not notice, by refusing to accept that he is what he is, namely a cuckold. The title of the book "Let my name be Gantenbein" seems to express the narrator's *desire* to attain to this happy state of affairs, which could enable him to live with the woman he loves without having to act out the consequences of his position as a cuckolded husband. But the inference from the mood of the book must be that the narrator has, in fact, found it impossible to carry this out. But then, the detailed image of a suicide's body slowly drifting down the river through Zurich, also turns out an unattainable dream of wish-fulfilment, and the novel ends with the narrator emerging from his musings with the recognition that "it is all as though it had never happened" and an acceptance of life as something which "pleases me". So, at the end, it seems, the narrator, having imagined the painful situation in all possible variations, has, by his imagination, healed his wound and emerged from his experience scarred but healed.

Mein Name sei Gantenbein is an impressive achievement, yet, in the light of Frisch's subsequent work, the play *Biografie. Ein Spiel* (1967. Biography. A Game. Ein Spiel could also merely mean : A Play. But Frisch has insisted that the subtitle is more than just a generic description and that it must be seen as a definition of the play as a party game) the novel merely seems like a preliminary experimentation for the far more elegant, lucid and satisfying dramatic work.

The "game" of the title derives from a remark made by Verchinin in Chekhov's *Three Sisters* : "I often think how it would be if one could live one's life once again, in full knowledge of the facts. How it would be, if the life one has lived through, were, so to say, merely the first draft, of which one's second attempt at life would be the clean copy. Each of us would then, I feel, try, above all, not to repeat himself . . . If I were to start my life again, I should not get married . . . no, no."

The hero Kürmann (which, in German, means the man who has a choice) is in fact given this chance by a character called "Registrator" (i.e. the recorder of his fate). Kürmann's marriage to a young intellectual woman, Antoinette, has turned out disastrously. The "Registrator" is giving him a completely free hand to re-live any situation he chooses in such a way as to *avoid* the disastrous course events have taken. But, try as he may, Kürmann cannot escape his fate—marriage to and painful betrayal by Antoinette. In the course of the play it gradually emerges that we are in fact inside Kürmann's own mind, while Kürmann lies in hospital dying from cancer. Finally, when all attempts on Kürmann's part have failed to change the course of events which followed the night when Antoinette remained behind after a party in Kürmann's flat and had to spend the night there, the "Registrator" reverses the situation and gives Antoinette the free choice. She merely decides not to stay and leaves. If *that* happened, Kürmann *would* have been free. But—would that have made that much difference, in view of the fact that he was destined to die of cancer seven years later. The play's last words are the "Registrator's" : "You are free—for seven years. . . ." The inference is clear : what would it have mattered in the end, in the face of the inevitability of death?

Biografie, however, is by no means a painful or tragic play. It is, as the subtitle implies, above all a *game,* a lightheartedly ironical examination of the hero's life and its turning-points. Again and again Kürmann returns to that fateful chance meeting with an unknown woman, the coincidence that brought them together and transformed their life. And it is clearly shown that, in fact, the development was wellnigh inevitable, that Kürmann's own character is his fate, that even with a different constellation of coincidences he would have involved himself merely in another set of equally unfortunate circumstances (his first marriage is shown to have gone wrong through his own passivity and weakness).

So light is Frisch's touch in this play, so great was its success with the public that the more intellectual critics were tempted to dismiss it as a purely commercial product, a "boulevard play". This, surely, is a form of snobbery, contempt for success merely as a symptom of vulgarity. *Biografie* is a play of considerable insight and profundity, a subtle and only seemingly effortless distillation of the experience so painfully outlined in *Mein Name sei Gantenbein.*

Biografie continues the fluid argumentative style of plays like

Die Chinesische Mauer or *Nun Singen sie Wieder* which shows the influence of Thornton Wilder, whose *By the Skin of our Teeth* made such a tremendous impact when it was staged in Zürich towards the end of the war. But it also contains a good deal of Pirandello in its exploration of what might have been, the interaction of destiny and coincidence. *Andorra* with its rigidly didactic stance and its trial structure shows the impact of Brecht, with whom Frisch had been linked by close ties of friendship during Brecht's stay in Zürich after his return to Europe from the United States and before his decision to settle in East Berlin (1947–9). Frisch has left an unforgettable pen picture of Brecht at this period in his published diaries. But in spite of his admiration for Brecht as a man, an artist and a champion of his political cause, Frisch did not follow him slavishly in his writing or in his stance as a public figure. In recent years he has increasingly taken part in the controversies of the day : notably in his polite but firm stand for modern literature in the debate provoked by a violent attack on the sordidness and lack of moral fibre of contemporary writers from the most revered traditional literary critic of Switzerland, Emil Staiger, which aroused a storm of protest and counter-protest in 1966. Although decidedly a man of the left, Frisch repudiates Stalinism and neo-Stalinism; he wrote the postscript to the German-language publication of Andrei Sakharov's important memorandum on "Progress, Coexistence and Intellectual Freedom" —the daring attempt of a Soviet scientist to draw the attention of his leaders to the dangers of the degeneration of Soviet society into a rigid, Byzantine, conservative totalitarianism.

It is this ability to remain flexible and undogmatic which gives Frisch his irony in tackling a myth like the Don Juan legend in the spirit of Cocteau, Giraudoux or Shaw. Frisch's existentialism also owes more to Kierkegaard than to the French or German schools of our own time. And it is in this easy mingling of European traditions that Frisch's essentially Swiss character emerges; indeed, in his preoccupation with the need for self-realization he shows the influence of the great Swiss novelist of the nineteenth century, Gottfried Keller, and his masterpiece *Der Grüne Heinrich*.

But however eclectic Frisch might appear if he is thus summed up in terms of literary models and influences, he is, basically, a highly original and personal writer, who has always strenuously refused to be classified or classed with any school or ideological grouping. And this precisely is what singles him out among most German-speaking writers of his generation : where most of them indulge in wild and woolly generalisations, Frisch always remains concrete and direct; where they go in for *Weltanschauung,* Frisch remains ideologically uncommitted; where they are baroque and excessive in their style, Frisch is simple, direct and yet full of lyrical power. Where they tend to offer panaceas and infallible solutions Frisch merely wants to define some questions that ought to be asked : "As a playwright I would consider my task to have been thoroughly fulfilled if one of my plays could succeed in so posing a question that from that moment on the audience could not go on living without an answer—without their own answer, which they can only give through their own lives. The general demand for an answer, a general answer, which is so often made so movingly, so reproachfully, perhaps, after all it is not as honest as those who ask it themselves believe. Every human answer as soon as it transcends a personal answer and pretends to general validity will be questionable, we know that all too well; and the satisfaction we find in disproving other people's answers consists in making us forget the question that bothers us; and that would mean : we do not really want answers we merely want to forget the question. So as not to become responsible."[8]

NOTES

1. Frisch: *Tagebuch 1946–9,* Suhrkamp, 1950, p. 275.
2. *Ibid,* p. 282.
3. *Ibid,* p. 411.
4. *Andorra,* scene 8 in Stücke II, pp. 258–9.
5. *Tagebuch,* pp. 33–4.
6. *Ibid,* pp. 31–2.
7. Frisch: *Stiller,* Suhrkamp, 1958, p. 570.
8. Frisch: *Tagebuch,* pp. 141–2.

SHORT BIBLIOGRAPHY

Plays
Max Frisch, *Stücke,* 2 vol. Suhrkamp, Frankfurt, 1961.
  Vol. 1 contains: *Santa Cruz, Nun singen sie wieder, Die chinesische Mauer, Als der Krieg zu Ende War, Graf Oederland.*
  Vol. II contains: *Don Juan oder Die Liebe zur Geometrie, Biedermann und die Brandstifter, Die, grosse Wut des Philipp Hotz, Andorra.*

Biografie. Ein Spiel, Suhrkamp, Frankfurt, 1967.
In English: Max Frisch, *Three Plays*, Methuen, London, 1962.
  Contains: *The Fireraisers, Count Oederland, Andorra*, translated by
  Michael Bullock.

Novels

Stiller, Suhrkamp, Frankfurt, 1954.
English translation: *I'm not Stiller* (Penguin Books).
Homo Faber, Suhrkamp, Frankfurt, 1957.
English translation: *Homo Faber* (Penguin Books).
Mein Name sei Gantenbein, Suhrkamp, Frankfurt, 1964.
English translation: *Wilderness of Mirrors* (Methuen, London, 1965).

Autobiography

Tagebuch 1946–9, Suhrkamp, Frankfurt, 1950.

Essays and Speeches

Öffentlichkeit als Partner, Suhrkamp, Frankfurt, 1967.

On Frisch

Eduard Stäuble, *Max Frisch, Ein Schweizer Dichter der Gegenwart*,
  Bodensee Verlag, Amriswil, 2nd ed. 1960.
Hans Baenziger, *Frisch und Duerrenmatt*, Francke, Berne and Munich,
  1960.
Michael Kustow, *No Graven Image* in *Encore* May–June 1962.

Friedrich Dürrenmatt

Friedrich Dürrenmatt

by H. M. WAIDSON

FRIEDRICH DÜRRENMATT, born on January 5, 1921 at Konolfingen, Canton Berne, is the son of the pastor Reinhold Dürrenmatt. When the family moved to Berne in 1935, Friedrich Dürrenmatt continued his secondary education there. In 1941 he began studying, in Zürich and then in Berne, and soon began writing; at one time he also thought of devoting himself to painting. He did not complete his university studies, but spent the years 1946–8 as a freelance writer in Basle. His play *Es steht geschrieben* was first performed at the Zürich Schauspielhaus on April 19, 1947. He married, in 1947, Lotti Geißler, an actress, and now lives at Neuchâtel with her and his three children. Apart from stage-plays, he has written mostly radio-plays and novels.

A glance at a few of the comments which Dürrenmatt has made about his plays and about drama in general may be of some preliminary relevance. Acting, magic and play, he says in the epilogue to *Frank der Fünfte,* are the origins of drama :

> Der Ursprung jeder Dramatik liegt vorerst im Trieb, Theater möglich zu machen, auf der Bühne zu zaubern, mit der Bühne zu spielen. Theater ist eine Angelegenheit der schöpferischen Lebensfreude, der unmittelbarsten Lebenskraft.[1]

He maintains that he does not interpret the world, for that is not the function of the creative writer, except incidentally and sub-consciously. The correspondence, if any, between what is shown on the stage and the outside world, is no business of the dramatist as a creative writer, but it is the duty of the critic to point to the existence of these two worlds and to show how far they are related to one another.

> Der Realität muß im Theater eine Überrealität gegenüber-stehen . . .
> . . . Dies alles enthebt den Kritiker jedoch nicht der Pflicht, gerade das zu tun, was ich mir verbiete, die Welt in meinen möglichen Welten zu entdecken.[2]

The assertion is then, roughly, that Dürrenmatt's plays originate in a series of "Einfälle", motifs or devices, but not in anything so formulated as an idea. In the comments at the end of *Die Physiker* Dürrenmatt states :

> Ich gehe nicht von einer These, sondern von einer Geschichte aus.[3]

He seems to be illustrating this method of imaginative writing in the construction of the radio-play *Der Doppelgänger*. Here the "author" tells the "producer" that he has a story to tell that lies close to his heart :

> Doch muß ich gestehen, daß ich nicht viel mehr von ihr weiß als das Motiv. Es macht dies aber nichts : Eine Handlung stellt sich immer zur rechten Zeit ein.[4]

The producer, the practical man with an eye to the expectations of the listeners, proceeds to try to persuade his author to name his hero, to give him a geographical setting, and generally to coax the action into common-sense shape; the author regards most of the producer's demands as irrelevant, but on the whole conforms to them, though without enthusiasm or conviction.

While emphatic in his belief that play-writing consists essentially in the dynamic urge of imaginative material in the dramatist's mind, and that a rigid structure of dramatic or philosophical theory is not part of the dramatist's essential craft, Dürrenmatt has made a number of theoretical statements which clearly have relevance to his creative writing. His essay on Schiller (1959) shows the affinities of his own writing to that of the earlier dramatist; the fact that Dürrenmatt had the occasion to make this speech (having been awarded the Schiller Prize by the city of Mannheim), he says, indicates that the civic advisers were already aware of this affinity. Dürrenmatt joins the name of Schiller with that of Brecht, and the links that he finds between them inevitably reflect some of his own dramatic preoccupations. Both Schiller and Brecht he sees as concerned with dramatic theory and its relationship with creative writing. He says of Schiller :

> Seine Dramatik beruht auf einer durchaus sicheren, handfesten Dramaturgie ... Diese Dramaturgie zielt auf das Rhetorische. Der Mensch wird in Szene gesetzt, um rhetorisch ausbrechen zu können. Operndramaturgie.[5]

Operatic and rhetorical elements are present in Dürrenmatt's work, as in that of Schiller and Brecht. The way in which Schiller brings about the downfall of his heroes is summarized in words which could apply equally to a number of Dürrenmatt's own plays :

Der Mensch scheitert am unnatürlichen Zustande der Welt . . . Der Mensch geht schuldlos zugrunde. Sein Opfer bleibt nur in einer inneren Weise sinnvoll.[6]

Dürrenmatt compares and contrasts Schiller and Brecht in their attitude to the state and to the idea of revolution, and, in expressing his concern about the impotence of the individual in face of a mass-organized world, he is also reflecting situations from his own work :

Für den Einzelnen bleibt die Ohnmacht, das Gefühl, übergangen zu werden, nicht mehr einschreiten, mitbestimmen zu können, untertauchen zu müssen, um nicht unterzugehen . . .[7]

By implication therefore Dürrenmatt sees himself as closer to Schiller and Brecht than, to quote the names he mentions in this context, Shakespeare, Molière and Nestroy.

The earlier essay *Theaterprobleme* (1955) emphasizes the spontaneous nature of drama writing and the subordinate position of dramatic theory and ideas :

Die Bühne stellt nicht für mich ein Feld für Theorien, Weltanschauungen und Aussagen, sondern ein Instrument dar, dessen Möglichkeiten ich zu kennen versuche, indem ich damit spiele.[8]

If it happens that his characters are concerned with problems of faith and philosophy, it is because Dürrenmatt finds it tedious to depict "lauter Dummköpfe", nothing but fools, and because human beings do concern themselves with such problems. Any dramatic theory, he says, will have only relative value, since it is bound to a specific environment. This is claimed to be true of Brecht as well as of Aristotle; if Brecht builds his dramatic theory into his philosophy of life, it often happens, and should happen, that "Der Dichter Brecht dem Dramaturgen Brecht durchbrennt".[9] In his appendix to *Die Wiedertäufer* Dürrenmatt comments that Brecht's alienation-effect is a form of opposition to tragedy as such, for "only the real affects us as tragic".

Theaterprobleme treats of a number of "practical problems" ("arbeitspraktische Probleme") which correspond to various devices that are used in Dürrenmatt's plays. One issue in the essay, however, which is repeatedly relevant to his own writing is the question of the possibility of creating tragedy for the modern stage. (It is echoed also in the query raised in the introduction to the tale *Die Panne* as to whether narrative is capable of existing today :

> Die Ahnung steigt auf, es gebe nichts mehr zu erzählen, die Abdankung wird ernstlich in Erwägung gezogen, vielleicht sind einige Sätze noch möglich . . .[10])

Dürrenmatt points out that the hero of tragedy traditionally comes from the highest social class and arouses our pity. With Lessing and Schiller the hero could come from the middle classes, and in the eighteenth century there was special emphasis on the element of pity; in the case of Büchner the implication seems to be that Woyzeck is the last tragic hero in German drama. Historical "Staatsdrama" in the manner of *Wallenstein,* it is argued, is impossible today because the state has lost its shape; political power has become so gigantic and uncontrollable that it ceases to be effective as drama. Tragedy depends on "Schuld, Not, Maß, Übersicht, Verantwortung" ("guilt, sorrow, proportion, perspective, responsibility"), but Dürrenmatt argues that these qualities are absent today, since events are on such a vast, unpredictable scale that no individual can be held responsible.

> Unsere Welt hat ebenso zur Groteske geführt wie zur Atombombe.[11]

Comedy then has more chance of success than tragedy, for it is formed on a social basis. It may be more effective to ridicule the tyrants of today than to criticize them by means of tragic pathos. As a contemporary form of "world theatre" which claims our serious attention there is that form of comedy which portrays tragic characters whom paradoxical, ridiculous and therefore comic events befall (c.f. the appendix of *Die Wiedertäufer*).

Dürrenmatt's first two plays may be seen as experiments in tragedy. There is a considerable quantity of clowning and parody in *Es steht geschrieben,* but the general treatment of its theme and the element of "Das Rhetorische" seem to point to tragedy, or at least to no conscious intention to avoid tragedy. *Der Blinde* is perhaps Dürrenmatt's most consistent tragedy. The blind Duke retains his faith in a supra-natural, ideal world in face of the destruction of his outward happiness and security, in a way that recalls Schiller's idea of the tragic hero in *Über das Erhabene.* Elisabeth Brock-Sulzer points out that *Der Blinde* was criticised at the time of its first production as being essentially undramatic; it is indeed a martyr-drama, with no outward opposition to the villain Negro da Ponte. She reminds us, however, that the element of theatre plays a large part in this play, though more as spectacle than as drama. Negro da Ponte causes a whole series of dramolets to be enacted before the unseeing eyes of the Duke; thus there is a set of plays within the play. But it seems as though Dürrenmatt became dissatisfied with the martyr-drama in this form; *Der Blinde* was withheld from publication for more than ten years, and in the meantime the author has hesitated to use the word "tragedy" with reference to his own plays. (*Der Blinde* is described in the published version as "Ein Drama".) The conscious evolution of a theory and practice of comedy on Dürrenmatt's part seems to have taken place after the first performance of *Der Blinde*. With *Romulus der Große,* the sunniest of Dürrenmatt's stage-plays and the closest to the traditional structure of drama, martyr-tragedy has merged into martyr-comedy; the hero, alone in his conflict with the evil and folly in himself and in the world at large, has now become the subject of comedy. But even so the possibility of his achieving tragic quality, of a traditional nature, cannot be excluded. Dürrenmatt writes in a note to *Romulus der Große* :

> Menschlichkeit ist vom Schaupieler hinter jeder meiner Gestalten zu entdecken, sonst lassen sie sich gar nicht spielen. Das gilt von allen meinen Stücken.[12]

However, his quality of humanity, though never absent from the author's intentions, is evidently expressed more sympathetically in some figures than others, and the mood of a play is indicated to some extent by the importance of the role assigned to the hero, the humane and suffering figure.

Es steht geschrieben has elements of horror, absurdity and vulgarity, plenty of action, plenty of speeches often containing paradoxical rhetoric, a variety of stage devices, great vitality. In the *Theaterprobleme* Dürrenmatt refers to a tendency on his part to attempt too much in the framework of one play :

> Es ist meine nicht immer glückliche Leidenschaft, auf dem Theater den Reichtum, die Vielfalt der Welt darstellen zu wollen. So wird mein Theater oft vieldeutig und scheint zu verwirren.[13]

This is particularly applicable to Dürrenmatt's first play, where it may be some time before it is recognized that Knipperdollinck is the hero (in the sense here of a model personality, with whom we may be expected to feel sympathy), since the outward action is often dominated by Bockelson, the newcomer to Münster who so violently affects its fate. It is Knipperdollinck, the rich merchant with settled domestic habits, who considers most closely the central theme of the play which is indicated in its title; literal obedience to the Bible's injunctions causes him to seize as an opportunity the importunate arrival of Bockelson at his house, to be impelled to divest himself of his possessions :

> Da steht geschrieben :
> Verkaufe was du hast und gib's den Armen, so wirst du einen Schatz im Himmel haben. . . .[14]

Knipperdollinck asks God for an answer : "Herr, du schweigst, und ich brauche eine Antwort," explaining his bewilderment : "Ich habe keinen Glauben, ich habe Gold".[15] (This statement anticipates the author's development of the theme in *Der Besuch der alten Dame* and *Frank der Fünfte*.) As the action proceeds, the two men change their parts; Knipperdollinck, the man of substance, gives away everything and in the practice of patient suffering acquires faith, while the beggar Bockelson steps into Knipperdollinck's discarded possessions and becomes further confirmed in his cosmic despair. There is a remarkable scene as the two men dance on the roof-top waiting for their city to fall to the Roman Catholic troops. In anticipation of certain death the two men let fall their differences and the driving force of their personalities and beliefs, and enjoy the dance in an aesthetic lyricism that includes the clumsy and ridiculous. If the main conflict of the play is on a personal level between Knipperdollinck and Bockelson, the wider tension is between the Anabaptist community and the established Empire and Church. The Anabaptists are all, in the context of this play, tragic-comic heroes and fools. Knipperdollinck and Bockelson are both clowns, swept on by living in a world where literal interpretation of the Bible is of prime importance. Thus Dürrenmatt's first play, while glorifying in Knipperdollinck the hero as martyr, at the same time contains strong elements of comedy, parodying the martyr as fool and clown.

Es steht geschrieben was revised and presented in new form as *Die Wiedertäufer* in 1967. Bockelson, now primarily a comic figure, is finally pardoned and taken on as a member of a cardinal's theatre-troupe. Our sympathies are directed also to the prophetic figure Matthison and to the humanist ex-monk, while the aged bishop of Münster "rebels" in the closing scene, leaving the audience with a final injunction and query :

Diese unmenschliche Welt muß menschlicher werden
Aber wie? Aber wie?[16]

Der Blinde is more unified in mood, a morality play, retelling the story of Job in the setting of the Thirty Years War. The Duke is close to Knipperdollinck, sharing his humility and his destination not to move away from the position he has taken up; both suffer deprivation from their possessions and then the loss of those members of their families closest to them, and at the end of each play both men still affirm their faith.

In *Romulus der Große* the situation of the martyr-hero confronted by vicissitudes of fortune is re-interpreted in the manner of comedy. Romulus, as last Roman emperor before the invasion of the Germanic barbarians, might be considered as the suitable central figure of a classicist tragedy, but Dürrenmatt depicts him as an anti-hero and clown. It seems as if the decaying Roman Empire is in conflict with the might of the advancing barbarians, but this apparent, outward, political conflict is shown ultimately as paradoxically non-existent. The contrast between the mood of the play's exposition and that of high tragedy is indicated in the scene where Phylax endeavours to instruct Rea to absorb the role of a tragic heroine, Antigone. The essential dramatic conflict is between Romulus and his own family and supporters. Much of the first three acts is on a level of persiflage and light banter, the witticisms and deliberate disrespectfulness of the Emperor arousing the indignation of his wife, daughter and entourage. The fourth act shows the elevation of the play, after comedy and then melodrama, in the attempted assassination of Romulus, to seriousness, as Romulus now contemplates the fulfilment of his self-appointed role of unheroic martyr. He differs from Knipperdollinck and the Duke in being free from a tendency to take himself too seriously in his role as sufferer. Romulus expects execution twice, but is spared the first time by sheer chance (as is also the case with Bockelson), the second time because he himself also has a conventional conception of the Germani. Apparently the first version of the play was consistently on a level of light comedy, but in the revised edition Dürrenmatt rewrote the last two acts to give Romulus greater dignity and heroism. As Dürrenmatt indicated in his postscript to the play, Romulus passes judgment on the Roman world in act three; but judgment is passed on him later when he is frustrated of his desired martyrdom, so that tragedy might be found in his inability to attain the dignity of this aim and in his being presented with comedy and pensioning-off. His wisdom lies in his willingness to accept an unheroic ending and to refuse to dramatise himself. As a character Romulus is much more rounded, warmer and more human than either Knipperdollinck or the Duke. What is more, his character gradually emerges as the play proceeds, undergoing development and purification.

Dürrenmatt takes up again in *Die Ehe des Herrn Mississippi* something of the grotesqueness of *Es steht geschrieben,* though in this instance he is more firmly determined to interpret it in a spirit of comedy. Elisabeth Brock-Sulzer regards *Die Ehe des Herrn Mississippi* as "sentimentalisch", that is, not spontaneous and evocative through direct human characteristics, but as "konstruiert", since its main characters are embodiments of ideas. It has been pointed out that Mississippi, Saint-Claude and Bodo von Übelohe may represent faith, hope and charity. These three main characters are united in their search for an absolute, in their desire to change the world and in their dissatisfaction with the policy of preserving the existing situation which is manifested in the figure of the minister Diego. Thus they are united by a gleam of what is regarded by others as fanaticism and folly, and hold together, symbolically at least, like the Anabaptists in face of the traditional forces of Church and Empire, or like the Duke when confronted by Negro da Ponte. Bodo von Übelohe resembles Knipperdollinck, the Duke and Romulus when he strips himself, or is stripped, of his riches until, possessing nothing, he embodies the ideal of poverty and powerlessness. Knipperdollinck and the Duke, in holding fast to rigid attitudes, are tragic martyrs; Romulus and Übelohe have no illusions about themselves, are willing to be regarded as clowns, and thus (from Dürrenmatt's point of view as apparently implied in these plays) can speak for ideals of wisdom or love. If Mississippi realizes that the action he is taking part in during a certain scene is comedy, he resents this and finds it humiliating :

Wie lange soll diese für beide Teile entwürdigende Komödie noch abspielen, gnädige Frau?[17]

Mississippi's role seems to be anticipated in a phrase from the early prose narrative, *Das Bild des Sisyphos* :

. . . auch schien unter seinen Worten jener Fanatismus zu glühen, den wir bei Menschen antreffen, die entschlossen sind, ihrer Idee die Welt zu opfern.[18]

Übelohe does not appear until the first section, previously dominated by Mississippi and Saint-Claude, is more than half over; subsequently he has a larger part to play and is allowed to survive, after Mississippi and Saint-Claude are dead, and to speak the epilogue. His desire to help mankind ("Dein Urwaldspital in Borneo"—"Your hospital in the primeval forests of Borneo") has crumbled, and his last illusion about mankind, his love for Anastasia, is soon lost :

Allein die Liebe ist geblieben. Die Liebe eines Narren, die Liebe eines lächerlichen Menschen.[19]

Übelohe's appearance finally, as Don Quixote in battered armour tilting at a windmill, sums up his conception of the play :

Eine ewige Komödie
Daß aufleuchte Seine Herrlichkeit
genährt durch unsere Ohnmacht.[20]

Romulus der Große, where the hero dominates most of the time, is more unified in its plot, theme and mood than the more disparate *Die Ehe des Herrn Mississippi.*

Ein Engel kommt nach Babylon, Dürrenmatt informs its readers, was intended as the preliminary action of a work which should culminate in the building of the tower of Babel, and is therefore sub-titled a "fragmentary comedy". As in *Die Ehe des Herrn Mississippi,* the stability of the state is threatened by revolution, though the rising is thwarted and the old order finally remains in control. The appearance of the Angel, with his bland belief in the perfection of earth as a planet, brings confusion and no visible improvement in the lot of the majority of Babylonians; his final leave-taking from the earth and the bewildered Kurrubi recalls the departure of the three gods in Brecht's *Der gute Mensch von Sezuan.* From the events in the first act especially our attention is directed to the figures of two comic beggars : Akki, the last surviving beggar in Babylon, and Nebukadnezar, the king who has assumed the guise of beggar for a short period. Dürrenmatt introduces an element of paradox into his conception of these two men. Akki, as a highly proficient beggar, is patron of numerous poets, and for a time becomes an unconventional executioner;

here we are reminded of Brecht's Azdak in *Der kaukasische Kreidekreis*. The gift of Kurrubi is intended for Akki; as the Angel says to her :

> Die geringsten der Menschen sind die Bettler. Du wirst demnach einem gewissen Akki gehören, der, wenn diese Karte stimmt, der einzige noch erhaltene Bettler der Erde ist.[21]

But Kurrubi is presented to Nebukadnezar, who desires her, as she now desires him. In one sense this is due to an error on the Angel's part, but in another sense (cf. Elisabeth Brock-Sulzer) it is fitting that Kurrubi should be linked with Nebukadnezar, for as king he is the first, and therefore the last man, while as a beggar he appears comic and clumsy in his efforts to compete with Akki; his power, though apparently unrestricted, shows itself in the third act as close to impotence. To realize the happiness offered by this gift of divine grace, Nebukadnezar would have to forego all wealth and power and become a humbler and also more comic character than Akki. The king has the most important and critical decision to make in the action of the play : to accept or reject Kurrubi. At the end of the first act he refuses her in favour of gaining power over ex-king Nimrod, while he loses her to Akki in the final act because he is unwilling to accept her unless she becomes his queen. Nebukadnezar is both tyrant and victim of his own tyranny, and some words of Mississippi seem to have relevance in this connection :

> So fielen wir, Henker und Opfer zugleich, durch unsere eigenen Werke.[22]

The play has a light, fairy-tale mood and a delicacy of charm in addition to satirical humour.

Dürrenmatt's prose fiction has reflected themes and moods of his plays, though at times in less tightly knit formal concentration. The stories and novels published in the 1950s are normally set in a contemporary Swiss milieu, while the earlier dramas are placed in remoter times and places. The short story *Der Tunnel* transforms an everyday train journey into a nightmare vision, while *Die Panne* describes an interruption in a car journey that precipitates unexpected confrontation with accusation and judgment. *Grieche sucht Griechin* (1955), with its prime emphasis on a love story, has remained on its own so far among the author's prose works. It is the three detective novels that have aroused the widest interest. *Der Richter und sein Henker* (1950) introduced the massive figure of Bärlach, the Swiss police officer who after years in Turkey and Germany has little time left, for health reasons, to settle accounts with his master-criminal antagonist. The wet late autumn in Berne and the Jura effectively sets the mood. In *Der Verdacht* (1951) Bärlach, a sick man, arranges to be transferred from the friendly care of his own doctor to another nursing home in Berne in order that he may confront a surgeon who was formerly engaged in inhuman operations in a German concentration camp. Dürrenmatt's outstanding novel is *Das Versprechen* (1958), sub-titled "a requiem to the crime novel". The author-narrator, having given a lecture in Chur on the art of writing detective stories, encounters Dr. H., retired chief of cantonal police in Zürich, who gives him a lift by road back to Zürich. This is the main framework to the story, related by Dr. H., of the fate of his colleague Matthäi whose obsession with the solution of a murder case brought about the collapse of his career and the downfall of his personality. Dr. H. reminds the author of the comforting pattern in traditional crime-stories, where the detective knows the rules and where justice is seen to be done. In this story chance plays a great part and the police do not always keep to the rules, he says, and demonstrates how Matthäi, at the age of fifty and about to be seconded to Jordan in an advisory capacity, gives a promise that he cannot keep; his rigid insistence on attempting to track down the murderer of a small girl loses him his place in the police force and later renders him incapable of comprehending the facts when they eventually emerge. This novel contains a number of tense episodes which appear as dramatic scenes, such as the dialogue between Matthäi and the child's parents, the scene of the villagers' mistrust of the police, the cross-examination of the wrongly suspected von Gunten, the interview with the psychiatrist, and the frustrated attempt to waylay the murderer with another child as bait.

> . . . die Situation war peinlich und grotesk, wir waren alle verlegen und kamen uns lächerlich vor; das Ganze war nichts als eine lausige, hundserbärmliche Komödie.[23]

Dr. H. reminds the author that it does occasionally "come to the worst", and that the absurd has to be reckoned with humbly.

The situation of the action in *Der Besuch der alten Dame* is comparable to that of earlier plays in that a powerful figure comes from outside and with his or her entry into a previously static community brings about confusion and conflict before disappearing from the scene at the end of the play. Claire Zachanassian brings the gift of her wealth, after having deliberately impoverished the community, as the Angel brought Kurrubi; or she can be seen as inflicting fear upon Ill, just as Negro da Ponte brought tribulations to the Duke. External forces start the action of these plays, and each of them contains a quality of irresponsibility and indifference to the needs and welfare of the community they disturb. The dissolution of the conventional world is threatened by Mississippi and Saint-Claude too, but is not achieved. The execution of Ill by his fellow-citizens at the orders of Claire Zachanassian recalls the death of Knipperdollinck and Bockelson in *Es steht geschrieben.* Claire Zachanassian is a static character, because she is outside the normal human order with her wealth and sense of purpose :

> Doch da sie sich außerhalb der menschlichen Ordnung bewegt, ist sie etwas Unabänderliches, Starres geworden, ohne Entwicklung mehr, es sei denn, zu versteinern, ein Götzenbild zu werden.[24]

Like the Angel in *Ein Engel kommt nach Babylon* the millionairess is remote from the people of Güllen. But Ill develops in the course of the action, while the citizens of the town change too. He becomes purified through guilt and suffering, but his family and fellow-townsmen become compromised through their guilt towards him. Up to the age of sixty-four Ill has lived unthinkingly, until Claire Zachanassian's ultimatum shocks him into a new awareness :

> Zauberhexchen ! Das kannst du doch nicht fordern ! Das Leben ging doch längst weiter ![25]

Anastasia and the Minister, in *Die Ehe des Herrn Mississippi,* succeed in preserving the *status quo* that lets them live in the present, but Ill is forced out of this position in the first act of *Der Besuch der alten Dame*. The second act shows the undermining of Ill's confidence and of his fellow-citizens' support of him and of the cause of "humanity". The crisis and turning-point occurs at the end of this act when he is unable to take the decisive step of entering the train :

> Einer wird mich zurückhalten, wenn ich den Zug besteige.[26]

By the third act he has overcome his anxiety and has turned from fear to readiness for repentance and atonement not through the compulsion of the other Güllen citizens, but through his own choice. In the first act Ill is identified with Güllen, subsequently he becomes separated from the other inhabitants of the town by his fear, while in the third act he acknowledges his guilt and is willing to accept death. The more surely he becomes resigned and ready, the less certain do the people of Güllen become, realizing something of the new guilt that is coming upon them. The Bürgermeister invites Ill to commit suicide to save the community from responsibility for his death :

Er wäre doch nun eigentlich Ihre Pflicht, mit Ihrem Leben Schluß zu machen, als Ehrenmann die Konsequenzen ziehen, finden Sie nicht? Schon aus Gemeinschaftsgefühl, aus Liebe zur Vaterstadt.[27]

But Ill, now stronger than the Bürgermeister in his newly found defencelessness, resembles Romulus standing alone against his family :

Bürgermeister! Ich bin durch eine Hölle gegangen. Ich sah, wie ihr Schulden machtet, spürte bei jedem Anzeichen des Wohlstands den Tod näher kriechen. Hättet ihr mir diese Angst erspart, dieses grauenhafte Fürchten, wäre alles anders gekommen, könnten wir anders reden, würde ich das Gewehr nehmen. Euch zu liebe. Aber nun schloß ich mich ein, besiegte meine Furcht. Allein. Es war schwer, nun ist es getan. Ein zurück gibt es nicht. Ihr *müßt* nun meine Richter sein. Ich unterwerfe mich eurem Urteil, wie es nun auch ausfalle.[28]

In his final *tête-à-tête* with Claire Zachanassian, Ill is cool and factual, much more her equal in the strength of his personality than in their first encounter in act one. He has become a suffering hero in the course of the action, having wrestled with himself for this quality in painful solitude. For Romulus, this quality was present all the time, but it was only fully revealed when his fellow-Romans left him. Ill begins as one of the drifting, conventional crowd, but is compelled to undergo a complete reversal of fortune and change of character. As Ill dies, he becomes the sacrificial victim so that the people of Güllen may be temporarily saved from poverty. The period of prosperity to which they proceed may only be an interlude before their judgment of Ill is caught up in a larger execution that may befall the whole community.

Humour in this play, which is sub-titled a "tragische Komödie", is for the most part demonstrated in the minor characters. There are the satellites of Claire Zachanassian, who have no personality since they have become humiliated to complete subordination to her will; hardly human, they are an extension of her personality and power. There are Ill's family and the other citizens of Güllen, whose gradual yielding to the will of the millionairess is satirically demonstrated. It could be argued that Ill is a tragic hero who has to undergo a searching process of emotional purification. At the same time Dürrenmatt has emphasized that comedy is integral to his conception of the play; as he writes in the "note" at the end of *Der Besuch der alten Dame* :

> Man inszeniere mich auf die Richtung von Volksstücken hin, behandle mich als eine Art bewußten Nestroy und man wird am weitesten kommen. Man bleibe bei meinen Einfällen und lasse den Tiefsinn fahren . . . Die alte Dame ist ein böses Stück, doch gerade deshalb darf es nicht böse, sondern aufs humanste wiedergegeben werden, mit Trauer, nicht mit Zorn, doch auch mit Humor, denn nichts schadet dieser Komödie, die tragisch endet, mehr als tierischer Ernst.[29]

Frank der Fünfte, "opera of a private bank", culminates in the killing of a bank magnate by his own son, after an exposition of the many crimes in which all members of the firm have been implicated. It is an essay in dynastic melodrama, and the parodistic prologue spoken by the personnel manager Egli draws a parallel with Shakespeare, insisting that a modern business milieu is as capable of showing "royal" action as any sixteenth-century play :

> Ein Relikt wie du, einer besseren schöneren Welt
> Stehn wir fürchterlich vor dir
> Henker zwar doch Götter schier
> Minder groß und blutig nicht
> Als die Helden von Shakespeare.[30]

The bank of Frank the Fifth has been left over from an earlier epoch, and finally when his régime is terminated his son is to modernise the undertaking by "a few years of brutal honesty" :

> Ich werde die Bank meiner Väter retten. Von jetzt an wird legal gewirtschaftet, einige Jahre brutaler Ehrlichkeit und wir tanzen wieder im Reigen der Großbanken mit.[31]

In an environment of total unscrupulousness there is little room for sympathy; the feigned death of Frank the Fifth is as melodramatic as his final disappearance at the end of the play. The illustrations of the bank's methods are indeed presented as being simplifications, since a detailed account, it is said, would be impossible to reconcile with the requirements of drama. In his desire to confess his past misdeeds Böckmann corresponds most closely to Ill in *Der Besuch der alten Dame* and to the earlier martyr-heroes. His discovery that he has cancer and that Frank the Fifth and Ottilie have been unwilling to permit the operation advised two years earlier, that they have children while he has remained alone, opens his eyes to a new interpretation of the world about him. Later, on his death-bed, Böckmann asserts his need to turn away from the life behind him :

> In jeder Stunde hätten wir umkehren können, in jedem Augenblick unseres bösen Lebens. Es gibt kein Erbe, das nicht auszuschlagen wäre und kein Verbrechen, das getan werden muß.[32]

This last wish is effectively frustrated by Ottilie and her husband. For Böckmann there is little or no opportunity to escape from the way of life he has lived so long; in this respect he differs from Ill.

In *Die Physiker* Möbius corresponds in some respects to Böckmann in *Frank der Fünfte,* though Möbius has a much more developed and significant part. Just as Böckmann finds it impossible to escape from his ties to the bank, so Möbius is apparently wholly identified with his fellow-inmates of the sanatorium "Les Cerisiers". The first act offers an exposition in which the three scientists appear to the audience as hardly differentiated in their roles. Beutler ("Newton"), Ernesti ("Einstein") and Möbius ("King Solomon") live together, are physicists with seemingly similar delusions, and as the act closes Möbius follows his companions' example when he too murders his nurse. Earlier in the act the separation from his children and his wife, who is newly married to a missionary, has allowed for Möbius' introduction to the audience as a charcter in the tradition of the suffering, clumsy figures in Dürrenmatt's previous works. A stage-direction describes him as :

> ein vierzigjähriger, etwas unbeholfener Mensch. Er schaut sich unsicher im Zimmer um . . .[33]

and he feels that as a father he has been inadequate :

> Ich bin froh, daß die Buben einen tüchtigen Vater gefunden haben. Ich bin ein ungenügender Vater gewesen.[34]

He attempts, in act two, to give himself up to the police-inspector, but with his two fellow-physicists realizes that "Les Cerisiers" has become increasingly like a prison. When he realizes the identity of

"Newton" and "Einstein", Möbius knows that he has been threatened with abduction from the agents of the two opposing major powers in world politics. He is an outstanding physicist, and thereby is liable to become the victim of the social-political consequences of his own discoveries; even if he "escapes" from the sanatorium, he will only become a prisoner of one of the two great states. As he explains his career to "Newton" and "Einstein", Möbius shows that he deliberately assumed the fool's cap, like King Romulus, believing that only through the assumption of madness would the world have a chance of being saved :

> Es gibt Risiken, die man nie eingehen darf : Der Untergang der Menschheit ist ein solches. Was die Welt mit den Waffen anrichtet, die sie schon besitzt, wissen wir, was sie mit jenen anrichten würde, die ich ermögliche, können wir uns denken.[35]

It is Möbius who persuades his two colleagues to give up their political missions and to remain voluntarily with him in the sanatorium. In this way, and no other, is there a remote possibility that the world may be saved, he argues, and that the murders they have committed may not be without meaning :

> Sollen unsere Morde sinnlos werden? Entweder haben wir geopfert oder gemordet. Entweder bleiben wir im Irrenhaus oder die Welt wird eines. Entweder löschen wir uns im Gedächtnis der Menschen aus oder die Menschheit erlischt.[36]

The three hope to be "mad, but wise, captive, but free, and physicists, but innocent". At this point the play attains a dignity comparable to the meeting between Romulus and Odoaker, and Möbius too may be seen as making a gesture of heroic self-sacrifice.

But Dürrenmatt ends *Die Physiker* on a note of sharp disillusionment. As "Einstein" says :

> Die Welt ist in die Hände einer verrückten Irrenärztin gefallen.[37]

Dr. Mathilde von Zahnd is a much more immediate danger to mankind than Odoaker's nephew in *Romulus der Große*. But Möbius is allowed the last words in the play, to confirm the central importance of his function in it; if Bodo von Übelohe concludes *Die Ehe des Herrn Mississippi* by seeing himself as Don Quixote, Möbius speaks as a King Solomon whose realm has lost all life :

> Ich bin Salomo. Ich bin der arme König Salomo. Einst war ich unermeßlich, reich, weise und gottesfürchtig. Ob meiner

Macht erzitterten die Gewaltigen. Ich war ein Fürst des Friedens und der Gerechtigkeit. Aber meine Weisheit zerstörte meine Gottesfurcht, und als ich Gott nicht mehr fürchtete, zerstörte meine Weisheit meinen Reichtum. Nun sind die Städte tot, über die ich regierte, mein Reich leer, das mir anvertraut worden war, eine blauschimmernde Wüste, und, irgendwo, um einen kleinen, gelben, namenlosen Stern, kreist, sinnlos, immerzu, die radioaktive Erde. Ich bin Salomo, ich bin Salomo, ich bin Salomo, ich bin der arme König Salomo.[38]

Der Meteor (1966) is a stark, paradoxical confrontation of life and death, fast moving and sharply contoured, as full of surprising and inventive sequences as any of Dürrenmatt's plays. It is a comedy; "There is nothing tragic about dying", the central figure says confidently at the beginning. Wolfgang Schwitter, Nobel prizewinner as an illustriously militant man of letters, comes back to life after he has been pronounced officially dead, and returns to the attic studio where he had attempted to be a painter forty years earlier. Like Claire Zachanassian he has the role of a powerful, hard figure, making an impact of confusion and disaster on a humanly ordinary community. Returned from the dead, he is even more separated from those he now meets than was the old lady. But his is no voluntary, long-planned visitation; it is an unexpected happening which gradually fills him with the horror that he may be condemned to life, and that the martyrdom of life may in his case not be terminated by death. The hot sunshine of the longest day is the background to the day of judgment. Schwitter may possibly be physically immortal, but already his reputation as a writer is crumbling. While longing for his own death, he brings death or misfortune to other people; wishing for passivity, he dominates and tyrannizes. The pastor Emanuel Lutz, who proclaims Schwitter's resurrection to be a miracle, himself dies. The young painter Nyffenschwander is killed when the landlord Muheim propels him downstairs, and consequently Muheim is taken into custody by the police. Schlatter, the doctor, sees his life in ruins on account of his inexplicably erroneous diagnosis of his patient's condition. Schwitter's most recent wife takes her life, while her mother, like Lutz, dies quietly as he confides to her :

> Da ließ ich mich fallen. Ich fiel und fiel und fiel. Nichts mehr hatte Gewicht, nichts mehr einen Wert, nichts mehr einen Sinn. Der Tod ist das einzig Wirkliche, Frau Nomsen, das einzig Unvergängliche. Ich fürchte ihn nicht mehr.[39]

His isolation increases hourly. He breaks up the Nyffenschwanders' marriage, and Auguste disappears. He has deprived his son Jochen of his fortune, and can only expect continued hatred from him. In the final Salvation Army sequence, when the "miracle" of his resurrection is being loudly celebrated, Schwitter asks them for mercy ("Seid gnädig, ihr Christen!"[40]) and death. Although it is difficult to take all the characters seriously as human beings, the macabre dance of death is presented with brilliant sharpness.

In opposition to Dürrenmatt's passive heroes stand the tyrants, executioners and men of ceremony. Together heroes and villains are absorbed by the problematic nature of life and by a strong desire to make it different, or at least not to accept it; the majority of people, of course, are not directly involved in the conflicts Dürrenmatt describes, and it may be part of the comedy that the dramatic tension often lies between people who, while violently in conflict with one another, have something in common which separates them from the unthinking majority. In *Es steht geschrieben* Charles V is shown as someone to whom the government of a vast empire brings none of the excitement that Bockelson acquires from his short-lived reign as "king" of Münster. The Bishop of Münster believes it to be his duty to persuade Charles V to destroy the Anabaptists, and in so doing asserts the right to sit in judgment over their state; but Dürrenmatt makes it clear that final judgment may take some quite other shape. Romulus is judged and condemned by his family and entourage; they are drowned as they try to escape, and Romulus remains alone. Mississippi and Saint-Claude are both executioners who are fanatically devoted to their cause. Nebukadnezar and Nimrod, as a pair of tyrants, are inexorably linked together. *Frank der Fünfte* shows the execution of an executioner. In this play, as also in *Der Besuch der alten Dame* and *Die Physiker,* the major antagonist to the suffering hero is an "old lady". Claire Zachanassian, it may be argued, has ultimately and in spite of herself, an ennobling effect upon her victim Ill. Frank the Fifth is supported and directed by his wife Ottilie; since during the course of most of the action he is ostensibly dead, she assumes leadership of the firm. She describes herself to Böckmann thus :

> Böckmann! Ich bin aufgerieben wie du von unserem Geschäft, eine alte Frau, die sich seit Jahren nur noch mit Morphium durch ein ekelhaftes Leben schleppt.[41]

Ottilie finally asks the President of the state, once her lover, to mete out justice and wind up the bank's affairs, but this is refused to her. As the President says to her :

> Nein, nein, erwarte von mir keine Strafe, erwarte von mir nur noch Gnade. [42]

Dr. Mathilde von Zahnd has a minor and apparently harmless role in the first act of *Die Physiker*. As last heiress of an old family, she may perhaps be eccentric, but in no wise dangerous :

> Schicksal, Voß. Ich bin immer Alleinerbin. Meine Familie ist so alt, daß es beinahe einem kleinen medizinischen Wunder gleichkommt, wenn ich relativ für normal gelten darf, ich meine, was meinen Geisteszustand betrifft.[43]

Her final revelation, that she is the sole possessor of Möbius' discoveries and thereby the most powerful person in the world, brings her into close kinship with Claire Zachanassian. Wolfgang Schwitter in *Der Meteor* brings disasters to those with whom he comes into contact, but nearly always by chance, and without the long-term calculations of Claire Zachanassian or Mathilde von Zahnd.

Dürrenmatt's interesting adaptation of Shakespeare's *King John* shows sympathy with the original play and at the same time an approach which makes it into a work of his own. In the last two acts especially Dürrenmatt goes his own way, omitting much that he found irrelevant and dispensing altogether with Shakespeare's call for English national unity. The Swiss author sees the English and French royalty and nobility, as also the papal representative, involved in stratagems and calculations that are indifferent to the general welfare of the people. As he explains in his note at the end of *König Johann* (1968), Dürrenmatt is converting a dramatized chronicle into a comedy of politics. The Bastard Falconbridge is given a much more central part in the action, becoming Blanche's lover and replacing Hubert as Arthur's keeper, as well as influencing King John's policies from an early point in their acquaintanceship. If Shakespeare's King John says "Why, what a madcap hath heaven lent us here!", Dürrenmatt develops the Bastard into a clown-hero who fails repeatedly in his attempts to introduce reason into high politics; his final retirement from public life will allow the political scene, in Pembroke's view, to continue "undisturbed by fools". Whereas Shakespeare's Bastard succeeds in the political world, Dürrenmatt's fails in his aims, attributing this to the folly of fate and chance :

Ich mischte
Mich in die Welt der Mächtigen hinein,
Versuchte sie zum bessren Ziel zu lenken.
Doch Dummheit zog den Wagen des Geschicks.
Und Zufall.[44]

In a speech to the audience Übelohe gives some hint as to the author's identity and purposes in *Die Ehe des Herrn Mississippi* :

So ließ der Liebhaber grausamer Fabeln und nichtsnutziger Lustspiele, der mich schuf, dieser zähschreibende Protestant und verlorene Phantast mich zerbrechen, um meinen Kern zu schmecken ... um mich nicht als Sieger, sondern als Besiegten . . . in den Tiegel seiner Komödie zu werfen : Dies allein nur, um zu sehen, ob denn wirklich Gottes Gnade in dieser endlichen Schöpfung unendlich sei, unsere einzige Hoffnung.[45]

In *Ein Engel kommt nach Babylon* this gift of grace is available to the beggar but not to the monarch. Nebukadnezar recognizes this already on first encountering Kurrubi :

So schlage ich zu Boden, was ich mehr liebe denn je einen Menschen, so trete ich dich mit Füßen, du Gnade Gottes, von der meine Seligkeit abhängt. . . .[46]

Nebukadnezar has wished to found a state on a combination of power and reason alone, with himself as its ruler :

Ich trachtete nach Vollkommenheit. Ich schuf eine neue Ordnung der Dinge. Ich suchte die Armut zu tilgen. Ich wünschte die Vernunft einzuführen. Der Himmel mißachtete mein Werk. Ich blieb ohne Gnade.[47]

Augias (*Herkules und der Stall des Augias*) presents to his son the "garden of his resignation" which he has cultivated in the midst of the all-pervasive dung, and tells him that the fruition of human endeavour is dependent upon grace, the presence of which cannot be compelled. These are a very few examples of the relevance in Dürrenmatt's work of the subject of grace, and the importance of this aspect has been shown by Fritz Buri in his essay in *Der unbequeme Dürrenmatt*.

The publication of a collected edition of the author's essays, reviews and sketches in the volume *Theater-Schriften und Reden* has made it possible to see his imaginative work in the context of a personal background; the pieces derive for the most part from the 1950s. He has described himself as not a village-writer, but a product of village life, and of the genuine Emmental as if conjured up by Jeremias Gotthelf. The difficulties of being a professional author are considered; how the Swiss author in particular has to wrestle with the problem of living in a small state and of thus being driven to becoming an "export-writer". In an essay on American and European drama Dürrenmatt enlarges upon the differences in social role of the author in the mammoth state and in the small unit where, he believes, the dramatist can take the state as it ought to be taken, as "a technical necessity and not a man-eating myth". The author from the more confined environment will expand this into a model for the larger, international world. Humour is indispensable in his conception of play-writing; if he is a moralist also, this will be as an afterthought, when interpreting himself. For the original conception of one of his plays is not sacrosanct, and after seeing various performances, with different producers' aims, there will come the urge to make changes and rewrite. More than once there is the expression of the belief that his writing must seek its themes in contemporary, everyday life. Amidst the reflections on drama and writing are striking pointers to more general issues, where the immediacy of imaginative vision can sparkle, the need for the preservation of peace, and the problem of living through its ordinariness (in this issue too there may be a specifically Swiss point of view); the present's trend to world-destruction as substitute for an earlier age's belief in revelation and a day of judgment; the short period of human history when seen in the context of the earlier saurians. Dürrenmatt's essays supplement his drama and prose fiction as a stimulating commentary, revealing further aspects of his lively, imaginative writing.

Die Welt ist als Problem beinahe und als Konflikt überhaupt nicht zu lösen.[48]

TRANSLATIONS

1. The origin of all dramatic art lies in the first place in the urge to make a performance possible, to practise magic on the stage and to play with the stage. A theatrical performance is a matter of the creative enjoyment of life, of the most direct vital energy.

2. In the theatre reality must be confronted with a supra-reality . . However, all this does not relieve the critic of the duty of doing precisely

what I do not allow myself to do, that is, of discovering the world in my potential worlds.

3. I do not start from a thesis, but from a story.

4. Yet I must confess that I don't know much more about it than the motif. But this doesn't matter: a plot can always be found at the right time.

5. His dramatic art rests upon a completely sure and practical dramatic theory . . . This dramatic theory aims at a rhetorical effect. A character is put on the stage so that he can break out rhetorically. Dramatic theory for opera.

6. Man founders because of the unnatural situation of the world . . . Man is destroyed in innocence. His sacrifice retains meaning only in an inward manner.

7. For the individual there remains impotence, the feeling of being passed over, of no longer being able to intervene and to have influence, of being compelled to go underground in order not to go under . . .

8. The stage does not represent for me a vehicle for theories, views of the world and pronouncements, but an instrument with potentialities of which I am attempting to get to know by playing with them.

9. Brecht the creative writer runs away with Brecht the dramatic theorist.

10. The misgiving arises that there is nothing more to relate, abdication is taken into serious consideration, perhaps a few sentences are still possible . . .

11. Our world has led to the grotesque just as to the atom-bomb.

12. The actor is to discover humanity behind each one of my characters, otherwise they cannot be played at all. This is the case with all my plays.

13. It is my not always felicitous passion to try to depict the richness and multifariousness of the world on the stage. In this way my play-writing often becomes ambiguous and seems to bewilder.

14. It is written: sell what you have and give it to the poor, and you will have treasure in heaven.

15. Lord, You are silent, and I need an answer . . . I have no faith, I have gold.

16. This inhumane world must become more humane. But how? But how?

17. How much longer is this comedy, which is so degrading for both sides, supposed to go on, madam?

18. Beneath his words it also seemed as if that fanaticism was burning which we meet in people who are determined to sacrifice the world to their idea.

19. Only love remains. The love of a fool, of a ridiculous person.

20. An eternal comedy, so that His majesty may light up, nourished by our impotence.

21. Beggars are the least among mankind. Consequently you will

belong to a certain Akki who, if this map is right, is the only surviving beggar on the earth.

22. Thus we fell, executioner and victim at the same time, through our own works.

23. . . . the situation was painful and grotesque, we were all embarrassed and seemed to ourselves to be ridiculous; the whole business was nothing but a lousy, wretched comedy.

24. However, since she moves outside the human order, she has become something unalterable and inflexible, without any further devolopment, unless it were to become petrified and to turn into an idol.

25. Little witch! But surely you can't ask for that! After all, life has been continuing on its way for a long time now!

26. Somebody will hold me back if I get on the train.

27. Now after all it is really your duty to terminate your life, to draw conclusions as a man of honour, don't you think? Even if only out of a communal spirit, out of love for your native town.

28. Mr. Mayor! I have been through hell. I saw how you all ran up debts and I felt death creeping more closely with every indication of prosperity: If you had spared me this anxiety and this horrible fear, everything would have turned out differently, we could be talking differently and I would accept the weapon. For your sakes. But now I shut myself in and overcame my fear. Alone. It was difficult, but now it is over. There is no going back. You *must* be my judges now. I submit to your judgment, whatever way it may go.

29. My work should be produced in a manner reminiscent of popular plays, I should be treated as a kind of self-conscious Nestroy, and that will take us furthest. Stick to my fancies and let the profundity go . . . The *Old Lady* is a wicked play, but precisely on that account it should not be played in a wicked manner, but in the most humane way possible, with grief, not anger, but also with humour, for nothing injures this comedy, which has a tragic ending, more than brutal earnestness.

30. A relic, like yourself, of a better and more beautiful world, we stand in our fearfulness before you, executioners, it is true, but almost gods, no less great and bloody than the heroes of Shakespeare.

31. I shall save the bank of my fathers. From now onwards everything will be run in a legal manner; a few years of brutal honesty and we shall once more take our part in the dance of the big banks.

32. We could have turned back at any hour or moment of our evil lives. There is no inheritance that may not be refused, and no crime that has to be committed.

33. A forty-year old and somewhat ungainly man. He looks round the room uncertainly . . .

34. I am glad that the boys have found a good father. I have been an inadequate father.

35. There are risks which one may never take: the destruction of humanity is one. We know what the world can do with the weapons

which it already possesses, and we can imagine what it would do with those which I make possible.

36. Are the murders we have committed to become meaningless?
Either we have performed sacrifices or committed murders. Either we stay in the asylum or the world becomes one. Either we blot ourselves out from the memory of men or mankind is blotted out.

37. The world has fallen into the hands of a mad doctor of mental diseases.

38. I am Solomon. I am poor King Solomon. Once I was immeasurably rich, wise and God-fearing. The mighty trembled at my power. I was a prince of peace and justice. But my wisdom destroyed my piety, and when I no longer feared God, my wisdom destroyed my wealth. Now the towns over which I ruled are dead, the kingdom which was entrusted to me is empty, a blue-shimmering desert, and somewhere the radio-active earth is circling senselessly and continually around a little yellow nameless star. I am Solomon, I am Solomon, I am poor King Solomon.

39. Then I let myself fall. I fell and fell and fell. Nothing had weight any more, nothing had value or meaning. Death is the only reality, Frau Nomsen, the only thing that is imperishable. I am no longer afraid of it.

40. Be merciful, you Christians!

41. Böckmann! I am worn out by our business just as much as you are, an old woman who for years has only dragged her way through a repulsive life with the help of morphia.

42. No, no, don't expect any punishment from me, expect from me only mercy.

43. Fate, Voss. I am always the sole heiress. My family is so old that it almost seems a small medical miracle if I may be considered to be relatively normal, I mean, as far as my mental condition is concerned.

44. I intervened in the world of the mighty, attempted to direct it to a better end. But stupidity was drawing the carriage of fate. And chance.

45. So the lover of dreadful fables and worthless comedies who created me, this tough-writing Protestant and lost dreamer, had me broken in order to enjoy my essence . . . in order to throw me into the crucible of his comedy . . . not as victor, but as one who is defeated: he has done this in order to see if God's grace, our only hope, really is infinite in this finite creation.

46. Thus I throw to the ground what I love more than any human being, thus I stamp on you with my feet, you grace of God, on which my salvation depends.

47. I aimed at perfection. I created a new order of things. I tried to destroy poverty. I wanted to introduce reason. Heaven disregarded my work. I remained without grace.

48. As a problem the world may be almost solved, as a conflict not at all.

SELECT BIBLIOGRAPHY

Dürrenmatt's chief publications to date (these have appeared mostly in the Verlag der Arche, Zürich, or in the Benziger Verlag, Einsiedeln and Cologne):

Stage Plays:
Es steht geschrieben, 1947 (revised as *Die Wiedertäufer*, 1967).
Der Blinde, 1948.
Romulus der Große, 1949 (edited by H. F. Garten, London, 1962).
Die Ehe des Herrn Mississippi, 1952.
Ein Engel kommt nach Babylon, 1953.
Der Besuch der alten Dame, 1956 (edited by Paul Kurt Ackermann, London, 1961).
Frank der Fünfte, 1959.
Die Physiker, 1962.
Der Meteor, 1966.
König Johann (nach Shakespeare), 1968.

Radio Plays:
Der Prozeß um des Esels Schatten, 1951.
Nächtliches Gespräch, 1952.
Stranitzky und der Nationalheld, 1953.
Herkules und der Stall des Augias, 1954.
Das Unternehmen der Wega, 1955 (edited by L. McGlashan and I. R. Campbell in *Drei Hörspiele*, London, 1966.)
Abendstunde im Spätherbst, 1957.
Der Doppelgänger, 1960.

Novels, stories, essays:
Der Richter und sein Henker, 1950 (edited by Leonard Forster, London, 1962).
Der Verdacht, 1951 (edited by Leonard Forster, London, 1965).
Die Stadt, 1952.
Grieche sucht Griechin, 1955.
Theaterprobleme, 1955.
Die Panne, 1956 (edited by F. J. Alexander, with *Der Tunnel*, Oxford, 1967).
Das Versprechen, 1958 (edited by Leonard Forster, London, 1967).
Friedrich Schiller. Eine Rede, 1960.
Theater-Schriften und Reden, 1966.

Some writings on Dürrenmatt:
Beda Allemann, *"Es steht geschrieben"*. In: *Das deutsche Drama*, edited by Benno von Wiese, vol. 2, Düsseldorf, 1958.
Hans Bänziger, *Frisch und Dürrenmatt*. Berne and Munich, 1960.

Elisabeth Brock-Sulzer, *Dürrenmatt. Stationen seines Werkes.* Zürich, 1960.

Elisabeth Brock-Sulzer, *Dürrenmatt in unserer Zeit.* Basle, 1968.

Edward Diller, "Friedrich Dürrenmatt's Theological Concept of History". *The German Quarterly,* vol. 40, 1967.

William Gillis, "Dürrenmatt and the Detectives". *German Quarterly,* vol. 35, 1962.

Peter B. Gontrum, *"Ritter, Tod und Teufel:* Protagonists and Antagonists in the Prose Works of Friedrich Dürrenmatt". *Seminar,* vol. 1, 1965.

Reinhold Grimm, "Parodie und Groteske im Werk Friedrich Dürrenmatts". *Germanisch-Romanische Monatsschrift,* vol. 42 (new series vol. 11), 1961.

A. J. Harper, "Dürrenmatt. A Way of Approach". *Germania,* vol. 2, 1962.

Christian Markus Jauslin, *Friedrich Dürrenmatt. Zur Struktur seiner Dramen.* Zürich, 1964.

Urs Jenny, *Friedrich Dürrenmatt.* Velber, 1965.

Peter Johnson, "Grotesqueness and Injustice in Dürrenmatt". *German Life and Letters,* new series vol. 15, 1961–2.

Gordon N. Leah, "Dürrenmatt's Detective Stories". *Modern Languages,* vol. 48, 1967.

Joachim Müller, "Max Frisch und Friedrich Dürrenmatt als Dramatiker der Gegenwart". *Universitas,* vol. 17, 1962.

Therese Poser, "Friedrich Dürrenmatt". In: *Zur Interpretation des modernen Dramas,* edited by Rolf Geißler, Frankfurt am Main, Berlin and Bonn, n.d.

Eugene E. Reed, "Dürrenmatt's *Der Besuch der alten Dame:* a study in the Grotesque". *Monatshefte,* vol. 53, 1961.

Der unbequeme Dürrenmatt, a collection of essays. Basilius Presse, Basle, 1962.

"Morality Plays". *Times Literary Supplement,* January 11, 1963.

General Bibliography *

A. General

Albert Bettex, "Swiss Literature" *in* Cassel's *Encyclopaedia of Literature,* v. I (London, 1953).

Guido Calgari, *Die vier Literaturen der Schweiz* (Olten, 1966). *The four literatures of Switzerland* (London, 1953). (Condensed version of above).

Oscar Ederle, *Das Schweizer Drama* (Lucerne, 1944).

Fritz Ernst, *Helvetia Mediatrix* (Zürich, 1939).

    European Switzerland (Zürich, 1951).

Robert Faesi, "Introduction to Swiss Literature" *in* ADAM, International Review, No. 174 (London, 1947).

Miron Grindea, *ed.*, "The country with four literatures" *in* ADAM, International Review, No. 275 (London, 1959).

Eduard Korrodi, *Geisteserbe der Schweiz* (Zürich, 1943).

Bruno Mariacher, and F. Witz, *Bestand und Versuch—Schweizer Schrifttum der Gegenwart.* An anthology in four languages. With biographical index and bibliography (Zürich, 1964).

Gonzague de Reynold, *Histoire littéraire da la Suisse au 18-ème siecle,* 2 vol. (Fribourg, 1909).

B. German-speaking Switzerland

Jacob Baechtold, *Geschichte der deutschen Literatur in der Schweiz* (Frauenfeld, 1919).

Albert Bettex, *Die Literatur der deutschen Schweiz von heute* (Zürich, 1950).

    Spiegelungen der Schweiz in der deutschen Literatur (Zürich, 1954).

Guido Calgari, *Die vier Literaturen der Schweiz* (Olten, 1966). Part I: Alemannische Schweiz.

Emil Ermatinger, *Dichtung und Geistesleben der deutschen Schweiz* (Munich, 1933).

Werner Günther, *Dichter der neueren Schweiz* (Berne, 1963, 1968).

Otto von Greyerz, *Die Mundartdichtung der deutschen Schweiz* (Zürich, 1924).

Walter Muschg, *Die Zerstörung der deutschen Literatur* (Berne, 1956).

Joseph Nadler, *Literaturgeschichte der deutschen Schweiz* (Zürich, 1932).

Virgine Rossel and E. Jenny, *Geschichte der schweizerischen Literatur* (Berne, 1910).

Karl Schmidt, *Aufsätze und Reden* (Zürich, 1937).

Swiss-German Dialect Literature. In: *The Penguin Companion to Literature*, Vol. 2: European. With bibliography. (Harmondsworth, 1969).
A. Zäch, *Die Dichtung der deutschen Schweiz* (Zürich, 1951).

C. French-speaking Switzerland

Alfred Berchtold, *La Suisse romande au cap du XXe siècle* (Lausanne, 1963).
Guido Calgari, *Die vier Literaturen der Schweiz* (Olten, 1966). Part IV: Französische Schweiz.
Charly Clerc, *L'âme d'un pays* (Neuchâtel, 1950).
Philippe Godet, *Histoire littéraire de la Suisse française* (Neuchâtel, 1895).
François Jost, *La Suisse dans les lettres françaises* (Fribourg, 1956).
Pierre Kohler, *Histoire de la littérature française*, vol. III (Littérature Romande) (Lausanne, 1949).
Edouard Martinet, *Portraits d'écrivains romands contemporains* (Neuchâtel, 1954).
Weber-Perret, *Ecrivains romands 1900–50* (Neuchâtel, 1954).

D. Rhaeto-Romanic speaking Switzerland

Arthur Baur, *Wo steht das Raetoromanische heute?* (Chur, 1955).
Giulio Bertoni, *La letteratura ladina dei Grigioni* (Rome, 1916).
Guido Calgari, *Die vier Literaturen der Schweiz* (Olten, 1966). Part II: Rätoromanische Schweiz.
Maurus Carnot, *Im Lande der Raetoromanen* (Zürich, 1934).
Casper Decurtins, *Geschichte der raetoromanischen Literatur* in Groebers "Grundriss der romanischen Philologie" II, 1961.
    Raetoromanische Chrestomathie (Erlangen, 1919).
Peider Lansel, *Musa Romonscha* (Chur, 1950).

E. Italian-speaking Switzerland

Guido Calgari, *Le quattro letterature della Swizzera* (Florence, 1968).
    Il libro del cittadino (Bellinzona, 1953).
    Ticino degli uomini (Locarno, 1966).
F. Filippini, *Una corona di ricci* (Bellinzona, 1953).
Giulio Rosse and Eligio Pometta, *Storia del Canton Ticino* (Lugano, 1941).
Scrittori della Svizzera italiana (Bellinzona, 1936)—a critical anthology.

Note: Bibliographies on individual writers at end of respective essays.